LIBRARIES WITHOUT WALLS 6
evaluating the distributed delivery of library services

LIBRARIES WITHOUT WALLS 6

evaluating the distributed delivery of library services

Proceedings of an international conference held on 16–20 September 2005, organized by the Centre for Research in Library and Information Management (CERLIM), Manchester Metropolitan University

EDITED BY
Peter Brophy
Jenny Craven
Margaret Markland

facet publishing

© The chapters: the contributors 2006
This compilation: Peter Brophy, Jenny Craven and Margaret Markland 2006

Published by
Facet Publishing
7 Ridgmount Street
London WC1E 7AE

Facet Publishing is wholly owned by CILIP: the Chartered Institute of Library and Information Professionals.

First published 2006

British Library Cataloguing in Publication Data
A catalogue record for this book is available from the British Library.

ISBN-13: 978-1-85604-576-6
ISBN-10: 1-85604-576-5

Typeset from editors' disks in 10/13 Caslon 540 and Zapf Humanist by Facet Publishing.
Printed and made in Great Britain by MPG Books Ltd, Bodmin, Cornwall.

CONTENTS

CONTRIBUTORS

María Luisa Alvite Díez, Professor of Library and Information Science, University of León, Spain

Ann Apps, IT Specialist, MIMAS, Manchester Computing, University of Manchester, UK

Chris Awre, Integration Architect, e-Services Integration Group, University of Hull, UK

Marie-Louise Axelsson, Subject Librarian for the Behavioral Sciences, Linköping University Library, Linköping, Sweden

Panos Balatsoukas, Greek State Scholarship Foundation (IKY) Scholar, Loughborough University, UK

Alison Brettle, Research Fellow, Institute of Health and Social Care Research, University of Salford, UK

Peter Brophy, Professor and Director, Centre for Research in Library and Information Management (CERLIM), Manchester Metropolitan University, UK

Jacqueline Chelin, Deputy Librarian, University of the West of England, Bristol, UK

Steve Cohen, Project Evaluator, Serious Assessments, Lexington, Massachusetts, USA

Chetz Colwell, Project Officer, Accessibility in Educational Media Group, Institute of Educational Technology, The Open University, UK

Jenny Craven, Research Associate, The Centre for Research in Library and Information Management (CERLIM), Manchester Metropolitan University, UK

Robert Davies, Senior Partner, MDR Partners, UK

Susan Eales, Programme Manager, JISC Executive, King's College, London, UK

Ken Eason, Director of the Bayswater Institute, London, and Professor Emeritus at Loughborough University, UK

Juliet Eve, Senior Lecturer, School of Computing, Mathematical and Information Sciences, Division of Information and Media Studies, University of Brighton, UK

Michael Fegan, Chief Technical Officer, Matrix, Michigan State University, USA

Emmanouel Garoufallou, Principal Lecturer, Technological Education Institution of Thessaloniki, and Director of Deltos Research Group, Greece

José-Marie Griffiths, Doctor, Dean and Professor, School of Information and Library Science, University of North Carolina at Chapel Hill, North Carolina, USA

Richard J. Hartley, Professor of Information Science, Head of Department of Information and Communications, and Director of The Information Research Institute (TIRI), Manchester Metropolitan University, UK

Yeu-Sheng Hsieh, Professor, Department of Agricultural Extension, National Taiwan University, Taiwan

Anne Jelfs, Learning and Teaching Development Officer, Institute of Educational Technology, The Open University, UK

Agnes Kukulska-Hulme, Senior Lecturer, Institute of Educational Technology, The Open University, UK

Li-Hsiang Lai, PhD Candidate, Department of Library and Information Science, National Taiwan University, Taiwan

Ross MacIntyre, Service Manager, MIMAS, Manchester Computing, University of Manchester, UK

Susan McKnight, Director of Libraries and Knowledge Resources, Nottingham Trent University, UK

Dawn McLoughlin, Academic Support Manager, Edge Hill College of Higher Education, Lancashire, UK

Elizabeth Mallett, Learning Resources Project Manager, Library and Learning Resources Centre, The Open University, UK

Anne Morris, Reader, Department of Information Science, Loughborough University, UK

Dianne Nelson, Faculty Librarian, University of the West of England, Bristol, UK

Ursula Nielsen, Senior Librarian, Linköping University Library, Linköping, Sweden

Bo Öhrström, Deputy Director, Danish National Library Authority, Copenhagen, Denmark

Ralph Quarles, Assistant Director of Information Technology, Indiana University Libraries, Indiana, USA

Dean Rehberger, Associate Director, Matrix, Michigan State University, USA

Jane Redman, Senior Assistant Librarian, University of the West of England, Bristol, UK

Blanca Rodríguez Bravo, Professor of Library and Information Science, University of León, Spain

Ellen Derey Safley, Senior Associate Director for Public Services and Strategy at the University of Texas at Dallas, USA

Pauline Shaw, Assistant Librarian, Health and Social Care, University of the West of England, Bristol, UK

Rania Siatri, Lecturer, Technological Education Institution of Thessaloniki, and Deputy Director of Deltos Research Group, Greece

Steven Smail, Programmer/Analyst, Indiana University Libraries Information Technology Team, Indiana, USA

Ruth Wilson, Academic Liaison Co-ordinator (Education), Edge Hill College of Higher Education, Lancashire, UK

Ming-Der Wu, Professor, Department of Library and Information Science, National Taiwan University, Taiwan

Claudine Xenidou-Dervou, Site Librarian, Physics and Informatics Department, and Co-ordinator, Steering Committee, HEAL-Link, Aristotle University of Thessaloniki, Greece

1
Introduction

Peter Brophy

The sixth conference on Libraries Without Walls marked the 10th anniversary of a series that began when the delivery of library services to distant users was in its infancy. Over the intervening period, not only has such a concept entered the mainstream of library practice but it has become the dominant service paradigm. What is more, a library operating in complex networked environments is simply one player among many. This is not to say that libraries are losing their role: the evidence seems to suggest that their networked services are in great demand, alongside a continued requirement for services based on the traditional media.

However, this observation itself raises the question as to just how robust the evidence base is for the continued relevance of the 'library without walls'. Previous conferences in the series (Irving and Butters, 1996; Brophy et al., 1998, 2000, 2002, 2004) had documented the achievements of many researchers and practitioners worldwide, but we felt it appropriate to step back and examine the evidence base. For the first time, therefore, this became the dominant theme of the conference.

Our keynote speaker, Sue McKnight, set the scene by providing a user (or customer) focus and challenging us to allow users to have direct input into library decision making. The user focus continued with a paper from Bo Öhrström showing how customer satisfaction needs to be considered alongside customer loyalty, and presenting a novel model for achieving this. A third paper focused on users from the perspective of accessibility, as Jenny Craven demonstrated critical issues for people with disabilities once services become distributed.

We then moved on to look at how libraries are evaluating the new generation of online services. Emmanouel Garoufallou and Rania Siatri examined this issue from the perspective of a Greek university, and Claudine Xenidou-Dervou showed the effects of a national initiative on another university in Greece. Richard J. Hartley reported on research into user behaviour when using large-scale union catalogues for resource discovery, while Ken Eason, Ross MacIntyre and Ann Apps examined user attitudes and behaviour in the context of electronic journal services. Dawn McLoughlin and Ruth Wilson then returned to a classic Libraries Without Walls theme with a paper on supporting distance learners.

A major topic of discussion at the conference concerned the assessment of impact, and a series of papers examined this issue from different perspectives. Alison Brettle addressed it in the context of health services; Dianne Nelson, Jacqueline Chelin, Jane Redman and Pauline Shaw related it to academic library evaluation; Juliet Eve reported on work to evaluate the UK's major investment in public library infrastructure; and, in a paper which probably provoked more debate than any other, José-Marie Griffiths unveiled a truly momentous study of the economic value of libraries in Florida. The final paper in this section, authored by CERLIM staff, reported on a study to develop longitudinal impact measurement methodologies.

Two papers on evaluation in the academic sector, one by Blanca Rodríguez Bravo and María Luisa Alvite Díez from Spain and the other by Ursula Nielsen and Marie-Louise Axelsson from Sweden, were followed by a report by Robert Davies on the state of public library, museum and archive development across Europe, using an innovative methodology developed in the PULMAN and Calimera projects.

Chris Awre, Ralph Quarles and Steven Smail reported on US–UK collaborative work examining the presentation of library services within complex, networked environments, and Li-Hsiang Lai, Ming-Der Wu and Yeu-Sheng Hsieh contributed a theoretical perspective seeking to develop a model of the digital library. An entirely novel approach to examining the sourcing of information was presented by another transatlantic team, Steve Cohen, Susan Eales, Michael Fegan and Dean Rehberger, within the context of the *Digital Libraries in the Classroom* programme.

The final section in these Proceedings reports on work with new media, including digital video and e-books. Elizabeth Mallett, Agnes Kukulska-Hulme, Anne Jelfs and Chetz Colwell presented a paper on an innovative digital video project, and Anne Morris, Panos Balatsoukas and Ellen Derey Safley looked at the evaluation of different approaches to e-book provision.

Taken as a whole, Libraries Without Walls 6 showed that not only is there a high level of innovation in our field, but that researchers and professionals are rising to the challenge of developing a robust evidence base – and the methodologies with which to build on the evidence already available. This suggests that the future for libraries that embrace the 'without walls' philosophy is bright.

References

Brophy, P., Fisher, S. and Clarke, Z. (eds) (1998) *Libraries Without Walls 2: the delivery of library services to distant users*, London, Library Association Publishing.

Brophy, P., Fisher, S. and Clarke, Z. (eds) (2000) *Libraries Without Walls 3: the delivery of library services to distant users*, London, Library Association Publishing.

Brophy, P., Fisher, S. and Clarke, Z. (eds) (2002) *Libraries Without Walls 4: the delivery of library services to distant users*, London, Facet Publishing.

Brophy, P., Fisher, S. and Craven, J. (eds) (2004) *Libraries Without Walls 5: the distributed delivery of library and information services*, London, Facet Publishing.

Irving, A. and Butters, G. (eds) (1996) *Proceedings of the First Libraries Without Walls Conference*, Mytilene, Greece, 9–10 September 1995, Preston, CERLIM.

2

Keynote address: Involving the customer in library planning and decision making

Susan McKnight

Introduction

There are many papers in this collection that provide a wealth of information and accumulated wisdom from the authors on the theme of evaluating the distributed delivery of library services. The reasons for evaluating service delivery are self-evident to this audience, and so do not need detailed explanation here. This keynote paper focuses more on the cultural issues, and the systems and processes that need to be in place to make evaluation worthwhile, rather than considering the evaluation of individual services.

Public, academic and special libraries provide services because of customers. Therefore, it makes sense to involve them in planning and decision making, so that the services provided meet their true needs.

Since the start of the Libraries Without Walls series of conferences, the emphasis has moved from the physical delivery of services to remote users to the focus being almost entirely on electronic services. These services are of benefit to all library customers, regardless of their physical location. However, it is important to remember that the services are for customers who may never – or only rarely – come to the physical library. Therefore, it is vital to remember that we should be providing services and solving problems for the disadvantaged and, by clever mainstreaming of those services, providing an improved service for all customers. The challenge is to identify the market segment – i.e. the users of distributed library services – and ask them what they need to be successful in their endeavours because of their interactions with the library.

The organizational culture

To involve the customer in library planning and decision making requires an environment where the customer is regarded as being at the centre of the service. A tangible way of doing this is to have clearly stated service statements or standards regarding what the library service will do on behalf of the customer, and to also spell out the responsibilities of the customer towards the service, including their role in improving it. However, although it is relatively easy to write a set of standards, it is very important to involve the customer in defining what ought to be included in the statements in the first place. At Nottingham Trent University, in the UK, we have just completed a drafting exercise to articulate service standards that reflect the 'hierarchy of values' as expressed by our customers, both students and academic staff. The values of the academic staff were identified and expressed in a hierarchy of importance, with 1 being the most important:

1 Easy access to materials where and when I need them
2 Comprehensive availability of relevant resources
3 Knowledgeable, friendly, accessible staff who help me
4 Proactive partnerships between academic staff and library
5 Inspiring environment which supports diverse needs
6 Opening hours that meet user needs
7 Managing multimedia and curriculum content
8 User-friendly loans policies and procedures
9 Good-quality, cheap photocopying and printing
10 Availability of reliable, up-to-date technologies and facilities
11 Timely, targeted training
12 Services clearly communicated to users.

These values were identified using the 'Customer Discovery' methodology developed and facilitated by an international consultancy, Enzyme International (see http://www.enzymeinternational.com/homepage2.asp), details of which are provided in the next section. Suffice to say here that the software used in the workshops provides a range of charts and graphs that indicate the relative importance of each value factor, and the impact of each on the overall 'hierarchy of value'. Similar charts are produced for the irritant values. Therefore, the data provided to library staff for the purpose of defining service standards are very informative.

For the customer-focused library service to be successful there needs to be a willingness on the part of staff to engage with customers and to actually listen to their perceptions, which are their reality. There are some clichés that need to be challenged: 'I know best'; 'We have done it like this for 20 years, therefore it must be right.' It is easy to make assumptions about the real needs and experiences of our customers, and we have to overcome this with a true engagement. The results of the Customer Discovery research, which uses a gap analysis approach whereby library staff vote on how they believe the customer will vote, certainly tests staff assumptions about how the library's services are perceived. A successful climate for service evaluation would involve a culture of continuous quality improvement, with innovation based on needs as articulated by the customer, rather than on the assumptions of library staff.

But who are the customers of the distributed library services? It is important to recognize that different customer segments have different drivers and experiences, so it is necessary to be clear as to which customers you engage with in the discovery process. For electronic library services we need to engage with the remote customers, not just those who are able to access the e-services from the physical library. Library services familiar with serving remote customers, for example academic libraries who have large numbers of distance education students, will understand that there is a staff culture that acknowledges and supports truly remote users, and this can be at odds with staff in the same library who service on-campus customers.

There also needs to be an unswerving commitment to actually do something as a result of customer feedback, unless management wants to encourage cynicism all round. There is no point in engaging with customers if there is no likelihood of changes being made as a result of the feedback. Therefore, the scope and focus of the customer discovery processes must be managed to ensure that there is a chance that improvements in service can be resourced and implemented.

Finally, on the issue of culture, management needs courage to focus on the real needs of the particular library service, rather than participating in regional/national/international benchmarking *per se*. Although there is certainly a place for benchmarking, which compares the same service criteria against similar library providers, the ranking information does not provide detailed information about what service improvements would actually benefit the library's customers the most. Some examples will explain: measuring the number of physical library seats available in a library per 100 customers may have no relevance if most of the customers are remote; in an academic library, measuring the number of library IT workstations per 100 customers may not provide meaningful information if the IT department provides public access resource rooms. Benchmarking the number of workstations may indicate sufficient provision, but if these are old, unreliable, and do not support relevant software applications the customers are not going to be satisfied.

Systems and processes

This section identifies some key systems and processes that need to be in place if the feedback from customers is to be maximized for their benefit. A brief description of customer value research is also provided, although a more complete description can be found in McKnight (2005).

Strategic and operational planning

There needs to be an overall framework that identifies the strategic directions of the organization, providing the long-term goals. This should reflect the commitment to providing excellent customer service. Ideally, the strategic plan is formulated with input from customer representatives, most likely at the Board or Library Committee level of the organization's governance. The operational plan identifies, on an annual basis, how the strategic plan is to be implemented. Included in the operational plan would be specific actions regarding obtaining customer input, and the follow-up analysis and implementation of changes as a result of the feedback.

Customer value research

There are a variety of ways and means of obtaining feedback from customers and there is no right or wrong way to do this. Customer value research, based on customer discovery workshops and interactive value modelling, is an ideal methodology for gauging customer satisfaction and feedback that can be used to directly inform operational planning. However, as indicated above, the results of this methodology cannot be used for direct comparisons with other library services.

Customer value research is predicated on a simple model or hierarchy of values. At one end of the spectrum the customer is angry. At the other, the customer is delighted by the unanticipated services that are available to them in their interactions with library staff, services and resources. In between, there are gradations of irritation and satisfaction based on the perceptions and needs of the customer. The hierarchy includes: Angry, Irritated, Frustrated, Basic, Expected, Desired and Unanticipated (Figure 2.1 overleaf).

In complex services sometimes we annoy customers and sometimes we delight. The total value is derived by taking away the 'irritation' factors from the 'delighted' ones and deriving a total score of 'value'. Using a simple example, a customer seeking information for an assignment may be irritated by an inconsiderate staff member who spoke off-handedly, but pleased that they were able to obtain the information they needed. The net value to the customer would be the 'value' of the information minus the 'irritation' of the rude staff member.

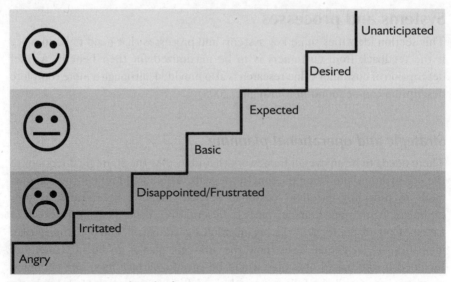

Figure 2.1   *Hierarchy of values*
Diagram reproduced with kind permission from Enzyme
International

Customer discovery workshops

The initial process involves conducting customer discovery workshops where customer groups (up to a maximum of 15 people) participate in facilitated
workshops. It may be appropriate to conduct workshops with different segments
of the customer base, as all groups have different needs and drivers. In the first
part of the workshops the participants identify and rate the irritants that they
perceive about the existing services. Then the participants are led through a
visioning exercise, where they are asked to imagine a time, three to five years on,
when they have been successful in their endeavours, and they are asked to identify what services, provided by the library, helped them achieve their success.
Wireless keypads are used to capture the customers' responses (votes) using
'Option Finder' technology. This exercise, through a prioritizing process involving forced pairing, leads to the identification of the services and resources that
are most valued. The participants are then asked to rate the current performance
of the library in delivering those identified services. This results in a hierarchy of
value elements and a gap analysis on perception of current performance, which is
later analysed to identify strategies to close the gaps. The gap analysis between
what is important and the customers' perception of current performance is very
useful. High performance on a lowly rated value factor might indicate over-ser-
vicing; poor performance on a highly rated value factor would be a priority area for
immediate remedial action to improve performance.

There is no leading of the customers as to what is important, as might be the case if they were asked to rank a standard set of services in order of importance. The customers describe their ideal service and the data collected at the workshop are captured in the customer's terminology, not library jargon. In the process, customers make suggestions for improvements by describing their future vision of success. This is very useful and often illuminating, as research indicates that customers do not compare our services with those of other libraries, but with those of bookshops, record stores, quick print services and coffee shops!

During the workshop, a small group of library staff observe the proceedings in silence. They also vote as to how they expect the customer to vote, thereby testing assumptions about what is and is not important. The gap analysis provided by 'Option Finder' is often revealing, highlighting that library staff are not always accurate in predicting the customers' perceptions.

One question that often arises is about the validity of the data. At Nottingham Trent University, in 2005, two customer research projects were undertaken. The Libraries and Learning Resources Division conducted customer discovery workshops with 60 students and 60 academic staff; the university conducted a Student Satisfaction Survey with over 3400 students. The key services identified (or hierarchy of values) were the same for both groups.

Decision making using interactive value modelling

After consolidating all the data from the customer discovery workshops, library staff who have been involved in the process come together in a final facilitated workshop to consider actions that would either reduce irritants and/or improve value factors. They estimate realistic improvement targets for the identified values and irritants and, using 'ithink' software, can plot the likely changes in customer satisfaction if the targets are reached. This process enables library staff and management to see whether the actions suggested will deliver real benefit to the customer, and this improves the quality of decision making.

It is not possible in this paper to fully describe the interactive value modelling exercise and the capabilities of the 'ithink' software. A more detailed description can be found in McKnight and Livingston (2003). This method of customer satisfaction modelling rates overall performance between positive 100 and negative 100. This is because the total value of all the irritants is subtracted from all the positive value factors. This does make the overall score more difficult to explain to stakeholders who are used to seeing a 'satisfaction rate' as a percentage, e.g. 70%. Using this model, a positive score of 30 is considered successful, as there will always be things that annoy the customer, however good the service is. The aim, over time, is to make sure that the irritant factors are not critical aspects of the service delivery.

The results of the interactive value modelling workshop are very high-level, and provide indicative data on which further consideration and planning must be based. An excellent way forward is to involve library staff from across the organization, as well as customer representatives, to work on detailed change strategies. For example, if loan policies were identified as a severe irritant, involving library staff from acquisitions, loans and reference services as well as a customer representative would bring a wealth of knowledge to the action planning exercise of reviewing the existing policies and recommending changes.

Library staff participate in this customer research, through active listening to workshop participants and providing an opportunity to follow up the issues raised; by seeking their analysis of the research findings as to what adds value for the customer and what are the irritations; and by their participation in teams established to define what change is required within the organization to deliver the customer value package. This creates an internal environment that is not only ready for change, but in which staff are driving the change from the ground up. Rather than being imposed by management from above, change is driven by the customer value propositions and the staff involved in implementing the change. In this way, there is a much greater chance of staff commitment and the change process, aimed specifically at delivering value to customers, is much more likely to be successful and sustained.

Communication and monitoring performance

Once library staff have analysed the customer research data and identified appropriate actions to either reduce irritants and/or improve value, it is very important to communicate the changes that are happening to customers, stakeholders and other library staff. It is also important to have systems and processes that enable regular monitoring, reporting and evaluation of performance against plans.

Service standards, as indicated earlier, should reflect the hierarchy of values from the customer's perspective. These can be published widely and performance against them communicated regularly to stakeholders and users. Whereas 'business as usual' activity is rarely articulated in operational plans, remedial actions or change strategies that are required to ensure compliance with agreed service standards to deliver on the customer value factors should be reflected there.

Individual staff performance reviews should be guided by the business imperatives articulated in operational plans and by the service standards. There should be an alignment, by cascading from the strategic plan at the top level through the library's enabling operational plan, and then to work group/team plans and on to the individual's performance planning objectives. In this way staff in all areas should be able to see how their daily activities contribute to customer satisfaction and the success of the library service.

A Library Committee which has customer representation can provide a formal channel for monitoring library performance against agreed plans. An annual report can be another vehicle for reporting on performance against standards. Less formal means include news articles in organizational magazines, a feedback website and targeted communications, including e-mail, to inform and engage customers and stakeholders.

Re-planning

Nothing remains the same. There is a constant need to evaluate actions and strategies, to check that the desired outcomes are being delivered, and that customers are receiving the basic and expected services consistently, and that some services delight and wow them. Having identified the customer value propositions through the discovery workshops, it is not necessary to undertake comprehensive workshops every year. Rather, experience indicates that an annual validation exercise, where the hierarchy of values and irritants is tested by way of an online survey, is all that is necessary.

Should new irritants or value factors be identified in the annual validation surveys, it would be necessary to undertake the complete customer discovery process again. This is to make sure that the hierarchy of values, which is reflected in service standards and operational and performance planning, is valid. Comparisons of two academic library services, one in Australia and one in the UK, that have used the customer value research methodology indicate that customer value propositions are very similar for the identical customer segments, whereas the hierarchy of irritants, despite including some similar concerns, reflects local situations (McKnight, 2005).

In an ideal world, library services would incorporate rolling surveys of customers to gain regular feedback on performance against the value propositions and the irritation index. The intention would be to minimize gaps between value and performance, to remove major irritations, and to match the level of resourcing and effort to the hierarchy of importance, such that low-valued (but yet still valued) services are provided with a minimum of effort or resources, and services that provide the greatest value are resourced appropriately to maintain customer satisfaction.

As indicated earlier, many different customer markets or segments are served by a library. Ideally, a library would undertake discovery workshops with a range of customer segments, to make sure that the value propositions are being addressed from the perceptions of the different customer groups.

The intention of the methodology outlined, coupled with a library staff culture of customer focus, is to strive for continuous quality improvement and innovation. Evaluation of services is undertaken so as to improve customer experiences, and to maximize efficiency and effectiveness.

Conclusion

Customer value research, which enables the customer to have a direct input into library planning and decision making, is used to improve library services. Using this methodology, planning is constantly informed by perceptions of current practices, and also by the aspirations and trends of the market. It is clear from the research that customers expect our services to develop more in line with commercial experiences they are having beyond the library, such as those provided by the large bookshop chains and online booksellers.

Having undertaken customer discovery research to identify the hierarchy of values, it might be easy to say, 'I could have guessed that' or 'I always thought that was so.' Rarely are there real surprises in the value factors. Library services are library services, after all! However, the confirmation of what is really valuable and the knowledge of the customers' perceptions of our services is a mighty management tool. The regular monitoring of performance against expectations and hierarchy of values enables close alignment of resources and services. Library staff can see how their services provide value, and they participate in the decision making about how to deliver on the customer value propositions.

Everyone benefits. Library customers have services and resources that help them achieve their goals; the library can demonstrate its value to stakeholders; library staff benefit from the praise that follows making customers happy. It becomes a self-perpetuating cycle of continuous improvement.

Professional associations are taking a lead in promoting the focus on customer experiences. Recently, the Australian Library and Information Association and CILIP, the Chartered Institute of Library and Information Professionals, published articles in their general association newsletters on this topic, perhaps reaching a wider audience than some of the scholarly refereed journals (Stanley, 2005a, 2005b; Brockhurst, 2005). IFLA (the International Federation of Library Associations and Institutions) promotes the concepts of evaluation, quality and performance measurement through its 'Quality Issues in Libraries' Discussion Group and various Sections' activities, for example the 2005 IFLA satellite conferences on Management, Marketing, Evaluation and Promotion of Library Services, sponsored by the Management and Marketing, Public Libraries and Library Theory and Research Sections (http://brgbib.bergen.folkebibl.no/ifla/), and the 6th Northumbria International Conference on Performance Measurement in Libraries and Information Services on The Impact and Outcomes of Library and Information Services: Performance measurement for a changing information environment, sponsored by the IFLA Statistics and Evaluation Section (http://online.northumbria.ac.uk/faculties/art/information_studies/imri/PM5/PM5.htm).

The papers from the Libraries without Walls 6 Conference will add significantly to the body of literature on this topic and provide a valuable resource to librarians who wish to evaluate the distributed delivery of library services.

References

Brockhurst, C. (2005) The Good, the Bad, and the Ugly, *Update*, **4** (7–8), 24–7.

McKnight, S. (2005) Customer Value Research. In *Management, Marketing, Evaluation and Promotion of Library Services Conference sponsored by the IFLA Management and Marketing, Public Libraries and Library Theory and Research Sections: papers*, http://brgbib.bergen.folkebibl.no/ifla/papers.html#26 [accessed 31 January 2006].

McKnight, S. and Livingston, H. (2003) So What do Customer Value Propositions and Strategic Planning have to do with Teaching and Learning? In *Educause in Australasia 2003: expanding the learning community, meeting the challenges, 6–9 May 2003, Adelaide*, Adelaide, Causal Productions.

Stanley, J. (2005a) Walk the Consumer's Journey: providing a rewarding experience for your customers, *inCite*, **26** (5), 6.

Stanley, J. (2005b) The Consumer's Journey, Step Two: journey of inspiration, *inCite*, **26** (7), 22.

3

Denmark's Electronic Research Library: evaluation of services through user surveys and usability tests

Bo Öhrström

Introduction

Denmark's Electronic Research Library (DEFF in Danish) is a co-operation organization for Danish reseach libraries. In early 2004 a new vision and mission formed the basis of a new strategy, and an action plan for 2004/5 was developed. DEFF's main target group is researchers, lecturers and students at institutions of higher or further education, and research institutions in the public sector.

One of the most important results of the activities over the years is the achieved level of library co-operation. All participants have learned to seek co-operation in areas such as operation and development in order to avoid duplicating work and to increase the value of individual efforts. An important area for co-operation is the evaluation of services through user surveys and usability tests, and these have been carried out for several years.

In the DEFF framework several evaluations examine the impact of electronic services on users, and this paper describes a large user survey from 2003 of three big Danish university libraries and usability tests of the websites of 11 of the biggest research libraries in Denmark.

The user survey exploits the European Customer Satisfaction Index (ECSI) model, which is a standardized instrument for measurement and can be used by different libraries across types and countries. At the same time it is a unique platform for benchmarking and a tool for prioritizing activities for improvement. It can even be used for comparison of results across libraries and other sectors (compared to banks, supermarkets etc.).

The usability tests of the websites of 11 of the biggest Danish research libraries are based on user interviews and user behaviour studies. Again the tests can give the individual university library important information about how to improve the value of the electronic library services to the users.

User survey and usability test co-operation

As mentioned above, one important area for co-operation is the evaluation of services through user surveys and usability tests. The specific reasons for co-operation are:

- Better exploitation of resources. There is increasing economy of scale in nearly all phases of the implementation of user surveys and usability tests. As an example, typically the libraries will get more value for money by co-operating on a standardized questionnaire with local adjustments.
- Better results. The libraries can demand a tailor-made product of higher quality, when the task reaches a certain size.
- Greater benefit from the results. For example, a rate of satisfaction of 67% does not contain much value unless it can be compared with the rate of satisfaction in similar institutions.
- Basis for extended co-operation. Co-operation in user surveys and usability tests can be a good starting point for benchmarking and for specific projects in the institutions with reference to the results. A poor result in a specific area can be improved with inspiration from the other libraries.

User survey of three libraries

Background to the user survey

In 2003 the Ministry of Culture asked the Danish National Library Authority (DNLA) to carry out a user survey of the ministry's three largest university libraries:

- The Danish National Library of Science and Medicine (DNLB)
- The State and University Library (SB)
- The Royal Library (KB).

The report containing the data analysis was finalized in July 2003 by two consultants, Anne Martensen and Lars Grønholdt of Copenhagen Business School (Grønholdt and Martensen, 2003).

The survey

There are several advantages in the method used: it builds on new methods and results in the area of customer and user surveys; it is a standardized measurement instrument, which can be used by different libraries across types (research and public libraries) and countries (Denmark, Sweden, USA, etc.); it is a unique platform for benchmarking and hence for quality improvement; and finally it is a tool to prioritize improvement activities.

The user survey was designed on the methods used in the ECSI, including the Danish Customer Index. The users in the survey were students, researchers/lecturers and external users. A questionnaire was distributed in March 2003, and the data analysis was based on both paper and online answers to the questionnaire. Completed questionnaires were received from the three libraries as follows:

- 404 users from the DNLB
- 620 users from SB
- 531 users from KB.

The model for library user satisfaction and loyalty

The model was developed earlier by Martensen and Grønholdt based on literature studies, focus groups among library users in a DEFF pilot project, and experiences from ECSI. The model is shown in Figure 3.1.

Application of the model gives answers to the questions: How satisfied and loyal are the users? and How are satisfied and loyal users created?

The model explains:

- The user's perceived value
- The user's satisfaction
- The user's loyalty.

It uses five determinants, each describing the user's library experiences, and in that way represents five quality dimensions (circled areas to the left). These determinants are:

- Electronic resources (electronic journals, search systems, databases, online catalogues, the library web, etc.)
- Printed material (collection of books, printed journals, etc.)
- Technical facilities (computers, printers, copying machines, etc.)
- Environment (atmosphere, design, opening hours, etc.)
- Staff service (staff skills, service, kindness, etc.).

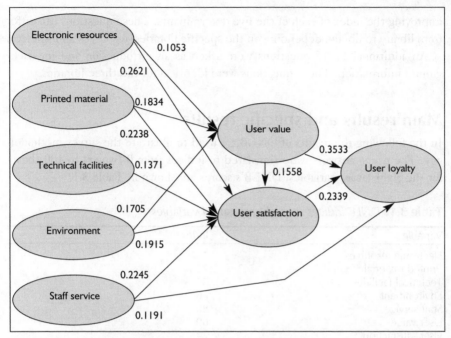

Figure 3.1   *User satisfaction and loyalty model (estimated model for DNLB)*

User satisfaction and loyalty depend on these five determinants and the perceived user value (user value, user satisfaction and user loyalty circled areas to the right).

The five determinants were identified in the above-mentioned DEFF pilot project. The eight variables (circled areas) are looked on as latent variables, which cannot be observed or measured directly. Every latent variable is made operational by two to three measured variables, corresponding to a total of 20 measured variables (i.e. 20 specific questions in groups of two to three). The numbers in each circled area indicate the index of the latent variable, i.e. the user's evaluation of the eight variables.

The arrows in Figure 3.1 illustrate the connections between the latent variables, and among other things they show how user satisfaction and loyalty are created. There are only arrows between variables where statistical analysis has proved a significant connection. The figure shows the estimated model and the specific numbers for DNLB.

The model is based on 20 generic questions, which allows the concrete estimation of the model and later comparisons between the libraries, and finally between the libraries and other branches.

An extra 42 questions were asked about the five determinants. The answers are used to choose which specific actions will have the biggest impact on improving the index of each of the five determinants. These questions can differ from library to library, depending on the specific libraries' resources and services.

An additional 11–12 questions were asked as an introduction and for background information. These questions were identical for the three libraries.

Main results and specific results

In the following the results of DNLB are used to illustrate the survey methodology. The users' answers were translated to indices from 0 (worst) to 100 (best) for the eight latent variables. DNLB's scores are shown in Table 3.1.

Table 3.1 *DNLB indices for eight measured variables*

Variable	Index
Electronic resources	71
Printed material	75
Technical facilities	77
Environment	76
Staff service	80
User value	69
User satisfaction	74
User loyalty	87

The trustworthiness of the results can be expressed by the fact that an index is estimated with a precision of $\pm$ two points. The indices show that the users express the highest score for staff service and the lowest for electronic resources.

These indices have been inserted in Figure 3.1 in the circles representing the variables, together with arrows having numbers that represent the calculated score of the connections between the variables. A score on an arrow specifies which effect a change of one point in a given index will have on the model's other indices.

The model shows that:

- User satisfaction is created in correlation between electronic resources, printed materials, technical facilities, environment, staff service and user value.
- User loyalty is created in correlation between staff service, user value and user satisfaction.

The explanatory power of the model is 66%, which fulfils the ECSI requirement of at least 65%.

As an example, it is possible to calculate the effect of an increase of one point in the determinant 'staff service' on user loyalty. An increase of one point in staff service will directly increase user satisfaction by 0.22 and directly increase user loyalty by 0.12. An increase of one point in staff service will indirectly, through user satisfaction, increase the user loyalty by $0.22 \times 0.22 = 0.05$, giving a total increase of $0.12 + 0.05 = 0.17$ in user loyalty.

The total effect of each determinant on user satisfaction and user loyalty can be calculated (Table 3.2).

Table 3.2 *DNLB effect on user satisfaction and user loyalty from five determinants*

Determinant	Effect on user satisfaction	Effect on user satisfaction (%)	Effect on user loyalty	Effect on user loyalty (%)
Electronic resources	0.2785	25.1	0.1024	18.9
Printed material	0.2524	22.7	0.1238	22.9
Technical facilities	0.1371	12.3	0.0321	5.9
Environment	0.2181	19.6	0.1113	20.6
Staff service	0.2245	20.2	0.1717	31.7

User satisfaction for DNLB is created as a reaction to:

- Electronic resources
- Printed material
- Staff service
- Environment
- Technical facilities.

User satisfaction is primarily created via electronic resources and printed material, although staff service and environment play a substantial role. Technical facilities play a minor role in the creation of user satisfaction.

User loyalty for DNLB is created as a reaction to:

- Electronic resources
- Printed material
- Staff service
- Environment
- Technical facilities.

In relation to user loyalty, the total picture changes from user satisfaction as staff service becomes the most central area. User loyalty is also created to a lower degree via electronic resources, printed material and environment, whereas technical facilities play a very minor role in the creation of user loyalty.

All these measurements can be used to prioritize quality improvements, and priority maps are the basic tools. The fundamental map is shown in Table 3.3.

Table 3.3 *Fundamental priority map*

High satisfaction	*Opportunities* 'Adjust resources'	*Strengths* 'Keep up the good work'
Low satisfaction	*Weaknesses* 'Observe position'	*Threats* 'Primary effort'
	Low importance	**High importance**

Every issue can be a:

- Strength – characterized by users attaching importance to it at the same time as they are satisfied by the library's performance
- Weakness – characterized by users not attaching any particular importance to it while at the same time being less satisfied
- Opportunity – characterized by the issue not being given particular importance, but the users are very satisfied
- Threat – characterized by the issue being important but the users not being particularly satisfied.

If the level of satisfaction is illustrated by the index value and the level of importance is illustrated by the specific effect of every variable, it is possible to draw up priority maps for user satisfaction and user loyalty. The map for user satisfaction (simplified without numbers on vertical and horizontal axes) for DNLB is shown in Table 3.4.

Table 3.4 *DNLB priority map for user satisfaction*

High satisfaction	*Opportunities*	*Strengths*
	Technical facilities Environment	Staff service
Low satisfaction	*Weaknesses*	*Threats* Printed material Electronic resources (71/25,1)
	Low importance	**High importance**

The map shows that DNLB's relative strength, in relation to user satisfaction, is staff service, and the threats are electronic resources and printed material, because their importance is high but their achieved index is low. Two areas are indicated as opportunities: technical facilities and environment. The next section shows that environment is a strength for user loyalty, so it is recommended that extra resources be allocated to this area in future. Technical facilities have a relatively high index, but the users attribute the area relatively low importance, so at the moment there is no reason to allocate more resources.

The map for user loyalty (simplified without numbers on vertical and horizontal axes) for DNLB is shown in Table 3.5.

Table 3.5 *DNLB priority map for user loyalty*

High satisfaction	*Opportunities*	*Strengths*
	Technical facilities	Staff service
		Environment
Low satisfaction	*Weaknesses*	*Threats*
	Electronic resources	Printed material
	Low importance	**High importance**

This shows that DNLB's relative strength is staff service and environment. For DNLB printed material is a threat, as the importance is high but the achieved index is low. Electronic resources are a weakness, and at the same time they are a threat to user satisfaction, for which reason it is recommended to prioritize this area together with printed material. Finally, technical facilities appear as an opportunity, but the importance is low with nearly no effect on the creation of user loyalty. Again, at the moment there is no reason to allocate more resources.

The specific actions concerning the selected areas for improvement are prioritized through analysis of the answers to the extra 42 questions. This enables the biggest impact to be obtained. A priority map for electronic resources in DNLB is shown in Table 3.6.

Table 3.6 *DNLB priority map for electronic resources*

High index	*Opportunities*	*Strengths*
	'Used in one total system'	'Internet guide is an efficient tool'
Low index	*Weaknesses*	*Threats*
		'Website is easy to navigate'
		'Website has relevant information'
		'Information about usage of electronic resources is understandable'
		'COSMOS is easy to use'
		'Adequate for my area of interest'
	Low relative importance for electronic resources	**High relative importance for electronic resources**

There is only one opportunity ('Used in one total system') and one strength ('Internet guide is an efficient tool'). There are five threats ('Website is easy to navigate', 'Website has relevant information', 'Information about usage of electronic resources is understandable', 'COSMOS is easy to use' and 'Adequate for my area of interest'). The threats should be attacked with more resources from DNLB to improve the index for the determinant electronic resources, and in that way improve user satisfaction and user loyalty.

Benchmarking

As mentioned earlier, the same questions are used to measure the eight variables in the model, and because of this the results can be used for benchmarking between the three libraries. Furthermore, benchmarking studies can be carried out between other Danish research and public libraries that have used the same model. If the model were to be used abroad, international benchmarking between libraries would be possible.

It is also possible to compare the satisfaction index with other ECSI satisfaction indices. The questions behind the library model are identical to those in the ECSI, including the Danish Customer Index. The loyalty index can also be compared with other ECSI loyalty indices. One loyalty question is identical with an ECSI loyalty question, whereas two differ a little but still allow valid comparisons.

Usability test of 11 libraries
Background for the usability tests

In the first half of 2004 DEFF financed usability tests of the websites of 11 of the biggest research libraries in Denmark. The project was managed by two consultants, Jens Sandberg Madsen and Julia Gardner from *UNI.C Usability* and documented in the report 'Det brugervenlige digitale forskningsbibliotek, Best practice rapport baseret på usability test of 11 store forskningsbibliotekers websteder' (Gardner and Sandberg Madsen, 2004).

The aims of the project were:

1 To prioritize the presentation of services on the libraries' websites through empirical research. The structure and functions of the research libraries' websites will be examined for their fulfilment of the users' expectations and needs. Furthermore, it shall be determined how the students' and the researchers' usage of the different resources can be improved.
2 To build up usability competence in the libraries researched. The consultants will assist the library staff with planning, carry out activities and analyse the

results. In a learning-by-doing workflow usability competencies are developed in the library staff.

3 To maintain the local usability competence. The project is designed in a way to encourage repeated evaluation and tests of the libraries' websites. A web forum is set up for continuing knowledge exchange.

The following describes the activities carried out in order to achieve the first aim.

All libraries allocated two or three members of their staff for the project, and in total 28 students, 23 researchers and four other users of the libraries participated. All were regular library users from different disciplines, with different levels of experience and age.

The methodology in the usability test was user interviews and user behaviour studies. The consultants and the library staff carried out five test sessions of 1½ hours each in every participating library.

All participating users had to work with a series of standard tasks and some local tasks for the individual library. Standard tasks could be omitted if the library did not provide the actual electronic service.

The workflow in a test session was initiated by a welcome session, where the aims for the test and the group's roles were presented. Afterwards users were interviewed about personal facts and their normal use of the library. The result was that some of the users' normal tasks were identified, and they were added to the prepared standard and local tasks. In this, they ensured that the user would not have to undertake tasks that were never performed in daily life. The actual testing was based on the think-aloud method, where the users' considerations and reactions were studied. Dialogue was allowed, but help was not. At the end, an interview was used for clarification and summary.

The overall aims for usability tests were:

1 Research in design. Does the product's content, structure and presentation correspond to the users' expectations and needs? Is navigation and searching functioning according to the users' wishes?
2 Research in usability and relevance. Do the users find that the product makes a difference in daily life? Does the product supply the users with new possibilities, and to what extent are special services used?

The conclusions centred on three challenges for digital research libraries:

1 Research libraries are not the only providers of information. Google is a significant competitor to the digital libraries, as it offers a complete and easily used entry for all queries. The simple user interface sets a standard for information

retrieval which is difficult to copy easily in other systems. Both students and researchers are big users of Google.

2 Electronic resources are not exploited efficiently. Users value electronic resources very highly, and the usage has increased every year. Users want to search at article level, but the large number of bibliographic databases with unclear content and different search interfaces confuses them. Fewer interfaces (or one) for article searching would improve the users' outcomes. The libraries' efforts in providing online help do not seem to be of much assistance.

3 The users do not know that their search results are not exhaustive. Most users are satisfied if they simply receive results. They are not aware, for example, that they could improve the results through subject-specific entries. Training, news and information campaigns will not have the expected effect when the users' problems start with inadequate construction of the user interface.

These observations resulted in recommendations for the design of the user interface. Two major recommendations were:

- Closer integration of website and catalogue to allow the user to shift seamlessly between tasks
- Fundamental tasks, such as ordering material, renewals, access to electronic journals, change of e-mail address, etc., should be possible in the catalogue.

Summary

The evaluations show that digital libraries have progressed far in recent years and extended their borders remarkably. However, there is still a long way to go to the seamless, personalized, digital library, and new competition to the research library changes the users' views on and requests for the library's services. User surveys and usability tests are indispensable tools for the guidance of libraries in their struggle to keep and possibly extend their role in the global information scene.

References

Gardner, J. and Sandberg Madsen, J. (2004) *Det brugervenlige digitale forskningsbibliotek, Best practice rapport baseret på usability test of 11 store forskningsbibliotekers websteder*, www.deff.dk/content.aspx?itemguid={82D05DC8-469A-44EB-96F1-04934A6A1903 [accessed 31 January 2006].

Grønholdt, L. and Martensen, A. (2003) *Brugerundersøgelse af universitetsbiblioteksfunktionen på Det Kongelige Bibliotek*, Statsbiblioteket og Danmarks Natur- og Lægevidenskabelige Bibliotek, www.bs.dk/content.aspx?itemguid={832D6A24-4DB1-454D-8C42-5A2A70C41A81 [accessed 31 January 2006].

4

Beyond the guidelines: assessment of the usability and accessibility of distributed services from the users' perspective

Jenny Craven

The concept of 'universal design' is not a new one. Organizations and individuals have become much more aware that the provision of accessible electronic information makes not only good ethical sense but also good economic sense. The issue has been driven further forward as a result of current and emerging disability legislation (for example the Disability Discrimination Act in the UK), which requires organizations and service providers to ensure equal access for all (or at least to take reasonable steps towards this).

Advice on assessing of the usability and accessibility of services is widely available. In the field of web accessibility, probably the best-known organization is the World Wide Web Consortium (W3C), whose Web Accessibility Initiative (WAI) provides a comprehensive set of guidelines and checkpoints to help ensure that websites embrace the concept of 'design for all'. These are available in a number of categories, covering guidelines for the accessibility of Authoring Tools (ATAG), User Agents (UAAG), and probably the most well-known: the Web Content Accessibility Guidelines, or WCAG. It should be noted that at the time of writing version 1.0 of the WCAG was still in use, and therefore has informed the findings reported here.

The WCAG Checkpoints are divided into a number of priority and conformance levels to help people assess the accessibility of their websites:

- Priority 1: A web content developer must satisfy this checkpoint. Otherwise, one or more groups will find it impossible to access information in the document. Satisfying this checkpoint is a basic requirement for some groups to be able to use web documents.

- Priority 2: A web content developer should satisfy this checkpoint. Otherwise, one or more groups will find it difficult to access information in the document. Satisfying this checkpoint will remove significant barriers to accessing web documents.
- Priority 3: A web content developer may address this checkpoint. Otherwise, one or more groups will find it somewhat difficult to access information in the document. Satisfying this checkpoint will improve access to web documents. (www.w3.org/TR/WCAG10/)

Priority levels are further defined by a level of conformance:

- 'A': all Priority 1 checkpoints are satisfied
- 'A-A': all Priority 1 and 2 checkpoints are satisfied
- 'A-A-A': all Priority 1, 2, and 3 checkpoints are satisfied. (www.w3.org/TR/WCAG10/)

Many organizations and institutions are adopting the WCAG and related documents as a benchmark for assessing the accessibility of their online services. In the UK, for example, the Cabinet Office e-Government Unit's *Guidelines for Government Websites* state that all UK government websites should, as a minimum, adhere to Priority 1 and 2 levels of the WCAG (version 1.0) (i.e. A-A compliant).

Accessibility can be assessed by a number of methods, such as those suggested by W3C on their Evaluating websites for accessibility page (www.w3.org/WAI/eval/). Having established the scope of the evaluation, these could include:

- Semi-automatic and automatic testing (using validation tools and accessibility evaluation tools)
- Manual evaluation using relevant checkpoints from the WCAG
- Usability testing of features (include people with different disabilities, technical expertise, users of assistive technology, etc).

Automatic accessibility evaluation tools are a popular way of assessing the accessibility of websites because it can be done quickly and often free of charge (Cynthia Says and WAVE are free online checking services). But this is only part of the process: the results can often be misinterpreted, and will not provide the whole picture in terms of accessibility. This was demonstrated in a formal investigation undertaken in 2004 by the Centre for HCI Design for the UK Disability Rights Commission, which evaluated the accessibility of websites for people with disabilities. One of the findings, identified by a panel of disabled users, was that the majority of problems experienced could not be checked using an automated checking tool, and therefore 'automated tests alone do not predict the experience of disabled people when using websites' (Disability Rights Commission, 2004).

Although widely used, the WCAG have often been criticized for being difficult to implement and even difficult to understand (although W3C is currently working on this to produce a second and more user-friendly version of WCAG). With this in mind, some individuals and organizations have decided to take a more holistic approach to web accessibility, rather than relying on existing guidelines and recommendations. One example described by Kelly et al. (2004) outlines broad issues for consideration, such as 'the purpose of the website, interoperability, cultural and resource issues' as well as usability and accessibility issues. The focus is to take a more pragmatic approach to accessibility rather than trying to achieve the 'holy grail' of W3C A-A-A compliance.

The W3C does, however, provide an important framework for ensuring accessible web design, development and assessment, and should be used to inform new developments rather than producing completely separate guidelines on accessibility and checking methods. This has been the focus of an EU Web Accessibility Benchmarking Cluster (a 'cluster' of three EU-funded projects) working together and in close liaison with the W3C/WAI to develop a harmonized European methodology for evaluation and benchmarking of websites: the Unified Web Accessibility Evaluation Methodology, or UWEM. The work will be based on the existing WCAG 1.0 guidelines and will be developed iteratively, involving evaluations with:

- potential users of the methodology (e.g. website developers, accessibility experts)
- users of websites (including people with disabilities) to cross-validate the checklist
- W3C/WAI and other public authorities (see www.wabcluster.org/).

As well as involving users in the development of the UWEM, the methodology itself will include a section on user testing protocols. This emphasizes to anyone considering or preparing to undertake web accessibility assessment that, whether they are using the WCA guidelines or other approaches, it is important to involve users and take into consideration their requirements.

This paper will now move on to consider a number of user-based studies and to describe how users are involved in the continuous development of one of the 'cluster' projects: the European Internet Accessibility Observatory (EIAO).

Findings from user-based studies have identified some interesting insights to web accessibility and usability that might have been overlooked if relying solely on automated or expert assessment. Abels et al. (1999) report on a two-part project to identify and implement user-based design criteria in websites. The user-based design gathered user input at three different times in the process.

The process began with information gathering to determine the criteria for the design process. Data were gathered through task-related information seeking and usage behaviour of a group of users. A focus group session was also run over half a day where the group used decision-making software to brainstorm and rank their ideas about positive and negative website features. Additional information from the task-related process was also gathered. The process identified 33 positive features and 18 negative features, which were grouped into six major criteria in order of importance:

* Use
* Content
* Linkage
* Structure
* Special features
* Appearance.

Another study, the Non-Visual Access to the Digital Library Project (NoVA) (Craven and Brophy, 2003), involved a group of sighted users and a group of blind users, who were asked to perform the same set of web-based tasks for comparison of user behaviour. They were observed by a facilitator and asked to provide a think-aloud protocol while performing the tasks. Pre- and post-task questions were asked in order to reveal what the users thought of the sites visited, how satisfied they were with the tasks performed, what they liked and disliked about the sites, problems encountered, and how they felt about the overall experience of using the web to find the information required of each task. The findings of this study highlighted the problems caused by poorly designed websites, and in particular the fact that people accessing the web using assistive technologies experienced greater problems, and in particular those using screen-reading technology. It also showed that where good training and support had been provided, people had a much better and more successful overall experience.

In their formal investigation of web accessibility the Disability Rights Commission (2004) tested 1000 websites using a software tool, then compared the results of detailed evaluation by 50 users with a variety of impairments. The study evaluated users' attempts to perform set tasks with assessment criteria of ease of use and success of outcome. Users also participated in focus groups and interviews to explore accessibility and usability issues further. A controlled study of six websites was also undertaken by groups of blind users and non-disabled users to assess the difference between the effects of inaccessible design and of the impairment. Focus group discussions concentrated on how people use the web, what they find useful, the variety of problems they encounter in accessing websites, and the problems associated with the assistive technology they use.

The study identified 585 accessibility and usability problems. The most reported problems relating to the WCAG checkpoints were as follows:

- Checkpoint 1.1: Provide a text equivalent for every non-text element.
- Checkpoint 2.2: Ensure foreground and background colour combinations provide sufficient colour contrast, etc.
- Checkpoint 6.3: Ensure pages are usable when scripts etc. are turned off, and if this is not possible provide an alternative.
- Checkpoint 7.3: Until user agents allow users to freeze moving content, avoid movement in pages.
- Checkpoint 10.1: Until user agents allow users to turn off spawned windows, do not cause pop-ups without informing the user.
- Checkpoint 12.3: Divide large blocks of information into more manageable groups where natural and appropriate.
- Checkpoint 13.1: Clearly identify the target of each link.
- Checkpoint 14.1: Use the clearest and simplest language appropriate for a site's content.

As a result of these findings the DRC recommended that the WCAG should 'provide better coverage of information architecture and navigation design issues in relation to accessibility', addressing in particular elements relating to the problems identified above (DRC, 2004, 47–8).

The EC-funded European Internet Accessibility Observatory (EIAO) has been exploring user requirements as a way of informing the development of a user-driven automated web accessibility tool. The initial findings have confirmed the importance of gathering users' requirements and perceptions of accessibility in order to look beyond the guidelines to provide an insight into web accessibility. The remainder of this paper describes the project and reports on the user requirements gathering process and results.

The EIAO is a three-year project co-funded by the European Commission, under the Information Society Technologies Sixth Framework programme (running from September 2004 to August 2007). The project aims to contribute to better e-accessibility for all citizens and to increase the use of standards for online resources by establishing a technical basis for a possible European Internet Accessibility Observatory (see www.cerlim.ac.uk/projects/eiao/). The 'Observatory' will consist of the following elements:

- A set of web accessibility metrics (WAMs) based on the WCAG 1.0 checkpoints (with a view to conversion to version 2.0 when appropriate)

- An internet robot (ROBACC) for automatically and frequently collecting data on web accessibility and deviations from web standards (i.e. the WAI guidelines)
- A data warehouse (ROBACC DW) providing online access to collected accessibility data.

Alongside the technical project partners, the Centre for Research in Library and Information Management (CERLIM) is leading two work packages relating to user requirements and user testing, which will be used to inform the technical development of the project and will also feed into work carried out in collaboration with the two other EC-funded projects (Ben-To-Web and Support-EAM) and in co-ordination with the World Wide Web Consortium Web Accessibility Initiative (W3C/WAI) with the aim of developing a unified website evaluation methodology.

User requirements were gathered from groups of users identified as those who might experience problems accessing the web. This could include people with disabilities, people using alternative devices (e.g. mobile phones), people whose first language is not English (but who have to access English-language sites), or people with a limited or slow connection. The project focused mainly on people with disabilities, although some were people using English-language sites whose first language was not English.

A mixture of qualitative and quantitative data was gathered to obtain a clear picture of perceptions, experiences, opinions and ideas. The data were gathered through a questionnaire and then follow-up interviews with a selection of respondents. Quantitative data included questions relating to disability, demographic data, and questions that required users to choose a frequency or rank a list of suggestions, for example asking users how often they use the internet: frequently, quite often, not very often, or very infrequently. They were also asked to rank potential problems with accessibility, for example whether missing ALT text was a serious problem, a minor problem, or no problem. Qualitative data were gathered from open-ended questions such as asking users what they liked about a website, what they disliked and the main barriers faced. After data analysis, follow-up interviews were conducted, picking out interesting and relevant themes and topics raised by users for further investigation.

Analysis of the questionnaire data showed that keyboard access (shortcut keys, tab navigation and/or keyboard navigation) was the most frequently cited accessibility problem experienced by the participants:

> Have to navigate using keystrokes when the page is designed to be navigated using the mouse. Have to listen to links, headings etc. one at a time rather than scrolling down to relevant link.

This was followed by problems with either lack of ALT text or poor use of ALT text:

> Moving away from no ALT text to inappropriate ALT text – e.g. file names, etc. Another good example is a Customer Services telephone number displayed as a graphic with the ALT text as 'Customer Services telephone number'! 'Click here, Click here – no good when using the links list in JAWS.'

Participants also cited problems relating to the organization of the page:

> Too many layers of pages in a site make it hard to find the information you want, tracking the information, etc. Not logical.

> Pages sometimes are too big so that you have to keep scrolling down and down.

And an inability to navigate the site:

> Navigation is a problem when using the in-built magnification because you can only view about two lines at a time.

> Nav buttons not in the same place and too small.

Also poor use of mark-up (e.g. titles and/or headings) for web pages:

> Title of page doesn't always correspond to what you have retrieved. You think the site should be about one thing, but the contents are something else.

> If each page is given a title it makes it much easier to know where you are in a website.

Other problems mentioned were confusing use of language, such as acronyms and abbreviations that are not fully explained; problems using multimedia; slow download times and having to download software; and being unable to personalize pages.

Participants indicated that they felt excluded from a number of elements found in web pages. The most frequently cited was images, followed by multimedia and forms. In the follow-up interviews participants talked about problems accessing FLASH, PDF and JavaScript, as well as specific problems associated with filling complex online forms when using a screen reader. Some participants also indicated problems using English-language websites when English was not their first language.

Regarding ways of improving accessibility, the most frequently cited suggestion (from a list of possibilities) related to the organization of the page or site ('a clear design with menus'); this was followed by the use of mark-up, such as titles to help inform the user about the content of the page; and forms that are easy to complete. Interestingly, although keyboard navigation and ALT tags were the most frequently cited problems, they were not the most popular suggestion for improving access.

In the questionnaire and interviews, participants were encouraged to raise any other accessibility issues that had not already been covered. Typical responses related to slow download times when not on broadband, and having to register on some websites before being allowed to access the information. Participants were also asked to talk further about specific websites they liked or disliked, and again they cited problems relating to page organization; navigation; use of text; lack of or inappropriate ALT text; incompatibility with their software; form filling; use of colour; and poor use of titles and headings. Interestingly, some of the websites identified were cited as both good and bad examples by different participants: this again demonstrates the diversity of user needs, perceptions and opinions.

As well as providing data on user requirements, the study also compared the problems identified by the participants with the WCAG checkpoints and priority levels. The purpose of this was to enable informed decisions to be made about which elements for checking should be made a priority for the first release of the software. The analysis revealed that a greater number of priority 2 and 3 checkpoints (as illustrated in Figure 4.1) could be linked to the problems identified by participants. Further comparison with the study conducted by the DRC (2004) show similarities with the problems identified in this study – in particular that fewer priority 1 checkpoints were identified as accounting for the problems reported.

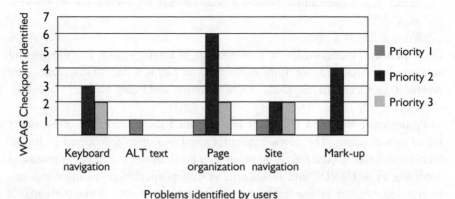

Figure 4.1   *Relevance of problems identified by users to WCAG 1.0*

The fact that more accessibility issues can be related to priority levels 2 and 3 of the WCAG (version 1.0) (as illustrated in Figure 4.2) suggests that there are differences between real users' needs and their perceptions of accessibility, and the formal recommendations such as those produced by the WCAG.

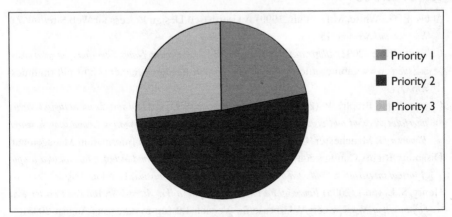

Figure 4.2   *Problems identified relating to WCAG 1.0 priority levels*

It is also interesting to note that in a recent document published by the W3C (Henry, 2005) designed to help organizations develop a business case for web accessibility, a list of WCAG checkpoints that 'directly increase usability to all users' is suggested, only one of which is a priority 1 level checkpoint, the majority being priority 2 (five suggested checkpoints) and 3 (seven suggested checkpoints).

The first iteration of user requirements gathering for the EIAO study was conducted on a relatively small scale, therefore the resulting analysis does not necessarily mean that those checkpoints not identified as relevant should be discounted, or that any significant statements should be made about the relevance of WAI guidelines and checkpoints in relation to responses in the study. It simply provides an initial picture of end-user requirements and their perceptions of accessibility, which can be fed into the development of the European Internet Accessibility Observatory and the development of the UWEM.

These results have, however, demonstrated how involving users can provide a broader picture of the accessibility of services delivered via the web, and shown the importance of looking beyond the guidelines towards what people really want from a web-based service. Once awareness of the diversity of user needs is increased there will be a greater understanding of the need for a more flexible and pragmatic approach to the design, delivery and assessment of distributed services.

The author wishes to express grateful thanks to all the participants who took part in the questionnaires and follow-up interviews.

References

Abels, E. G., White, M.D. et al. (1999) A User-based Design Process for Web Sites, *OCLC Systems and Services*, **15** (1).

Cabinet Office (2002) *Illustrated Handbook for Web Management Teams. Guidelines for government websites*, www.cabinetoffice.gov.uk/e-government/resources/handbook/html/htmlindex. asp.

Craven, J. and Brophy, P. (2003) *Non-Visual Access to the Digital Library: the use of digital library interfaces by blind and visually impaired people. Library and Information Commission Research Report 145*, Manchester, Centre for Research in Library and Information Management.

Disability Rights Commission (DRC) (2004) *The Web: access and inclusion for disabled people. A formal investigation conducted by the Disability Rights Commission*, London, DRC.

Henry, S. L. (ed.) (2005) *Financial Factors in Developing a Web Accessibility Business Case for your Organisation*, www.w3.org/WAI/bcase/fin. Version 1.0 (up-to-date as of August 2005).

Kelly, B., Phipps, L. and Swift, E. (2004) Developing a Holistic Approach for E-Learning Accessibility, *Canadian Journal of Learning and Technology*, **30** (3).

World Wide Web Consortium (1999) *Web Content Accessibility Guidelines*, www.w3.org/ TR/WCAG10/.

5
Online services versus online chaos: evaluating online services in a Greek academic library

Emmanouel Garoufallou and Rania Siatri

Introduction

In recent years Greek academic libraries have moved from providing only traditional services to the provision of hybrid services, keeping a balance between traditional and electronic services. The financial support that Greek libraries received from the European Commission (EC) assisted them in employing electronic services to meet the demands of our information society. Currently some academic libraries are undergoing the process of assessing their new electronic services in order to evaluate their use and improve their efficiency. One such is the Central Library of the Higher Technological Educational Institution of Thessaloniki (ATEI-T). This paper presents the outcome of an ongoing independent study carried out during 2005 by the Deltos Research Group, which aims to investigate user satisfaction with online library services and accessibility issues relating to library websites.

Community support framework programmes for Greek libraries

The process of modernizing library services began in 1996, when Greek academic libraries participated in the Second Community Support Framework (SCSF) programme and its special Action of the Operational Programme for Education and Initial Training (EPEAEK in Greek: www.epeaek.gr). Before the SCSF programme, libraries' lack of information technology (IT) and electronic information resources (EIR), qualified staff and financial resources hindered their efforts to provide adequate services. In addition, the existing teaching and learning methods inhibit library development, and university structures and processes often act as barriers to new ideas and influences introduced by a few professional librarians (Krikelas, 1984; Birk and Karageorgiou, 1988; Skepastianou, 1993; Keller, 1993; Zachos, 1995; Garoufallou, 2003; Garoufallou and Siatri, 1999).

The SCSF programme aimed to modernize and develop library services and establish new IT-based services, to automate library functions, to enrich their collections, to complete retrospective cataloguing, and to increase the number of qualified personnel. New studies show that Greek academic libraries, with support from the SCSF programme, have managed to overcome many difficulties and move towards a more electronic environment (see, for example, Garoufallou et al., 2004).

Nowadays, Greek academic libraries participate in the Third Community Support Framework (TCSF) (second EPEAEK), which runs from 2000 to 2006. The programme focuses on developing portals, digital libraries, digitizing collections, and improving services based on the EIR.

Higher Technological Educational Institution of Thessaloniki (ATEI-T) and its library

The institution

The ATEI of Thessaloniki was established in 1970. It is the second largest ATEI in Greece, consisting of five faculties: Agricultural Technology, Business Administration and Economics, Food Technology and Nutrition, Health and Medical Care, and Technological Applications. In total there are 25 departments, with more than 20,000 students. There are 450 academic staff and over 1000 full-time (FT) or part-time (PT) non-permanent academic staff with fixed-term contracts, and 230 administrative staff. The main campus is located in the area of Sindos, Thessaloniki. Since 1999 ATEI-T has established three new campuses in three different towns and regions (Nea Moudania, Kilkis and Katerini), each housing one department.

The library

The library of ATEI-T was established in 1974. Today it has approximately 30,000 volumes and 250 printed journals. The library operates with 12 members of staff, eight of whom are librarians, three administrative staff and one computer scientist. The SCSF has had a great impact on the library since it assisted in the establishment of new services based on new technology, such as the electronic reference desk and the index ArxeionWeb. In seven years the number of holdings has doubled, and currently four librarians and the computer scientist work under the EPEAEK programme. Moreover, the library now provides an IT area with 15 PCs available for booking, two of which provide access to the library OPAC and 13 to the internet, although students do not have access to word processors. At institutional level each department has its own computer laboratories, used mainly to support classes. The absence of drop-in centres negatively affects the use of electronic library services. There are 9369 enrolled users, of whom 3047 used the library at least once between 1 January and 30 June 2005.

The library established a website in 1999 (www.lib.teithe.gr) and revamped it in spring 2004. By using its website as a platform, the library moved traditional services to the electronic environment, developing new electronic services and improving the existing ones based on IT. The library now provides access to its OPAC, databases, electronic journals (approximately 3500), an online reference desk and an index called ArxeionWeb. In addition, it works on the development of tools for user education.

It is worth at this point paying extra attention to the online service ArxeionWeb, which is the first of its kind in Greece. ArxeionWeb indexes articles from Greek scientific journals held by the library. The project began in 1998 and the index became available to users in 1999. In 2000, the software was upgraded with an easy-to-use interface and IP recognition. In order to enrich the database, librarians input bibliographic data from Library and Information Science (LIS) students' dissertations on indexing. So far 13 journal titles have been indexed, and the library aims to index all 45 Greek journal titles to which it subscribes. It is worth noting that the service is heavily used by users from public libraries, especially the Public Library of Thessaloniki.

The library and the TCSF programme

The ATEI-T library participated in the TCSF (second EPEAEK) with a budget of 1,424,000 euros. The object of this was:

- to establish a digital library environment by upgrading the library OPAC, organizing web resources, developing ArxeionWeb, and providing online information regarding the curricula of different departments
- to further develop the reference services by developing services for users with disabilities, and by developing services targeting mainly off-campus users
- to expand online user education programmes and support staff training in IT and electronic services
- to market the library's services via its website, by publishing materials and organizing a conference on library assessment

- to assess library services
- to enrich the library's collections and create special and short-loan collections.

Study on user satisfaction by Deltos Research Group

Deltos Research Group is a non-profit organization established in 1993 by information professionals. It is the only information and library science research group in Greece, and aims to:

- develop research in LIS
- publish Greek LIS materials such as books, as the bibliography is limited
- participate in research projects
- provide consultancy services to libraries, museums, information centres and other organizations
- organize seminars, workshops and other activities for Greek information professionals.

Part of Deltos' activities is a research project that investigates the use of and user satisfaction with online services in all three central libraries of the universities of Thessaloniki. In this paper we present the preliminary results of the survey that involved the library of ATEI-T. The survey was conducted between January 2005 and May 2005 and 314 questionnaires were distributed, 84 to academics and 230 to undergraduates.

The first part of the study was concerned with the use of library services. This study showed that, of the 84 academics, three used the library services weekly by visiting the library, 31 of them monthly and 30 rarely (once or twice per year). None of the academics used online services on a weekly basis from their own office or a remote PC, whereas 38 used them on a monthly basis and 26 used them rarely. It is worth noting that of the 84 academic staff, 20 (23.8%) never used the library and did not participate any further in the research. The majority of the academics mentioned that they encountered problems when using online library services, electronic information resources (EIR) and information technology (IT). Only a few of them who were involved in research projects felt that they did not encounter any problems when using IT and EIR. Of the 230 students, 29 used the library services on a weekly basis by visiting the library, 53 monthly, and 108 rarely. None of the students used online services on a weekly basis from a laboratory, their own PC or an internet café; seven used them monthly and 24 rarely. Of the 230 students, 40 (17.4%) never used the library. Students who used online services stated that they encountered many problems because their training was inadequate. However, the majority of students, users and non-users of online services indicated that they knew how to use and search the web via a search engine, and do so on a regular basis, thus indicating a preference for the web over the library. Unfortunately, this indication was also recorded for the academic staff.

The most popular online services among both academics and students, in order of preference, was the OPAC, followed by the electronic journals, online databases and the ArxeionWeb. As indicated earlier, the use of these services is low. The survey showed that 37 users used the library OPAC monthly (all students and the majority of academics), and 19 used the electronic journals monthly (the vast majority were academics). Two typical quotations illustrate user attitudes towards online services and librarians. Academic 63 stated that 'if I want something I ask librarians to fetch it for me . . . there is not a need for me to use electronic services'; student 141 mentioned that 'reference librarians usually find the required information for me'. Both comments make it clear that users prefer to ask librarians to retrieve the required information, rather than taking the time to learn and use the online services. Some users commented on the frustration they felt when using online services and EIR. Three typical quotations illustrate this: academic 57 said that 'we are deserted in an electronic environment'; student 29 said that 'neither the institution nor the library provides points of access in order to use EIR', stating clearly what users need in order to access the library's online services. Finally, a comment from academic 16 raises the problem of inadequate training on online services: 'Whatever I have learned, I learned it by myself. I believe the library is building online services and at the same time is building "walls" around them in order for users not to use them. Librarians tend to abandon what they build in electronic form.'

It is worth mentioning that the study indicated that students prefer both online and hands-on training, whereas most academics feel reluctant to attend a training course organized by the library, preferring to use online training materials.

Evaluating the library's online services

From the survey, we identified four online library services that users preferred using most often. These were the library OPAC, the electronic journals, the databases and the ArxeionWeb service. Users were asked to evaluate each in terms of reliability (whether the information provided is reliable), ease of use, accessibility and stability (is the service stable and accessible at all times?) and finally usefulness (how useful is the service for each user?). Users marked their answer on a scale from 1 to 5, with 1 being most dissatisfied and 5 being very satisfied. All users had made use of these services at least once. Table 5.1 provides the average score for each service on each issue. In each row the first number is the average score of academic staff and the second is the average score of students.

Table 5.1 *Evaluation of online services by academic staff and students*

	OPAC	E-journals	Databases	ArxeionWeb
Reliability	3.81 (academics)	4.18	4.09	2.54
	2.00 (students)	4.36	4.36	3.96
Easy to use	2.81	3.36	3.27	2.09
	1.86	1.96	2.16	2.16
Accessibility/Stability	4.81	4.72	2.09	2.63
	1.93	4.56	2.00	4.43
Usefulness	4.90	4.83	4.80	4.72
	4.90	4.10	3.90	4.90

Some general observations from Table 5.1 are: a) the academic staff have a more positive view of the library's online services; b) all services have a low average score in this evaluation process; and c) all users believed that these online services are very useful, with the OPAC scoring 4.9. Both groups of users believed that all online services were difficult to use, with the OPAC and the ArxweionWeb scoring lower than the other two services. The majority of users felt that the difficulties they experience were derived from lack of training. It was indicated earlier that users felt that the library developed online services without taking their needs into account. This is a source of frustration and disappointment to users, as student 91 stated: 'I do not want to use online services . . . each time I feel incapable of doing a simple job and that's very annoying.' Moreover, students felt that the OPAC interface was not simple, and the web page with the searching tools contained too much information, which is confusing for users.

Users believed that the OPAC could not be regarded as reliable as in many instances the same search provided different results. Following up this intriguing result and investigating the subject further, we concluded that many users, especially students, confused the web searching tools with the OPAC searching tools, as the web search box is next to the OPAC search box. Often users do not pay attention to whether they use the web or the OPAC search box, and as a consequence the results can be confusing. Another point worth mentioning is that students stated that the OPAC was not an accessible service (score 1.93), based on the fact that the library provides only two PCs with access to its OPAC and that there are no computer laboratories available for students at the institution. It is evident that this can cause disappointment. On the other hand, academics believe that the service is accessible (score 4.81), as they access it from their own desks. Both academics (score 2.09) and students (score 2) believed that online databases are not an accessible and stable service. Commenting on this issue, they said that databases are not 'always available for use', and that the library does not 'always provide access to the service'. Thus, some users stated that the library does not pay any attention to this service because it provides 'only a few databases that do not cover the subject areas of all faculties'. These negative comments are derived from the fact that the renewal of subscriptions for a small number of databases was delayed for two months at the beginning of 2005. However, the library failed to inform users that some databases were not available at the time, and as a result many users continued their attempts to access them unsuccessfully, experiencing feelings of confusion and frustration: 'the library does not value both users and the online services'. It became obvious that removing this service from library's website, and at the same time failing to inform users, in many instances damages the credibility of the library.

Accessibility issues relating to the library website

The Deltos Research Group tests libraries' websites in order to propose ways of improving their accessibility and effectiveness and to increase the value of online services. The evaluation is in two parts: evaluating the website using five criteria; and using the evaluation tool WebXACT from Watchfire.

Evaluation using five criteria

Five criteria were selected to test the website: the aim (whether the website has a clear aim), the content (check various issues concerning the website content), the precision in syntax (grammar), its currency (how current are the web pages) and its accessibility (e.g. navigation of website). The evaluation took place in May 2005, and showed the following:

1 Aim: the website has a clear and distinctive aim, presenting a brief description of its main objectives and its mission.
2 Content: the content is satisfactory in general. The website uses a mix of Greek and English languages. Unfortunately, sometimes English terms are used in Greek sentences, especially in online training tools. Moreover, web pages such as the OPAC use both Greek and English terms in a way that confuses the user. Furthermore, many broken internal links were found.
3 Precision in syntax: a very satisfying outcome as the website demonstrated the correct use of grammar with no spelling mistakes.
4 Currency: unfortunately many pages are not updated regularly. For example, the databases' web page had not been updated for 464 days, the home page for 43 days, and the pages in English, French and German had not been updated since 2001, having retained the previous design of the website.
5 Accessibility: the website has good navigation and uses adequate navigation tools. On the negative side, the web pages in other languages do not work; there is no text-only option, and no alternative description for images.

Evaluation with WebXACT

WebXACT is a free online tool from Watchfire (webxact.watchfire.com) that tests single pages of web content for general, quality, accessibility and privacy issues. It uses four accessibility test options: the Section 508 (www.access-board.gov/sec508/guide) and the W3CWCAG (W3C Web Content Accessibility Guidelines) A, A-A, and A-A-A compliance (www.w3.org). For the purpose of this study we used the W3CWCAG-A-A-A compliance guideline. From the survey we identified the four most visited pages of the library's website: the home page, the OPAC, the electronic journals and the databases. Using WebXACT, we scanned these four pages in order to identify and report information on general issues (e.g. information concerning the total download size, the last update and a metadata summary); quality issues (e.g. content defects such as broken links and spelling errors, search and navigation and page efficiency); accessibility issues (e.g. provides a report according to W3CWCAG with priority 1, 2 and 3 automatic and manual checkpoints); and privacy issues (e.g. information about visitor tracking).

The data were collected during May 2005 using WebXACT. In the space available we have quoted only a small fraction of the data in order to illustrate some key issues, presenting a general report for all four pages. The evaluation shows that 35 broken links were identified in all four pages. None of the pages examined provided metadata descriptions, and there were missing elements of alternative (ALT) text in all pages. Moreover, in all pages the last updates were rather dated, varying from 43 days for the home page to 464 days for the databases. It has to be said that the system found errors and warnings in all four pages. Table 5.2 provides the report of accessibility issues according to W3CWCAG-A-A-A compliance with priority 1 (the most important errors and warnings), 2 and 3 (less important) automatic and manual checkpoints.

Table 5.2 *Report of accessibility issues of the library's web pages*

	Errors	Warnings
	Automatic/manual checkpoints	Automatic/manual checkpoints
Priority 1	10/44	48/213
Priority 2	19/92	129/292
Priority 3	13/75	67/81

From Table 5.2 it becomes apparent that in the most regularly used library web pages many errors and warnings were recorded. Nevertheless, it has to be acknowledged that the most vital accessibility issues are those of the priority 1 errors, which in this case are fewer. When it came to priority 2 errors, the majority were encountered in the web pages of the OPAC and electronic journals. Finally, in priority 3, less important accessibility errors are recorded; the home page had 49 warnings.

Conclusions

It became evident from this study that the Greek educational system and the academic environment do not support the use and the advancement of libraries. However, libraries have managed to overcome most of the difficulties they have faced over the years in moving to an electronic environment. The ATEI-T library obtained extra funds from the CSF and was given the opportunity to demonstrate a capacity for rapid development of the library services based on IT and electronic information resources. These new services were evaluated in this study.

The study indicated low use of online services by students as much as by academics. The users in many instances expressed feelings of dissatisfaction and frustration when using the services, which derive from a lack of knowledge on how to use them. It has to be said that the library does offer user education, but apparently needs to promote these sessions more effectively and also to provide leaflets to act as a reference point for first-time users. Additionally, paying attention to detail can prove most rewarding. For example, at the time of the study users did not have access to some of the databases because the subscriptions had expired. This resulted in users ranking the reliability of this service as very low. A simple warning message on the database web page would have made all the difference for the users, and consequently for the library, as it would have scored much better in the evaluation. Use of the WebXACT tool recorded a number of errors and warnings in all W3CWCAG priority levels. However, this is also an issue the library can overcome very easily.

This evaluation is one of the first of its kind in Greece; it has demonstrated that the library provides remote access to services via its website without properly taking into account accessibility issues. This has a snowball effect, as it increases the number of problems the library encounters and creates dissatisfaction among users, affecting the reliability of these services and making users feel more reluctant to use online services in the future. A lot of work needs to be done in the provision of electronic services in order to increase user satisfaction ratios and to enable users to access the services more frequently. There is a need for a constant effort to regain the trust of users. These problems cannot be solved in a day, but need to be worked on within the frame of the strategic plan for the development of online services.

We believe that the library has to take into account the following issues in order to improve accessibility and enhance the provision of online services: it has to develop a strategic plan concerning the development of its website and online services; it has to employ its website as 'a service of services', and not as a storage device for housing services; all institutional stakeholders need to be involved and to use the results from recent evaluation projects as a tool to further the development of online services; finally, the library must design a more effective promotional campaign for its services and invest in user training.

Disclaimer

The views expressed in this chapter are those of the authors and do not necessarily reflect, or even agree with, the official policies of the institution for which they work.

References

Birk, N. and Karageorgiou, D. (1988) Academic Libraries in Greece: a new profile, *Libri*, **38** (2), 81–93.

Garoufallou, E. (2003) *The Impact of the Electronic Library on Greek Academic Libraries and Librarians*, PhD thesis, Manchester Metropolitan University, Department of Information and Communications.

Garoufallou, E. and Siatri, R. (1999) The Impact of Information Technology on Greek Academic Libraries and Librarians: preliminary results. In Clapsopoulos, G. and Hagiala, N. (eds), *Organisation and Collaboration of Academic Libraries in the Digital Age, Proceedings of the 7th Greek Conference of Academic Libraries*, Volos, University of Thessaly Library, 49–67.

Garoufallou, E., Siatri, R. and Hartley, D. (2004) Virtual Learning Environments and Greek Academic Libraries. In Brophy, P., Fisher, S. and Craven, J. (eds), *Libraries Without Walls 5: the distributed delivery of library and information services*, London, Facet Publishing, 66–75.

Keller, D. H. (ed.) (1993) *Academic Libraries in Greece: the present situation and future prospects*, New York, Haworth Press.

Krikelas, J. (1984) Academic Libraries in Greece, *International Library Review*, **16** (3), 235–46.

Skepastianou, M. (1993) *Promotion of Preservation and Conservation in Greek Libraries with Special Reference to the Education of Greek Librarians*, PhD thesis, University of London.

Zachos, G. (1995) University Libraries in Greece: the present situation, *Alexandria*, **7** (3), 155–69.

6

The Hellenic Academic Libraries Consortium (HEAL-Link) and its effect on library services in Greece: the case of Aristotle University library system

Claudine Xenidou-Dervou

About HEAL-Link

The Hellenic Academic Libraries Link (HEAL-Link) was established in 1998. It began as a project funded by the Ministry of Education (with part EU funding) as a horizontal action aiming to promote co-operation within the academic library community in Greece. One of the action lines was to study possible co-operation between the academic institutions to face the problem of the ever-increasing cost of subscriptions to print journals. Until then, the academic libraries dealt with this problem by cancelling more and more subscriptions every year.

A study undertaken in 1999 in three disciplines (physics, chemistry and computer science) in five universities proved that the journal collections of the corresponding departments were so limited that they could not support most of the research areas or the graduate study programmes of those departments. With a very limited national journals collection, academic libraries depended heavily on interlibrary loans from abroad, mainly from the British Library, with a high cost which they passed directly to the users. Thus, most researchers who could not themselves finance their need for journal articles were dependent mainly on requesting them from colleagues abroad. It goes without saying that most Greek academic libraries, in their effort to sustain their journals budgets, had hardly any subscriptions to bibliographic databases.

As a result the aim to co-operate in print journals collections was abandoned and replaced by the effort to co-operate in common access to electronic journals. In 1999 HEAL-Link signed a three-year licence agreement with five major publishers for access to all their journals , as well as a small number of bibliographic databases. For the first three years the academic libraries were obliged to keep their print subscriptions with the above-mentioned publishers, while HEAL-Link covered the access fees. Thus all members of HEAL-Link had access to 3500 full-text journals and to 12 bibliographic databases, which was a vast improvement over the previous situation.

In 2002, at the end of the three-year period, the eight institutions having the vast majority of the print subscriptions could no longer sustain the cost of the subscriptions to the five publishers, and HEAL-Link had no more funds from the horizontal action to support the access fees. The Council of Rectors of Greek academic institutions accepted the proposal of the steering committee to move to electronic only by aiming to sign as many licence agreements as possible and cancel all print subscriptions to the corresponding publishers. For archive reasons one print copy would be deposited at the National Documentation Centre. It was decided that the cost would be distributed according to an algorithm that is more or less the same as that used by the Ministry of Education to distribute funding to academic institutions. A committee of rectors visited the Ministry and asked for the budgets of the institutions to be top sliced at Ministry level and the amount to be given to HEAL-Link to cover the cost of the licence agreements. The Ministry decided not to further cut the budgets of the already under-funded institutions and provided extra funding to cover the budget of HEAL-Link. So in 2003 HEAL-Link signed agreements with 12 major publishers and its members gained access to about 8000 journals. In November 2004 the Ministry agreed to continue funding of HEAL-Link for the next three years, until December 2008.

According to the Greek constitution, higher education in Greece must be public. Today there are 22 universities in Greece and 15 technology educational institutes (TEIs). Also members of HEAL-Link are the 18 research institutes of the General Secretariat for Research and Development of the Ministry for Development, the National Library, the Academy of Athens, and a small number of publicly funded research institutions from other ministries. Two of the academic institutions, namely the University of Athens and the Aristotle University of Thessaloniki, are by far the oldest and largest. In fact, of the 22 universities these two have half the student population and half the number of academic staff.

Aristotle University library system: the past

Aristotle University of Thessaloniki (AUTH) has 43 departments in almost every discipline, from medicine, science and engineering to law, philosophy, theology, education, theatre, cinema, etc., and its library system is a librarian's nightmare. There is one central library and 45 departmental libraries. Most departments have their own library, and some departments in the school of philosophy have more than one, whereas the School of Medicine, which is the largest in the university, with 700 faculty members, has one very small library. The central library has a big reading room with 1000 seats, runs the union catalogue and controls the journals budget. The central library committee decides how the journals budget will be allocated between the different departments, and the departments decide which journal subscriptions they will keep. All journals are delivered to the central library; once they are checked into the system they are distributed to the departmental libraries. To make things worse, the departmental libraries are not under the administration of the central library but belong to their departments. So most departments have their own library committee and the departmental libraries act totally independently of each other. Apart from some basic rules, such as using the union catalogue, Library of Congress subject and classification scheme and MARC21 for cataloguing, they are free to run their libraries as they wish. As a result they have different opening hours, different checkout rules for the books, different library identification cards, etc. Until two years ago, students could borrow books only from their own library (if they could at all). Getting a book from another departmental library was considered an interlibrary loan (many libraries were unwilling to lend books to other than their own students). Obviously the level of service varied greatly from library to library, and with the exception of a very small number of science libraries the profile of the library system was very low. The users basically had no expectations from the libraries. Most of the undergraduates never used them, as they receive one book per course they attend free of charge. Incidentally, it should be mentioned that students at Greek universities do not pay tuition fees.

However, even the dysfunctional environment described above is a vast improvement from that before the 1980s, when there were no libraries and the books and journals were gathered in professors' offices. This still happens more or less in the School of Medicine even today. It would make managerial sense to combine similar libraries together – e.g. the five libraries of the Science School could become one – but the departments are afraid of losing control and are dead against any such mergers.

Although Aristotle University had and still has the largest collection of print journals in Greece (about 2500-3000), this is not enough to cater for the diversity of subjects of the different university departments and the journals are scattered around 60 different locations. In 1997 the library had a huge deficit in its journals' budget and hence the science, medicine and technology departments saw their budgets cut by half. As an example, the physics department went from 200 subscriptions to 54 in just one year. Thus HEAL-Link was a relief for researchers in the university, and although the library did not conduct a marketing campaign, its use was mostly spread by word of mouth. By 2002 Aristotle University was the heaviest institutional user of HEAL-Link. When in 2003 a large number of the print journals were cancelled and replaced with electronic ones, and the number of HEAL-Link e-journals increased from 3500 to 8000, no-one complained.

Aristotle University library system: the present

In 2002 the universities were asked by the Ministry of Education to submit proposals for funding (partly EU money) to upgrade their library services. Aristotle University grasped the opportunity to do what was virtually impossible to do physically: to unite the library services. The proposal was focused on providing the following services:

- Electronic reference and interlibrary loans
- Electronic course packs
- Electronic dissertations
- Digitization of special collections
- User training
- Continuing the retrospective conversion of the special collections of the central library
- Offering a unified environment for all e-resources (federated searching)
- Uniting all services under one library portal
- Creating guidelines common to all departmental libraries
- Introducing the concept of subject libraries.

The group that would realize these services under the guidance of a co-ordinating committee of four departmental librarians (supervised by the chairman of the library committee) was made up of about 30 librarians who were hired in 1997 and had spent five years doing cataloguing and retrospective conversion of the university collections. Training those librarians in group work and introducing them to the concept of the services that were about to be created was the biggest challenge. For most of them the job of a librarian was to carry out perfect cataloguing. There needed to be a shift in their priorities from technical services to user services. Extensive training was provided by colleagues from abroad, and although most of the librarians rapidly became familiar with the new technologies, several of them were not convinced that the new services would be used and would be of value to the users. The librarians were divided into seven work groups, each having to realize one of the action lines above.

Common guidelines

One of the most time-consuming tasks was the simplest: to create guidelines for operation that would be enforced and followed by all departmental libraries. All departmental librarians were invited to take part in the committee that would prepare the first draft of the guidelines. Once again, it was proved that human beings prefer to complain instead of getting involved to make things happen. The committee that was formed worked for almost a whole academic year to finally compromise on a common draft. This was submitted to the central library committee for approval and then was sent to the Rector's office. Finally, a year and a half later, the guidelines were approved by the governing body of the university, so that they became a rule and had to be enforced. As a result, today a student receives a library card from one of the libraries that gives them the same privileges at any library in the university. There are common rules for lending the books, so that the users will no longer be confused, and all departments must make at least one-third of their collection available for lending. The fines, charges for photocopies, interlibrary loans (ILL) and any other services are now common around the campus. As all libraries do not offer the same array of services, the concept of the subject library was introduced and one of the existing libraries was appointed to act as subject library with the obligation to offer services beyond their own department. So far, three such subject libraries are in operation: one at the Science School, one at the School of Economics, Business and Law, and one at the School of Philosophy. All of them depend on the new central library services to offer support and infrastructure. Although common operating rules are a very old concept in most if not all libraries abroad, creating them was one of the most difficult tasks, because it had to change the status quo of decades and involve all levels of university administration. Undergraduate and graduate students are very pleased with the new developments, as they were the ones with the most problems in obtaining access to other departments' libraries.

Electronic reference service

The next most difficult task was the creation of electronic reference services. Aristotle University chose to subscribe to QuestionPoint by OCLC, and because we were one of the first users we had several technical problems to solve, and still do. But the most difficult aspect was not the electronic part of the service but rather to create a reference service that until then had not existed as such. As mentioned above, the university library system had a very low profile and was not established as the place to turn to for information needs (with the exception of a few departmental libraries). It took some time for the librarians in the working group to familiarize themselves with the resources, both print and electronic, of the university and to feel confident enough to answer reference questions. Also, it takes time to change the very low image of the library and build a relationship of trust with the users; the signs, though, are very encouraging.

Electronic course packs

For electronic course packs the university decided to choose Blackboard as the software platform (after an international tender). This was a totally new concept for the university. Some professors had personal home pages with information for their students, but most were still dependent on the traditional style of teaching. The work group had a difficult task indeed, first to inform the academic community, market the concept, train the professors and support the users. Today about 200 different courses are on Blackboard, with about 3000 registered users (students). Although there is still a long way to go, it is steadily spreading among faculty members. Many more professors are willing to use it to supplement their teaching, but their usual comment is that they do not have the time to prepare the material for the courses online.

Electronic dissertations and digitization projects

Creating a database of electronic dissertations and our digitization project have been two of the least problematic action lines. Human interaction with users is less in both work packages and the problems were mostly technical. The software chosen was CDSware, developed by CERN, the Nuclear Research Institute in Switzerland. The guidelines of the Open Archives initiative were followed from day one, and MARC21 and Dublin Core were chosen for the metadata. Today 566 dissertations are online. The support of the university administration was very important for the success of this work package, as the university made it mandatory for doctoral candidates to submit their dissertations to the central library in electronic format.

The same software was used for our digitization project, the aim of which was to digitize 20 years' worth of clippings from Greek newspapers and magazines, with articles of literary criticism of Greek authors. The project will complete within its timeframe (until 2006) and provides the university library with valuable experience on digitization. Based on this experience, the library submitted a proposal to the Ministry of Culture for funding for the digitization of two collections of the School of Philosophy, both involving manuscripts of modern Greek authors, and a special collection of the central library with artefacts and books dating from the 15th century. The proposal received funding and the new project is under way.

These projects are very important, not only because they brought to light the collections of the School of Philosophy that had not been accessible until then, but also because they help the humanities faculty and students to change their attitude towards electronic resources. Up to that point, HEAL-Link had not had much to offer the humanities, so these users had not become familiar with the new electronic environment. The digitization projects are changing this attitude. Finally, equally important is the fact that material in the Greek language will become available on the internet, whereas until now most (if not all) of the material had been in English. This is very important for the preservation of our culture and language. Apart from the library's digitization project funded by the Ministry of Culture, two more projects have been funded by the university. It was very gratifying that both called for technical support, training and consultation from the library. So the image of the library services is changing and the library is becoming a trusted party on campus.

User training in federated search

Since 2003, when the university cancelled its subscriptions to the print journals that are now accessed electronically through HEAL-Link, the library has been able to subscribe to more electronic resources to better support the different disciplines, mostly the humanities. Today the academic community has access to over 10000 electronic journals and a significant number of bibliographic databases. It is becoming difficult not only for the users, but even for the departmental librarians, to know where to search to find the information on demand. Even though a work package has been established that provides training in the use of library services, either in the central library or on location around campus, the number of users attending the courses is very small and does not seem to have increased during the past two years. The work group is therefore trying to find alternatives by preparing online tutorials, simple guidelines, etc. It very soon became clear that federated search software was needed, so that the users would not be confused or disappointed and turn away from the library portal. The software chosen was MuseGlobal, so that the users could take advantage of the library's electronic resources and seamlessly search the library catalogue, the e-journals, the bibliographic databases, and the databases that are created locally.

Library portal

All the above virtual services operate under the umbrella of the library portal. The portal is supported by a work group of two librarians who try to satisfy the needs of all those whose work is represented. They have also recently completed an A–Z list of all journals, both electronic and print, that the university has access to, either through HEAL-Link or by its own funds.

It should be mentioned that all the work packages receive technical support from a group of three computer experts, who have been successful in dealing with a number of challenging technical tasks over the past two years. The most important problem has been the implementation of the Greek character set in the software that was purchased or used. This is much more complicated than it sounds, and things become even more difficult as support is not offered locally but, in most cases, from the USA. Even the difference in time zones made things slower than anticipated.

Conclusion

Today, two-and-a-half years after the project for creating new library services began, the academic community of Aristotle University of Thessaloniki has equal access to all libraries on campus and can obtain services wherever they are. Even though there are still discrepancies between the quality of services provided by the departmental libraries, users can access equal services using the virtual system through the library portal. The library system that was operating according to the standards of the past century and was decades behind the developments of libraries abroad until three years ago, has now taken a huge leap into the 21st century. This would have been a disaster if the users had not been using HEAL-Link for their information needs since 1999. Not only did this give users the opportunity to become familiar with online library services, it also provided the whole Greek academic community with an information foundation to stand on and to expand to new services. Without the electronic resources provided by HEAL-Link, any other service would not attract users as it could not satisfy their information needs.

Further reading

Xenidou-Dervou, C. (2001) Consortial Journal Licensing: experiences of Greek academic libraries, *Interlending and Document Supply*, **29** (3), 120–5.

Xenidou-Dervou, C. (2003) Moving from Print to Electronic: a survival guide for Greek academic libraries, *Serials*, **16** (2), 145–52.

7

Information seeking in large-scale resource discovery environments: users and union catalogues

Richard J. Hartley

Introduction

Union catalogues have been part of the library scene for many years, during which there has been renewed interest as a result of the emergence of the networked environment. This paper presents the results of a study of the use and users of union catalogues which was undertaken as a part of a larger study of interoperability between physical and virtual union catalogues in the UK (http://ccinterop. cdlr.strath.ac.uk). The research sought to improve our understanding of the way in which people searched union catalogues, and to discover something of their preferences and expectations.

The paper reports the aims of the research, the methods used, and some of the results achieved. The results and their implications are then discussed.

Background

The context of this research was a project to investigate the feasibility of linking the physical union catalogue COPAC with the virtual union catalogue, the so-called clumps, which have been developed in the UK over the past decade. The project was known as CC-interop (COPAC, clumps interoperability) and full reports can be located at http://ccinterop.cdlr.strath.ac.uk. COPAC is a physical union catalogue of 27 national and university libraries which was developed and maintained at the University of Manchester (http://copac.ac.uk). It was created by a process of record merging, which has been described elsewhere (Cousins, 1997). Various virtual OPACS have been created in the UK using Z39.50 technology to enable simultaneous searching of one or more OPACs. The clumps relevant to this project are CAIRNS, the Cooperative Academic Information Retrieval Network for Scotland (http://cairns.lib.gla.ac.uk); InforM25, the virtual union catalogue of the London region (http://www.m25lib.ac.uk); and RIDING, the virtual union catalogue of the Yorkshire region (http://riding.hostedbyfdi.net/riding.indexhtml). The research reported here was undertaken by CERLIM, alongside technical investigations undertaken by the CC-interop partners, and concentrated on user behaviour and attitudes to union catalogues. Using recorded searches, interviews and focus groups it complemented earlier questionnaire-based investigations undertaken by Stubley and others (Stubley and Kidd, 2002).

Methods

The research used three types of data collection undertaken by the libraries of the universities of Leeds and Strathclyde, and at the London School of Economics:

- Paid volunteer searchers undertook a number of searches on two different union catalogues which were recorded using screen logging software.
- The searchers were interviewed about their search experiences and their requirements of union catalogues.
- Three focus group discussions were conducted with library staff in which their views about searchers' use of union catalogues, their own use of union catalogues, and their views on the development of union catalogues were explored.

The searches used manufactured but realistic queries which replicated several search types identified for us by the Project Advisory Group. These were:

1 A search where the user needed to find a common item in a library close to them (to ascertain whether libraries were selected before carrying out the search)
2 A search where the user was given a lot of information about a book or a journal (to observe which search option was selected)
3 A search where the user needed to find an obscure or unique item, or an item for which they had been given partial information, such as a possible author name, or part of a title or subject (to observe the strategies employed by the user to locate the item)
4 A general subject-type search (which may give a large results set).

Using data from a COPAC search log and personal experience, real query statements were created. These were presented as mini-scenarios, as shown below.

You urgently need to get hold of a copy of *Clinical Medicine* edited by Parveen Kumar and Michael Clark. You need to get the most up-to-date edition you can find in the nearest library.

You are doing some research into monasticism and are interested in books on monks behaving badly. Someone has told you about a book that was published some time in the late 1990s. They aren't sure of the title, but think that the author might be Justice or Jestice.

A full list of the queries used can be found in either Booth and Hartley (2004) or Hartley and Booth (2006).

Scandinavian research has suggested both increased use of simulated work tasks and their validity in this type of research (Borlund, 2000; Vakkari, 2003).

The 34 volunteer searchers were academics, researchers or postgraduate students; all performed four searches: two each on COPAC and the local 'clump'. Different searchers received the queries in a different order and undertook searches on the different systems in a different order, to minimize the impact of any possible learning effect.

Searchers were not given any training prior to undertaking their search tasks, but were allowed to explore both union catalogues prior to searching. There was no time limit on the task and the decision to terminate the search rested solely with the searcher. They were asked to spend as much time on the search as they would do in a 'real world' situation. Reasons for stopping were that:

- the searcher was satisfied that the appropriate search result had been achieved
- the searcher was not satisfied but did not want to proceed further
- the searcher was not able to proceed further
- the searcher was fed up and wanted to go to the next task.

Immediately after searching, all the searchers were interviewed about their experience, exploring:

- search options used, and why
- whether the 'select libraries' feature had been used
- ease of understanding the retrieved results
- error messages and feedback from the service
- search problems faced
- ease of system use
- satisfaction with the search and the search session
- features liked or disliked with the union catalogues used

- general feelings about services used
- previous use of union catalogues.

In addition, data were collected from three focus groups of librarians at each of the universities. The groups ranged in size from eight to 12, and consisted of both professional and semi-professional staff with experience and responsibilities in both technical and user services. Focus groups were used for this rather than interviews, because it was expected that as knowledgeable users their comments would generate informed discussion and hence more valuable data.

Results

A selection of the results is presented here, starting with demographic data concerning the searchers, followed by outcomes from the searches, the interviews, and finally the focus groups.

Table 7.1 *Profile of volunteer searchers*

Gender			FT	PT
	Female	20		
	Male	14		
Age groups	21–30	19		
	31–40	4		
	41–50	5		
	51–60	5		
	61–70	1		
Occupations	Postgraduate (education)		1	
	Taught Master's student		4	3
	Research student		9	2
	Research staff		8	2
	Academic staff		3	1
	Admin staff		1	
Subject	Accounting and finance	2		
	Archaeology	1		
	Biology	1		
	Counselling	1		
	Economics	3		
	Education	5		
	English	1		
	Environmental science	2		
	Genetics	1		
	Information management	1		
	Linguistics	1		

Continued on next page

Table 7.1 *Continued*

	FT	PT
Marketing	2	
Media and communications	1	
Medicine	1	
Neuroscience	1	
Philosophy	1	
Politics	2	
Psychology	3	
Sociology	3	
Statistics	1	

Table 7.1 shows that the searchers spanned a range of subject specialisms, ages and academic types, whereas Table 7.2 demonstrates the predominance of use of search engines over 'traditional' resource discovery tools. There was an almost complete lack of awareness of the concept of union catalogues among the volunteers.

Table 7.2 *Volunteer searchers' use of electronic resources*

Internet search engines	
Every day	28
4–5 times a week	1
Once or twice a week	5
Bibliographic databases	
3–4 times a week	3
Once or twice a week	13
Every other week	6
Once or twice a month	5
Less than once or twice a month	6
Haven't used any yet	1
Online library catalogues	
Every day	3
3–4 times a week	3
Once or twice a week	15
Every other week	6
Once or twice a month	4
Less than once or twice a month	2
Never	1

The searches were examined for:

- features used
- whether users selected libraries to be searched or used the default
- whether help pages were accessed
- search options chosen
- the number of attempts per search

- whether the search was abandoned
- common errors.

Research in an operational environment is at the mercy of system changes, and unfortunately major changes were made to the RIDING system soon after data collection, thereby rendering analysis of use of that system pointless. Therefore, the results refer only to CAIRNS, COPAC and InforM25. Fuller results are presented in the complete report and in Hartley and Booth (2006). However, it can be noted that:

- out of 228 searches, 30 were abandoned without getting results
- numerous spelling errors occurred, some of which were not noticed and some of which produced results, for example Econimics, Bryon, Liguistics, Parlement, Shapespeare
- in all systems considerable use was made of the facility to restrict a search to specific libraries
- the CAIRNS Refine search option proved popular
- the COPAC Help feature was well used, as was the ability to restrict output to English-language material
- the InforM25 Map was well used
- in searching for books, there was almost equal use of author, title and ISBN as search criteria
- in searches for periodicals, there was most use of ISSN followed by title
- different searchers used a wide range of search criteria, both singly and in combination.

Turning to users' comments about union catalogues, the most obvious feature was the impact of Internet tools, in particular Google and to a lesser extent Amazon. For example, one searcher commented: 'I would like to see something a bit like you get on Google, where you can . . .'

There is now an expectation that search tools will be easy to use, as typified by the comment: 'If I cannot learn to use a search tool very rapidly then users would go to Google or Amazon', or 'If I can't get the hang of what I am doing in the first half an hour then I'd reject the package and look for something else.'

In addition, there was also some interest in greater information about book content, which presumably results from experience with Amazon. Evidence of the requirement for a rapid system response was provided by the number of abandoned searches.

Although there were occasional exceptions, most searchers were unwilling to wade through a large number of retrieved items. They reported various means of dealing with large numbers of hits including:

- narrow search
- find out more about topic then try again
- give up and use the web instead.

Information professionals may believe that progress has been made in screen design, but users still report problems with onscreen language. Examples quoted included:

- Miniclumps
- Holdings
- Tag
- Z39.50
- Anything (COPAC search option).

Finally, it was very obvious that users do not like the presence of duplicate records in search output – fortunately, they do not have to develop matching algorithms to remove genuine duplicates and only genuine duplicates!

Turning to the findings from the focus groups, it was no surprise to find that librarians were well aware of the concept of union catalogues and quoted a range of tools that stretched far beyond those used in this project. They also expressed limited trust in the outcome of searches – in the case of a physical union catalogue because of problems associated with maintaining currency, and with virtual union catalogues a mistrust of the efficacy of Z39.50 searches. Their views on user awareness of union catalogues validated our decision to exclude undergraduates from our research, as exemplified by the comment: 'I would say that I don't think students are particularly aware, but some researchers might be.'

The librarians believed that researchers use union catalogues either for known item location or for the acquisition of bibliographic details. Librarians in London did not think researchers would travel outside London to gain access to material; in Strathclyde it was felt that they would travel within the Scottish urban belt; and in Leeds there was the belief that academics would travel to access material.

In discussions about the need for union catalogues the view was expressed that union catalogues of serials are the most important, followed by catalogues of rare books – though there was no agreement on what was meant by a rare book. There was no enthusiasm for subject-based union catalogues and limited interest in regional union catalogues. Finally, there was little evidence in these focus groups of concerted efforts to either market union catalogues or to raise awareness of their existence. The exception was LSE, where there were posters and bookmarks promoting InforM25.

There were numerous constructive comments about features wanted in union catalogues. These included:

- ability to sort by date
- ability to sort by title and by author
- ability to place own library first
- ability to sort geographically
- ability to link search output to interlibrary loan software
- ability to pass search results to reference management software.

Comments and observations

The COPAC usage data show that there is clearly a demand for union catalogues, though of course it is currently insignificant compared to the use of search engines. However, this does raise the question of how much greater that use could be if there was a greater awareness of these tools among potential users. This emphasizes the need for a concerted effort to market union catalogues, and indeed other resource discovery tools, to their intended audience.

It is apparent that designers of resource discovery tools such as union catalogues need to take greater account of users, their expectations and their use of language. There thus needs to be a review of language to remove jargon from screens, responses need to be speedy, and there needs to be an on-screen indication to users when query processing is taking place.

The enthusiasm for a serials union catalogue reinforces the recent investment in the creation and continued development of the UK's national serials union catalogue SUNCAT. In addition, it may be worth trying to identify what is meant by a rare book and concentrating book union catalogue development in that area.

Given the ease with which users are likely to give up using resource discovery tools, it may be well worth recalling the oft-quoted Mooers Law, namely:

> An information retrieval system will tend not to be used whenever it is more painful and troublesome for a customer to have information than for him not to have it.

Conclusions

It is important to reiterate a point made earlier in this paper. This was a small study which involved only 34 users and 26 librarians. It would therefore be dangerous to draw too many firm conclusions from this single study. More research is clearly required in this area. This would seem to be important, because at present there appears to be a mismatch between the investment going into the creation of research support tools and either the awareness of potential users of the existence of these resources or their willingness to use them.

Although it is easy for researchers to argue that more research is required, it is possible to offer some recommendations to various groups based on these findings, albeit that the number of participants was limited. Thus the following recommendations are made, and those to whom they are directed are indicated in brackets.

- There appears to be a marked lack of awareness of various research support tools such as union catalogues among their intended users, with the possible exception of InforM25 at LSE. It is important to increase the awareness of and publicity for a range of publicly funded tools such as COPAC and InforM25 (academic librarians and information service funders and providers).
- Fast and Campbell (2004) provide evidence that, in the context of one university, users understand the functions of different tools but still prefer search engines. This phenomenon needs to be investigated more widely and the reasons behind it understood (researchers, academic librarians).
- Some information tools seem to be better used than others. There is a need to understand why (researchers, academic librarians and information service providers).
- On-screen language needs to be checked to ensure that it is comprehensible to users (system suppliers, information service providers and academic librarians).
- Consideration should be given to the implementation of spell checkers at the search stage, as there continues to be evidence of spelling errors in search input. Consideration should be given to the use of spell checkers at data input, as incorrectly spelt search terms often produce results (system suppliers, information service providers and academic librarians).
- The popularity of search engines appears to be based on their speed of response and apparent ease of use. These features need to be built into information tools emanating from the information community. The notion of making a tool as much like other web services as possible should be fully explored (system suppliers, information service providers, and academic librarians).

A considerable investment of time and money goes into the development of union catalogues and other tools. If the maximum benefit is to be derived from these tools it is important that there be a better understanding of users and their needs. In addition, there is a need for greater awareness on the part of users of the tools available and their functionality. Much has been achieved, but there is scope for further achievement by both researchers and practitioners.

Acknowledgements

This research was funded by JISC through the LSE library. Thanks to colleagues Gordon Dunsire and George McGregor (CAIRNS), Shirley Cousins and Ashley Sanders (COPAC) and John Gilby and Fraser Nicolaides (InforM25) for their co-operation during the research, but most of all to Helen Booth for undertaking much of the data collection.

References

Booth, H. and Hartley, R. J. (2004) *User Behaviour in the Searching of Union Catalogues: an investigation for Work Package C of CC-interop*, http://ccinterop.cdlr.strath.ac.uk/documents/ finalreportWPC.pdf [accessed 31 January 2006].

Borlund, P. (2000) *Evaluation of Interactive Information Retrieval Systems*, Abo, Finland, Abo Akademi University Press.

Cousins, S. A. (1997) COPAC: the new national OPAC service based on the CURL database, *Program*, **31(1)**, 1–21.

Fast, K. V. and Campbell, D. G. (2004) 'I Still Like Google': university student perceptions of searching OPACs and the Web, *ASIST2004 Proceedings of the 67th ASIST Annual Meeting, Providence, Rhode Island*, Information Today Inc., 138–46.

Hartley, R. J. and Booth, H. (2006) Users and Union Catalogues, *Journal of Librarianship and Information Science*, **38** (1), (in press).

Stubley, P. and Kidd, T. (2002) Questionnaire Surveys to Discover Academic and Library Staff Perceptions of a National Union Catalogue, *Journal of Documentation*, **58** (6), 611–48.

Vakkari, P. (2003) Task-based Information Searching, *Annual Review of Information Science and Technology*, **37**, 413–64.

8

A 'joined-up' electronic journal service: user attitudes and behaviour

Ken Eason, Ross MacIntyre and Ann Apps

From attitudes to usage

This paper is an exploration of what happens when a service is provided that users have said they want. We have been able to study users who have the opportunity to go seamlessly from electronic discovery of an article title to its full electronic text, an opportunity many of them had been asking for. We might expect that, where attitudes are positive, there would be a rapid take-up of the service. However, attitude research has consistently found that a positive attitude does not necessarily translate into action. In the information systems domain we could hypothesize, for example, that there are many barriers that might prevent usage developing.

A model of user behaviour that has stimulated much user attitude research in relation to the use of information systems is the Technology Acceptance Model (TAM) (Davies, 1993). This relatively simple model depicts attitudes towards using a service as the product of perceived benefits (the 'pull') and perceived ease of use (the barriers to use). Many attitude surveys have been inspired by the TAM. For example, studies of user attitudes to internet shopping have demonstrated that perceived benefits are tempered by concerns over the trust users can have in handing over financial information.

TAM researchers have focused on the factors that affect attitudes, rather than the usage patterns that result. They have not looked at what gets used and how usage develops over time, but we know from many studies that use of a service is often very selective. A study of branch banking staff, for example, found that most clerks used only five of the 36 features of a service that gave them access to information in a customer's account (Eason, 1984). Similarly, a study of the use of telephone #* services showed that users typically used only one or two of the many services available (Eason and Damodaran, 1986). Why do users select some features and ignore others? We have had an opportunity to follow the attitudes and usage patterns of the users of a major bibliographic record system over a four-year period. As a result, we have been able to follow the way attitudes have translated into behaviour and the factors that have influenced this translation.

The Zetoc service

Since its launch in September 2000, the Zetoc service (http://zetoc.mimas.ac.uk) has become a popular electronic resource for UK academics and others who need to keep up to date with developments in their field of study. It provides table of contents information for the journals and conference proceedings held by the British Library, a database that currently includes more than 25 million records. It is funded by the Joint Information Systems Committee (JISC) and provides free access to staff at UK universities, and is provided by MIMAS at the University of Manchester. In its initial form the service provided 22 facilities that enabled users to undertake a variety of activities:

- Access via the Zetoc website to search the British Library database
- Z39.50 facilities to transfer records to bibliographic systems such as EndNote
- E-mail alerts, to receive table of contents details of new issues of selected journals, etc.
- Ordering facilities for interlibrary loans and other routes by which the user can order a printed copy of the full text of an article.

In its first two years the service became very popular. By 2002 there were 12,394 users registered to receive e-mail alerts and approximately 40,000 searches of the database each month.

Evaluating the Zetoc service

The user response to the Zetoc service was evaluated in four ways. Macro-information was obtained from the usage logs of different facilities at each institution. Unfortunately, this information cannot be linked to individual user behaviour, and to study this, two electronic questionnaires were distributed to users. Finally, an interview study was undertaken to provide qualitative information. This paper focuses on the interview study because it provides richer information on usage behaviour. However, a summary of the results of the log data and the questionnaire studies is presented below to provide a broad context within which the interview data can be placed. Further details of the questionnaire surveys are provided by Eason et al. (2003, 2005).

The initial survey

During 2001 the first evaluation of user responses to Zetoc was carried out. An electronic questionnaire seeking evidence of usage and attitudes attracted 655 responses from over 100 higher education institutions. Usage was explored by asking which of the 22 facilities in the system people had used. Attitudes were examined by asking what features in the current service were valuable, and what hopes the users had for the future development of the service. The results showed that 83% of the sample (the 'passive majority') used from one to five of the features available. Most of them thought of Zetoc as a British Library e-mail alert service and made little use of the rest of the facilities. The remaining 17% used from six to 18 of the facilities. We called these the 'active integrators' because they were busy linking what they could do with Zetoc with other services they used.

The users were mainly academics, researchers, postgraduate students and librarians, and there were significantly more postgraduates and librarians among the 'active integrators'. The attitudes towards Zetoc were very positive: it was seen as a single resource that enabled users to keep up to date with broad areas of interest. The average number of journal alerts was 13 per user, but many set far more. The biggest disappointment was that, when an article of interest was found, there was no way within the system to obtain electronic full text. The service had features for ordering printed copies of articles, but these were rarely used. When they found an article of interest, users left the service to get the full text. The major hope for the future was that the service would be able to provide a direct route from an article title to full text on their desktop: they wanted a joined-up electronic service.

Studying the use of 'joined-up' facilities

From 2002 onwards a series of enhancements that implemented OpenURL Technology in Zetoc made electronic join-up a reality. This technology enables direct communication between two services and made possible two changes to the Zetoc service. First, university libraries with metasearch portals, which enable federated searching across their resources, could provide their users with direct access to the Zetoc database without the need to access the Zetoc website. The opportunity to use this method to search the database led to a rapid increase in usage, leading to 46,229 searches in March 2005. Secondly, OpenURL technology makes it possible for Zetoc to link directly to electronic full texts or abstracts of articles held by other services. A 'more information' about a selected article feature was included in Zetoc to tell users what electronic or other information is available, and whether it might be able to provide direct access to it. The use of this service has grown from 4954 (November 2002) to 13,306 in March 2005. The service operates in two ways. When a university registers with Zetoc its OpenURL 'resolver' which may possibly but not necessarily be part of a metasearch portal, the 'more information' feature is able to list the specific resources that can provide the full text of, and other services relating to, an article, which are available to a user at that university. When the university does not have an OpenURL resolver a 'default' service shows the user where an electronic abstract or full text is available, but it cannot tell whether the user will be able to access them. The use of 'more information' in the default mode has been more or less stable since 2003 at 9000 per month, but as more universities registered their resolvers with Zetoc, the use of the OpenURL resolver route grew from 594 in March 2003 to 4625 in March 2005. In a relatively short period the use of these facilities at a particular group of institutions has increased significantly.

A second questionnaire survey was undertaken in 2003 to examine how usage had changed with the implementation of these enhancements and to assess changes in attitudes to Zetoc. It yielded 167 responses and was followed by an interview study of 26 users. Both samples were questioned about the benefits they sought from Zetoc. Top of the list was being able to keep up to date across many journals, and second was the hope that they would be able to get from the title of an article to electronic full text. Of these 193 users, 118 (61%) were aware of the enhancements to the service and had made some use of these services. Of this group, 79 (67%) thought the service was 'better', 34 (29%) that it was 'the same', and five (4%) 'worse'. Those who considered the service had improved included 93% of users at universities with their own resolvers and 81% of users at the older, more established universities. Those who said it had not improved included 53% of the users at newer universities and colleges, most without their own resolvers.

Three factors seem to explain these differences:

- Many 'passive' users had not noticed the new facilities and had not used them.
- Some users are achieving their dream of a seamless route to electronic full text: one user called it 'magic'. They were successful for one of two reasons. First, if they were at a large, established university with many subscriptions to electronic journal resources they often got access to the articles they wanted. Second, if their university had a resolver linked to Zetoc, they were told whether or not they could get electronic full text.
- Some users are looking for electronic full text but are not being so successful. The user of the default 'more information' facility may be told of a source of full electronic text but may not be allowed access. This happened particularly when

their institution had limited subscriptions to electronic resources. Some users in the survey had been disappointed often enough to be developing negative attitudes towards the service. The promise of electronic full text was proving an illusion.

Users in all these categories had expressed positive views about the seamless delivery of full text, but now that it was available were reacting in different ways. It was clear that the context in which they were using the service was having a powerful effect, and to examine this in greater detail we undertook an interview study.

Examining user strategies

Interviews were conducted at six universities, three of which had resolvers linked to Zetoc and three that did not. The interviews obtained structured information about the use of Zetoc, but explored in an unstructured way the users' strategies to locate relevant information and obtain full text. From the data, the use of Zetoc could be placed in the context of the other services made use of. Twenty-six interviews were conducted – sufficient to identify a number of different strategies if not to provide statistical evidence of their occurrence in the population at large. Table 8.1 summarizes the strategies and their occurrence in the different universities.

Table 8.1 *User strategies*

Universities	With resolver 3		Without resolver 3		Total 6	
User strategy	No.	Av. Zetoc score	No.	Av. Zetoc score	No.	Av. Zetoc score
Passive: ad hoc	2	1.8	3	1.7	5	1.7
Passive: traditional	1	7.0	3	6.1	4	6.5
Active: fragmented	7	7.5	4	5.5	11	6.5
Active: integrated	6	10.0	0	0	6	10.0
Total	16	7.6	10	5.9	26	6.9

The sample included nine users who adopted a passive strategy, i.e. they had existing ways of getting information and were not actively looking for other methods. The 'passive: ad hoc' users had low Zetoc scores, i.e. used very few facilities; mostly they had set up some e-mail alerts and 'let the system do its work'. Often they could not find the time to follow up the e-mails. These users were typically academics with many pressing duties. As one reported, 'the e-mails tyrannize me; they come when I cannot follow them up and I'm left feeling guilty and out of touch.' The 'passive: traditional' users were more organized about looking for new articles, which they did mostly by traditional means such as visiting the library.

However, they were not looking for new services.

Users with passive strategies were present in universities with or without resolvers. It is likely that these strategies are as prevalent in the population as the passive users in the first survey. They are less well represented in the interview sample because it proved hard to get people to agree to be interviewed on things they make little or no use of.

There were two strategies by which users were actively seeking to make more use of electronic resources. Both made use of the enhanced facilities and exhibited quite high Zetoc scores. The first strategy we labelled 'active: fragmented' because users already used a range of electronic resources, both for discovery and for obtaining full text, and they added particular links via Zetoc when they found they worked. They were building idiosyncratic electronic library facilities for themselves in a rather haphazard way. These users were evenly split between institutions with and without resolvers, and used whatever worked for each journal of interest. This is the group that expressed most frustration when they located electronic resources that they could not access. The final group were all at large established universities with a resolver linked to Zetoc and considerable electronic resources. We called this strategy 'active: integrated' because, as a result of regular success in using Zetoc, the users had built it into their routine of keeping up to date. Some research students were, for example, using the service to compile an electronic full-text library of the articles they needed for their research.

From attitude to usage revisited

These evaluations confirm the central tenet of the Technology Acceptance Model that a positive attitude to benefits and relative ease of use will lead to use of a service. There are many users for whom the Zetoc enhancements are helping to make the integrated electronic library a reality, and they have enthusiastically embraced the new facilities. There are many others, however, whose positive attitudes have been tempered by a variety of barriers to use. There are two kinds of barrier, those related to service delivery and those related to the working practices of the users themselves.

Service delivery barriers

The providers of Zetoc can set up a route from discovery to delivery of electronic full text but cannot control whether it will work for a particular user in a particular location. The integrated electronic library is a product of many services working together, and success for a user depends also on the electronic subscriptions of the host institution, the links made by the host to the Zetoc service, and the service offering the relevant full text article. When all these services work together the result may be the 'magic' experience of getting from discovery to full text 'in a few clicks'. When it does not work well the user may have a fruitless and time-wasting experience, and this may discourage further use of the facilities. It may also harden attitudes on the basis that the electronic library is more myth than reality.

The barrier of existing working practices

At any one institution there are wide variations in usage behaviour, and to explain this we have to understand the context within which each user operates. What was most evident from the interviews was that every user had established a set of methods and resources by which they kept up to date in their field of study. These may be paper based or electronic and may be more or less efficient, but they are above all what Winograd and Flores (1987) call 'ready to hand'. This is a concept from the philosopher Heidegger (1977), which emphasizes the way in which people undertake their everyday tasks by using tools and techniques so familiar to them that they do not have to think about them. They can then concentrate on the job in hand. Most users are not in the business of regularly reviewing how they get information and whether there are new services that might help them. This is particularly so for the 'passive users', who are probably in the majority in the Zetoc population and who have mostly yet to explore the 'joined-up' facilities.

If existing working practices dominate user behaviour, what then leads to the exploration of new opportunities? There appear from the interview data to be two basic routes. The first is what Winograd and Flores (again borrowing from Heidegger) call the 'breakdown': when something goes wrong or is a little different from the norm. The user is then pushed to explore beyond their usual practice. They still have a goal to achieve, which means they will not want to stray far. In the case of Zetoc, the reason so many quickly discovered the new facilities was that in the normal course of following up a reference they found a 'more information' facility on their screens. It was an easy step to try it, and if it worked a great new facility was immediately 'ready to hand'. If it did not work, and a time-wasting diversion ensued, the further use of the facility might be in question. The important consequence of this way of learning about a new service is that it is fragmentary. The user explores one facility on a particular occasion: it is not a systematic exploration of all that Zetoc has to offer, and it explains why people add incrementally to their working practice rather than making a full evaluation of what is available.

The second route that some of the more active users took was to attend a course on Zetoc, or otherwise to study the new service as a whole. There is some evidence that librarians and research students often took this route. These are users who for professional or advanced training reasons were prepared to make time to understand the new electronic resources. Unfortunately, this group is a minority; the more likely route to greater use of electronic resources is the localized examination of a particular facility for a particular purpose.

Conclusions

Although the focus of this research was the Zetoc service, our attempts to understand user behaviour have focused on its place in the array of services that are the users' 'ready-to-hand' working practices. Although the TAM reflects the major benefits and barriers that shape attitudes, it says little about the mechanisms by which some facilities become used and others do not, and why some users make restricted use whereas others are much more active. The rapid growth of the use of Zetoc for seamless access to electronic full text in some places but not others has revealed some of the mechanisms by which positive attitudes are or are not transformed into usage. First, the local service delivery can make this a rewarding or a frustrating experience. Second, and perhaps of greatest significance, most users will only try new services as minor variations on normal practice that are easy to explore. They will then make a comparative evaluation against normal practice in a particular instance, and if this is successful will add this increment to their practice. An interesting challenge for developers is how to deliver what are for them complete systems but for users are a source of add-ons to the resources they use.

References

Davis, F. D. (1993) User Acceptance of Information Technology: system characteristics, user perceptions and behavioural impacts, *International Journal of Man–Machine Studies*, **38** (3), 475–87.

Eason, K. D. (1984) Towards the Experimental Study of Usability, *Behaviour and Information Technology*, **3** (2), 133–43.

Eason K. D. and Damodaran L. (1986) Usable Customer Interfaces. In Griffiths, J. (ed.) *Local Telecommunications*, London, Peter Peregrinus.

Eason, K. D., MacIntyre, R., Apps, A. and Ashby, M. A. (2003) Early Integrators and the Passive Majority: an evaluation study of a large web-based bibliographic reference database, *Proceedings of the Digilib Conference, Espoo, Finland, September 8–9*, 2003.

Eason K., Harker, S., Apps, A. and MacIntyre, R. (2005) Towards an Integrated Digital Library: exploration of user responses to a 'joined-up' service, *Lecture Notes in Computer Science*, **3232**, 452–63.

Heidegger, M. (1977) *The Question Concerning Technology*, New York, Harper & Row.

Winograd T. and Flores F. (1987) *Understanding Computers and Cognition*, Boston, Addison-Wesley.

9

Climbing the ladders and sidestepping the snakes: achieving accessibility through a co-ordinated and strategic approach

Dawn McLoughlin and Ruth Wilson

Introduction

The provision of services and resources to students who are based away from mainstream provision has been a reality for many more higher education institutions in the last few years. If this is combined with the fact that courses are delivered in centres not owned by a college or university, another level of complexity is added. The challenge has been to try and match the expectation of students and academic staff with the realities of service provision within limited budgets and staffing complements. This paper explores the themes of distance student expectations and the tensions these may engender for service providers attempting to meet those expectations. This is illustrated by focusing on the development of a foundation degree in teaching and learning support at Edge Hill College of Higher Education, within the context of the national picture of the Government's foundation degree agenda, which is firmly fixed in the idea of local delivery. Learning Services at Edge Hill College have developed a 'lifecycle' approach to the provision of resources, skills and learner support. The paper will outline the developmental process, from initial assumptions through modifications to the position to date.

Context

The Government's agenda: foundation degrees and teaching assistants

In February 2000, David Blunkett (then UK Secretary of State for Education and

Employment) announced the launch of the foundation degree, a new concept in vocationally orientated, more flexible provision in the higher education sector. This was as a result of a number of Government reports that stressed the need to widen participation and develop a culture of lifelong learning, and was part of the government's vision to increase participation rates in higher education (Department for Education and Skills, 2004 and Department for Education and Employment, 1997). The key features of foundation degrees are that they are delivered by consortia, including higher education, further education and employers. The finished programme can be designed to meet the needs of a particular sector or occupation and will deliver a mix of academic knowledge, work-based learning and key generic skills. Greater flexibility in delivery and opportunities to progress to an honours degree programme were key aspects designed to suit the vocational learner.

In 2000, Howson noted a rise in the number of teaching assistants. For example, the numbers in primary schools had risen by 40% between 1996 and January 2000, and indications were that they would continue to increase. At this time those employed in this role had varied skills and training and few had formal qualifications in terms of their teaching role. The development of further training and the option to progress to the teaching profession would be well received, according to research carried out by Bourne et al. (1999). Edge Hill College grasped the opportunity that was presented in the above climate, and in 2001 the foundation degree in teaching and learning support was developed for teaching assistants.

The case study that follows looks at how this foundation degree was supported across a range of locations, and how this evolved from an operational approach to a strategic lifecycle model.

Case study

Edge Hill

Edge Hill College of Higher Education is a medium-sized higher education institution in the northwest of England with over 12,000 students taking a wide range of diploma, undergraduate, postgraduate and continuing professional development courses. The Faculty of Education comprises three main areas of work:

- Initial teacher training
- Foundation degrees in teaching and learning support for teaching assistants
- Professional development and postgraduate work.

Learning Services

In 2001 the then Information and Media Services department covered support for students in information and communication technologies (ICT), information skills, and the provision of learning resource centres, along with media facilities and support for classroom equipment. In 2003 the department evolved into Learning Services, with the addition of e-learning development, study skills, and support for students with specific learning difficulties, such as dyslexia.

Learning support for information literacy is offered through Learning Services, which has a strong and active working relationship with the faculty. The development of support for students is discussed between the faculty and staff of Learning Services, and in this new programme the Academic Liaison Advisor was part of the course team during the validation process.

The distance learning lifecycle approach: throwing the dice and starting out

The development of off-campus support was born out of a combination of developments in all the faculties, across health, education and franchise provision at further education partners.

Learning Services provided a variety of resources and support for off-campus students, until it became evident that there was a need to develop a more co-ordinated approach that would incorporate a number of key elements to ensure consistency and ensure efficient use of staff time. What emerged was the VISTA service – Virtual Student Access – which covered the following:

- Postal loans of books
- Reservations
- Document delivery of journal articles
- Interlibrary loans
- Enquiries and 'ask a question'
- Access to the library catalogue
- Access to general and subject resources
- Access to other UK academic libraries.

VISTA is only available to specific courses that are based away from the college, and students register to access the service.

From generic to tailored: lots of rungs in the ladder

The operation of the VISTA service was monitored by a group of staff involved in its day-to-day running, and was refined via user feedback as more students accessed its resources. The service was piloted and evaluated by a control group, though not tested extensively with larger numbers, and was a starting point on which to build.

Foundation degree teaching and learning support

Initially, on validation in 2001, the foundation degree was based at the Ormskirk campus and students had access to the facilities and support on campus. In 2002, provision was expanded to cover centres in the northwest of England. Initially this covered four centres in Greater Manchester and Merseyside, based in a school and three city learning centres.

The uniqueness of the course is characterized by its flexibility and innovation to suit students' circumstances, evident in the part-time nature, delivery at local providers, and the integration of online learning. The foundation degree intake was initially 75 students, although the target had been 25, and currently there are 850 students registered; to date (September 2005) there are eight centres.

The students attracted to the course are mainly mature and mostly in teaching assistant posts already. They are often time-poor and have little history of study and relatively low ICT skill levels.

The key steps

There were a number of key events or steps that had a significant impact on the services and support we provided, which caused a change in direction. The following outlines these, describes what they are, and what the effect has been.

Operational to strategic

The VISTA service was an operational response that grew out of a need to co-ordinate and standardize the services provided. The group that co-ordinated the service was charged with getting it up and running, looking for solutions to specific issues, and developing the elements of VISTA. It was essential in that it put the ladder in place, but the question then arose of how the rungs of off-campus support would be developed in the medium to long term to meet the increasingly complex provision, as described previously. In 2003, after a year of operation, a decision was made at senior level that a strategic approach was needed, prompted by the increasing number of outreach sites and students, together with the knowledge that it was unlikely that a significant increase in resources would be available. Learning Services needed to ensure that resources were being deployed to achieve maximum effect within a finite budget. A senior manager now chaired the new group and the remit was as follows:

The remit will involve developing a strategy for off-campus support covering all areas and will look beyond the operational issues of VISTA and take a more holistic approach to support. The new Off-Campus Steering Group will provide a forum for taking actions forward and planning strategic developments. The key parts of the remit will be development, co-ordination, publicity and awareness raising.

The group reports at a senior level and has signalled a shift in the level of influence, as the membership is now of more senior staff. One of the most significant developments to come from the group has been a strategy for off-campus provision that would cover all areas. The aims of this strategy are:

- to ensure that all current activities are drawn together to ensure quality, consistency, and further development in line with user needs
- to ensure that all students receive equity in terms of the provision of learning support systems and services
- to ensure a standardized approach to the implementation and development of support systems and access to resources
- to ensure that students are fully supported in their use of resources off campus
- to further develop the corporate identity away from Edge Hill sites, with students feeling an integral part of the college community
- to promote the dissemination of information about off-campus students, both within Learning Services and to those departments we work closely with to ensure an awareness of support needs, e.g. Student Services, Business Network Systems
- to ensure greater collaboration with partner organizations to further develop the support mechanisms currently in place
- to ensure further development in response to a changing curriculum and to support changing user needs.

The strategy is a crucial document that underpins the co-ordinated approach across the service. Its first annual action plan specified the following objectives:

- Identifying systems for monitoring and review
- Auditing current provision, reviewing and improving marketing and publicity
- The development of service-level agreements for partner organizations
- Reviewing statistics and reporting mechanisms
- Reviewing the systems for first-level support
- Exploring issues around the equity of skills support and development.

A pattern has emerged to monitor the progress of the strategy of annual objectives at the start of the year, and an annual report at the end to review and evaluate progress.

A lifecycle has started to emerge – strategy, aims, objectives and an annual report – but this is only part of the picture. It deals with the services that Learning Services provide once an outreach centre is up and running. It is divorced from the earlier part, the negotiation and setting up of an outreach centre, and the later part, the student experience and how that feeds into the lifecycle. To have a truly complete lifecycle these parts need to be included, as illustrated in Figure 9.1, and this became our aim.

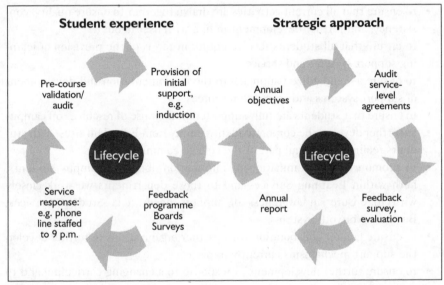

Figure 9.1   *Complete lifecycle*

Evaluation and feedback mechanisms

A key component of the lifecycle model for the student experience is the use of monitoring and review mechanisms. Our model is one that is developing and is based on our off-campus monitoring and review strategy 2004–2006, which outlines current provision and puts forward a strategic plan for the future identifying a range of mechanisms, such as:

• suggestions scheme
• recommendations
• survey

- annual report
- e-mail
- liaison activity.

The strategy was useful in that it drew together existing mechanisms, and this assisted in identifying any gaps. What was at first a one-off survey of off-campus provision has now become an annual event that picks up on issues with documentation sent out to students, the services we offer, communication, e-resources, IT support, accessing other libraries, and also asks for suggestions on what improvements the students would like to see. In response to their suggestions, we have introduced a welcome pack and newsletter. If specific issues are highlighted then action is taken. For example, a student at the Whiston outreach centre said: 'Most of the students have not been able to get online despite numerous attempts during sessions.' In this case a member of staff arranged to visit the centre and deliver a session on electronic resources. This approach is supplemented by actively seeking feedback from students whenever staff visit an outreach centre, and this is then channelled back to relevant managers. This can include WebCT – the virtual learning environment – ICT support and study skills, and uses both formal and informal methods to ensure accountability and responsiveness across all areas of the service.

Support for a faculty rests with identified individuals in each of the teams providing support, and regular meetings occur between these staff to ensure a co-ordinated approach and good communication, both within the service in relation to the support for the faculty and also from the service out to the faculty. This is done by exchanging information on new developments and producing newsletters and reports, which are then disseminated to academic staff, students and committees.

The nature of the location of the outreach centres, initially in premises owned by other organizations, meant that there was no facility to have book collections. The increasing availability of e-journals and e-books was seen as a potential 'lifesaver' for our foundation degree students. A number of key texts were purchased in 2002, backed up by induction sessions with workbooks to provide hands-on opportunities to locate and explore the e-resources, particularly e-books. This proved relatively successful with these students being consistently at the top of the usage figures. However, this did not remove the need or desire for printed material. Feedback through student consultation groups and the survey made it evident that the provision of e-books did not provide all that the students needed. Postal loans, although used by a significant number of students, did not satisfy all their needs either. In 2004 small book collections were set up at two locations. These are managed by students and have been positively received. Having e-resources available round the clock adds to the resource mix and provides students with more opportunities for access.

At the same time as the monitoring and review strategy was drawn up for all off-campus activity, a service-level agreement specifically for Faculty of Education outreach centres was also made. This aimed to establish and clearly articulate the responsibilities, communication channels, services and support, and to provide a framework for the review and ongoing development of such support. This has informed and influenced the establishment of new service-level agreements for our further education partners.

Resources and staffing

Our support for off-campus students was initially covered by existing staff and budgets. This increased the need to review existing roles and determine whether there were any areas of declining activity, where roles might be refocused to provide aspects of off-campus support. This occurred in our interlibrary loans team, which had a reduction in the number of requests received. A member of staff could now be released to spend part of their time providing a dedicated evening telephone helpline to off-campus students.

Existing academic liaison staff provided learning support, though as student numbers and centres increased this became more difficult. To supplement this, a pool of associate staff was created who could be called upon to deliver learning support sessions at points of increased demand. To maintain quality assurance it is paramount that these staff are inducted, observe, and are shadowed by existing staff to define and reinforce standards. An online resource of lesson plans, workbooks and guidance notes supports the face-to-face interaction, and a system of peer review provides a means of identifying areas of good practice and areas for development.

A significant development in 2005, as centres in Lincolnshire, Shropshire and the Isle of Man are on the horizon, is the creation of posts specifically to support outreach centres. The increase in number of locations, their geographical spread and the large number of students now off campus necessitated this. Currently, a post that covers both Learning Services and Student Services is being advertised which aims to strengthen the provision and co-ordination of support. This centres on four key areas:

- The co-ordination of Learning Services and Student Services support activity at outreach centres
- The delivery of learning support at outreach centres across the range of ICT, information literacy and study skills
- The management of specific Learning Services and Student Services projects for outreach work

- The provision of an effective support structure and information service for students at outreach centres in liaison with central support services and the Students' Union.

The role will fortify the existing holistic approach and ensure that the many-faceted demands of all outreach students are met. This post signifies a shift to more hybrid posts to 'join up' support and activities as appropriate to the learning experience. Other posts will hopefully follow as the benefits are demonstrated and appreciated.

The future

The creation of the hybrid post arose out of the realization that the Student Services and Learning Services were both grappling with similar issues in terms of support for students off campus. This realization developed from the sharing of information and approaches between the two services, and has included input from the Faculty at an off-campus 'away day'. Furthermore, this has been built upon by the development this year of the 'Learning Services and Student Services Partnership Framework', which sets out the approach across the two services to providing access to learning resources, learning support and student support, and guidance to those off campus. This framework is structured into three sections:

- Partnership audit – to ensure that the learning infrastructure is in place from the beginning of the partnership, and that it meets the needs of the students and trainees
- Partnership relationship – the development of the relationship between the relevant services to ensure that the service-level agreement works effectively, and that monitoring and evaluation inform enhancements. This will be underpinned by a regular audit cycle
- Learning Services and Student Services collaboration – to ensure that a joined-up approach is taken wherever possible, leading to the more effective use of resources and a more seamless approach for students, trainees and partners.

This document is predicated on the need for a joint approach by the two services, the Faculty and their partners, and that the learning infrastructure is key to the quality of the learning experience, wherever the students are based. Furthermore, that the learning infrastructure is a fundamental part of the approval of any new partnership, and ongoing monitoring and evaluation is essential to ensure the quality of the student experience. This framework is to be used as the starting point to ensure that relevant discussions take place at the planning stage to allow for the agreement of roles and responsibilities, the setting-up of service-level agreements and any additional resources requirements. It has now provided the final piece in our lifecycle.

Conclusions: empty board, no rules

The development of the 'lifecycle' approach has been a fragmented process and has been like playing a game on an empty board with no rules. There are now, though, clear frameworks, documents, and monitoring and evaluation built into the development of provision for off-campus students, with clear structures and responsibilities outlined. In effect, we have mapped out the issues and pitfalls in off-campus provision and have confidence that we know the landscape. We are working in partnership with the Faculty to plan audits for the new provision, with service-level agreements developed in a timely manner. There is a joined-up approach to off-campus support across Learning Services, and the creation of a hybrid post to incorporate Student Services provision has linked up two services within the college to maximize the use of staffing resources.

Our incremental approach has been based on good management and the best use of resources. We have developed pilots, monitored them, and scaled them up based on the evaluation and links to service, Faculty and institutional goals. There has been a realization that one size does not fit all, though there is a need to co-ordinate services and standards; this has been achieved through the development of a menu or framework of possible support options. This can then be considered in relation to the setting and client group. This will ensure that our services are accessible to students wherever they are based, and this has been achieved by the development of a strategic lifecycle approach.

References

Bourne, J., Smith, K., Kenner, C., Barton-Hyde, D. (1999) *Career Ladders for Classroom Assistants: research report*, London, TTA.

Department for Education and Employment (1997) *Higher Education in the Learning Society [Dearing Report]*, London, HMSO.

Department for Education and Skills (2004) *Foundation Degree Task Force Report to Ministers: a summary*, London, DfES.

Howson, J. (2000) Rise and Rise of Support Army, *Times Education Supplement*, (8 December), www.tes.co.uk/ search/ story/?story_id=341679 [accessed 25 July 2005].

10

The impact of library and information services on health professionals' ability to locate information for patient care

Alison Brettle

Background and introduction

Throughout the UK North West Health region the library services provided to health professionals who need information for patient care are varied. Some libraries promote their mediated search services, whereas some focus on training health professionals to locate information for themselves; others have implemented specialist posts such as dedicated library trainers and clinical librarians. As services are rarely evaluated, little is known about which are effective or cost-effective, or the impact they have on the health professionals' ability to locate information for patient care. Furthermore, there are a number of problems and a lack of validated tools with which to evaluate health library services routinely (Brettle, 2003). This paper outlines some of the issues involved in evaluating the impact of health library services (particularly the provision of information skills training). It then goes on to describe a research project that evaluated the impact of library and information services on health professionals' ability to locate information for patient care.

Evaluating health library and information services

Evaluation is essential in determining whether services are useful and effective. There is little point in providing services if they are of no use to the intended users, nor if they are not delivering what they are meant to. Although health librarians are being urged to evaluate the services they provide, there are a number of issues that should be considered before embarking on any evaluation, including an awareness of the limitations of the available tools. One of the main areas of service provision for health libraries is information skills training to enable health professionals locate evidence for practice. Before describing a research project that involves evaluating the effectiveness of information skills training compared with mediated searches, this paper will consider some of the issues involved in evaluating information skills training.

There are four main problems or issues involved in evaluating health library and information services (and these may not be restricted to health libraries): these should be considered before beginning any evaluation.

1 What is being measured? Is it satisfaction with the training session, or is it whether the training makes a difference? Before carrying out any evaluation, it is important to be clear about what exactly is being measured and what you want to get out of the process.

2 What are the standards? What makes a good training session? Is it the venue, the teacher, or the way the subject is taught? Are there any standards that can be used to measure against? A number of information literacy standards have been developed (Association of College and Research Libraries, 2000; Council of Australian University Librarians, 2001; NHS Information authority, 2001; SCONUL, 2003), but none of them addresses precisely the skills that are needed for health professionals to locate information for evidence-based practice.

3 Whose perspective is being measured? Is the training successful from the point of view of the trainer, the person being trained, or the organization as a whole? Different stakeholders are likely to have different perspectives on what is important and what makes the training successful.

4 What method(s) or tool(s) should be used in the evaluation? The method or tool should aim to measure whether you have achieved the objectives of the training or the aim of the research. It should therefore cover the work contained in the training session or the aims of the research. The tool should be reliable (repeatable over time, providing consistent data) and the measure should be valid (that is, measure what you want it to measure); and finally the measure should be feasible for your use. For example, if you wanted to carry out routine evaluation the measure should be easily incorporated into your training session, not take much time to administer, and you should make sure you have the resources to obtain and interpret the results. If the evaluation is being carried out as part of a research project there is likely to be more time and resources available for data analysis and a more detailed tool could be used.

Potential tools that can be used for evaluation include:

1 User surveys. These are relatively quick and simple to administer, can be used for small or large sample sizes, and can be used to find out users' views of the

training and its impact on their skills, and to follow up training over the longer term. They are often used to provide feedback about sessions. However, they obtain subjective views rather than objective data. In relation to training, they do not measure the impact of training or whether skills have changed.

2 Quizzes and questions. Quizzes and questions can be used before and after training to determine how much users have learned. However, they are only likely to be useful and practical on smaller samples, are pertinent to a specific training session, and are likely to test knowledge rather than actual skills.

3 Recall and precision. Recall and precision are commonly used to measure the quality of a literature search. They may be useful in evaluating small-scale projects or sessions by examining each search undertaken and comparing against a gold standard or consensus of a 'good-quality' search. This standard must be agreed before using the measure. Recall and precision may not cover all aspects of the training that you want to evaluate, and are not likely to involve the users' perspective.

4 Skills checklists. A checklist of skills is used to mark against a 'test' literature search. This provides an objective measure of the skills learned and can be used before and after training for comparison. They are time-consuming to use and analyse, and are therefore more likely to be feasible for smaller groups or as part of research or one-off evaluations, rather than routinely. A number have been developed, but they are software specific and there is limited evidence about their reliability and validity. Unless users have been involved in the development of the checklist, it is unlikely that it will take their perspective into account.

5 Assessments. Users are given an assessment after training to provide an objective measure of what has been learned. These are usually only likely to be useful if the training has been carried out as part of a course.

6 Use of skills after training. The use of skills learned can be a proxy measure of the effectiveness of training. If users continue to use their skills after training, it can be argued that the training has been useful/effective. Conversely, if users do not use their skills then there is little point in undertaking the training. However, this does not take into account whether the skills are being used correctly, or whether users are putting into practice what they have learned.

7 User satisfaction with search results after training. Satisfaction with results after training is another proxy measure of effectiveness. If users are satisfied (particularly compared with their satisfaction before training), this could be an indication that training has had an impact on their searches. Satisfaction with results does not necessarily mean that a search was effective: a user may be satisfied with any results (particularly if they have searched fruitlessly in the past), but the results they obtain may not be the most appropriate to answer their questions.

It can be seen that all the above tools have their limitations. There are few practical, usable tools specifically aimed at evaluating health information skills training in routine practice. For research purposes there are few that have been tested for their validity and reliability (Brettle, 2003).

Effective Methods of Providing InfoRmation for patIent Care (EMPIRIC)

The issues relating to evaluation described above were taken into consideration when devising the methodology for the EMPIRIC research study. The study was commissioned by the North West Libraries Health Care Unit (HCLU), which is responsible for the strategic provision of health library services in the northwest of England. The project aimed to investigate the effectiveness and cost-effectiveness of different approaches to providing information for patient care, namely information skills training and mediated searches, from the perspective of the library staff, dedicated trainers and health professionals.

Six key research questions directed the study:

1 Does information skills training improve the ability of health professionals to search for evidence?
2 When and why do health professionals rely on librarians to search for evidence? Is this appropriate, acceptable and effective?
3 Are dedicated library trainers an effective method of enabling health professionals to understand and apply their searching skills to locate information?
4 What factors affect health professionals' ability to locate information for practice?
5 Which is more cost-effective, information skills training or librarian-mediated searching?
6 How can libraries best meet the needs of health professionals?

Methods

The study was designed in three distinct phases. Each phase informed the next, and the data gathered were analysed before moving on to the next phase. Ethical approval and individual Trust R&D approval was obtained before phase two of the study began.

Phase one aimed to contextualize the research and involved administering a baseline questionnaire to all the healthcare libraries throughout the North West region to provide an overview of library services. A comprehensive literature review was undertaken to examine the effectiveness of information skills training and librarian-mediated searches. **Phase two** involved a questionnaire survey to provide details on the nature of searching and training, and obtain the perspectives of key participants (library staff, dedicated trainers and health professionals). Outcome measures used included user perceptions, user satisfaction, and use of skills after training. Questionnaires were sent out to a total of 115 library staff, 15 dedicated trainers and 780 health professionals across 26 sites. **Phase three** involved presenting and feeding back the findings to expert workshops comprising librarians and health professionals. A combination of both qualitative and quantitative methods was applied in all three phases. Cost analysis was undertaken on the data obtained during phase two. Data were analysed using SPSS and thematic analysis.

Results

The results described below relate to the responses received from health professionals across the North West region. Other results from the project, including the responses from library staff, dedicated trainers and the cost-effectiveness analysis, can be found in Brettle et al. (2005) and at www.fhsc.salford.ac.uk/hcprdu/.

The response rate to the questionnaires received from health professionals was 31.5% (243 responses). Comparison with the baseline data survey showed that the sample was representative. The nature of the services provided to health professionals, their perceptions of those services, and the results relating to the effectiveness of the services are presented below.

Who uses mediated searches and why?

Over half (54%) of respondents use mediated search services, and most respondents request between one and four searches in a 12-month period. Mediated services are used because they save time, improve knowledge or evidence-based practice, and in turn improve patient care. Those health professionals who do not use mediated services either preferred doing searches themselves, or were unaware that the service existed.

Are mediated searches effective?

Over 80% of health professionals were satisfied or very satisfied with all aspects of mediated searches, indicating that the service is effective. Analysis of the qualitative data showed that successful mediated searches depend on clear search questions or the librarian knowing and understanding what the health professional wants (it is unclear whose responsibility this is). The majority perceived that library staff are more efficient at searching than health professionals, but fewer believe that using library staff to carry out searches is an efficient use of resources. A third (32%) of mediated searches are carried out with the health professional and librarian working together; furthermore, an overwhelming majority of respondents believed that working together increases the chance of retrieving better-quality information. Despite receiving training, 66% of respondents continued to request mediated searches. Health professionals provided clear evidence (via a range of examples) that information from mediated searches has positive or highly positive effects on their continuing professional development, research and patient care.

The nature of information skills training provision

The majority of health professionals received information skills training via small group sessions, but a significant proportion is carried out on a one-to-one basis.

The nature of searching following information skills training

The majority of health professionals use their information skills frequently (on a weekly or monthly basis) after training. The most frequently used resource is electronic databases; however, the use of Google or other search engines is almost as high. When asked about factors that constrained their use of information skills, health professionals reported time as the biggest constraint, but one in five cited poor access to computers/the internet. Barriers to implementing or applying evidence include time constraints, the cost of change, restricted resources, a culture resistant to change, lack of authority to implement change, negative attitudes and a lack of confidence.

Effectiveness of information skills training

Training is perceived as most effective in improving users' knowledge of resources and confidence. It is seen by one in three respondents as less successful in improving search skills and reducing the amount of time taken to find information. Indeed, one in five health professionals indicated that their skills remained poor despite training, and a third reported that their confidence prevented them using their information skills. The majority of health professionals are satisfied with the training they receive and use their skills frequently (on a weekly or monthly basis). Almost two-thirds of health professionals report being satisfied with the information they receive from their own searches. There is a split between the number of health professionals who have difficulty in finding information and those who do not, however, this does not appear to depend on whether or not they have received training. Health professionals provided clear evidence that information is being used to change, influence or inform patient care both directly and indirectly, and they report that information obtained from searches has a positive or highly positive effect on patient care, research and professional development.

Perceptions relating to training

The majority of respondents believed that health professionals should have the skills to search for themselves and should undergo information skills training, and that training was not a waste of resources. However, they also believed that such training is only useful if the health professionals have the time to use the skills learned.

Expert workshops

Two workshops were held, one comprising librarians and one comprising librarians and health professionals. All participants acknowledged and confirmed the findings of the study. A number of issues were questioned, and then addressed in the discussion of the final project report.

Conclusions

The quantitative and qualitative data obtained as part of the EMPIRIC project provide a comprehensive picture of how health library services in the northwest are perceived from the users' point of view. Furthermore, the results of the study provide evidence as to the effectiveness and cost-effectiveness of information skills training and mediated searching. The two expert workshops held with library staff and health professionals confirmed the findings and analysis of the data collection survey.

The evidence showed that for the majority, information skills training is effective in that it improves confidence and knowledge of resources. Although there is less evidence relating to improvement in skills, the majority of users are satisfied with the results of their searches and continue to search relatively frequently. There remains a significant number (about one-third) however, who are less confident, who do not perceive their skills to have improved and who struggle to find information.

In terms of mediated searches, health professionals rely on librarians to search for evidence for information for professional development, research and patient care because it saves them time. Mediated search services are appropriate, acceptable and effective.

Users continue to search post training and some prefer to undertake their own searches rather than request mediated searches. However, training, practice, enjoyment, time and access to computers affect health professionals' ability to locate information for practice.

Outcome measures and methods used in the study

A range of quantitative and qualitative measures and methods were used in the study. This combined approach enabled the research team to evaluate the impact of library services on health professionals' ability to find information for patient care. The limitations and advantages of these methods are discussed below.

The use of a questionnaire survey enabled the collection of both quantitative and qualitative data to gauge perceptions and the effectiveness of services. This was a good way of obtaining results from a large sample spread across the North West region. The response rate from health professionals was not particularly high (31.5%), but included 243 responses and was therefore considered enough to be significant and compared favourably with a number of other studies (Dalton et al., 2002; Robinson, 2004; Yeoman et al., 2003).

When selecting outcome measures for the study it was essential to select those that could be used with a large sample and which would be valid and reliable. It was considered that two proxy measures of effectiveness, use of search skills post training and user satisfaction, were the most feasible. Use of search skills post training was selected as it was considered that there would be little point in providing training if users did not continue to use their skills. User satisfaction was also relevant and feasible to use in this situation. In the case of mediated searches, if users are satisfied with all aspects of searches then they can be considered effective. If users are satisfied with the results of their searches, it could be argued that it is not necessary to measure their actual skills to determine whether the training has been effective. The measures used were not perfect measures of effectiveness, but were appropriate for this study design. Assessing skills objectively for such a large number of subjects and across the region would not have been feasible or appropriate within the remit of the project, nor would it have been feasible to undertake objective assessments on all the mediated searches carried out in the region.

The data obtained from these proxy measures were combined with quantitative and qualitative data about users' perceptions of the services they received. Although asking for users' perceptions is limited in terms of measuring effectiveness, as it provides subjective views rather than objective data, when combined with the measures outlined above it enables a picture of the overall effectiveness of the services to be built. Furthermore, the qualitative data provided an insight into users' beliefs and needs, which is useful for service development and planning.

References

Association of College and Research Libraries (2000) *Information Literacy Standards for Higher Education*, www.ala.org/ala/acrl/acrlstandards/standards.pdf [accessed 18 August 2005].

Brettle, A. (2003) *How Can We Evaluate Information Skills Training*, oral presentation at 2nd International Evidence Based Librarianship Conference, June, Edmonton, Canada.

Brettle, A., Hulme, C. T. and Ormandy, P. (2005) *Effective Methods of Providing InfoRmation for patIent Care (EMPIRIC Project): report three, data collection and analysis*, Salford, University of Salford, Health Care Practice R&D Unit.

Council of Australian University Librarians (CAUL)(2001) *Revised version of CAUL's Information Literacy Standards*, www.caul.edu.au/info-literacy/InfoLiteracyFramework.pdf [accessed 18 August 2005].

Dalton, P., Kane, D., Faux, J. and Nankivell, C. (2002*) An Interim Formative Evaluation of the Worcestershire Health Informatics Programme Libraries and Access to Evidence Projects*, Birmingham, Centre for Information Research (CIRT), Faculty of Computing, Information and English, University of Central England, Birmingham.

NHS Information Authority (2001) *Health Information Competency Profiles for the NHS*, www.nhsia.nhs.uk/nhid/pages/resource_informatics/hi_competencyprofiles.pdf [accessed 18 August 2005].

Robinson, S. (2004) *Health Information East London Training Evaluation*, London, Health Information East London, 11, 22.

SCONUL (2003) *Information Skills in Higher Education: a SCONUL Position Paper*, www.sconul.ac.uk/activities/inf_lit/papers/Seven_pillars.html [accessed 18 August 2005].

Yeoman, A. J., Cooper, J. M., Urquhart, C. J. and Tyler, A. (2003) The Management of Health Library Outreach Services: evaluation and reflection on lessons learned on the VIVOS Project, *Journal of the Medical Library Association*, **91** (4), 426–33.

Further reading

Brettle, A. (2005) *Effective Methods of Providing InfoRmation for patIent Care (EMPIRIC Project): report two, literature review*, Salford, University of Salford, Health Care Practice R&D Unit.

Brettle, A., Hulme, C. T. and Ormandy, P. (2005) *Effective Methods of Providing InfoRmation for patIent Care (EMPIRIC Project): report three, data collection and analysis*, Salford, University of Salford, Health Care Practice R&D Unit.

Phillips, S. (1993) *Evaluation*, London, Facet Publishing.

Williams, J. L. (2000) Creativity in Assessment of Library Instruction, *Reference Services Review*, **28** (4), 323–34.

11

We know we are making a difference but can we prove it? Impact measurement in a higher education library

Dianne Nelson, Jacqueline Chelin, Jane Redman and Pauline Shaw

Introduction

UK academic libraries are expected to demonstrate that their services provide value for money. One way to do this is to measure the impact our services have on users. Impact is quite hard to define. Generally, if something has impact it results in a change of some kind, e.g. in attitude or behaviour, or as Payne and Conyers (2004) expressed it, 'Are we making a difference?' Impact is also difficult to measure (Everest and Payne, 2001). A number of studies have looked at ways of doing this, such as The Centre for Research in Library and Information Management – CERLIM's Longitude project, which aimed to develop a toolkit of impact assessment techniques for measuring changes over time (Craven and Brophy, 2004). One of the latest impact measurement projects, aimed specifically at the UK higher education (HE) sector, is the Library and Information Research Group (LIRG) and the Society of College, National and University Libraries (SCONUL) Impact Implementation Initiative. This paper describes the University of the West of England (UWE) Library Services' participation in the Initiative, and reflects on our methodologies and outcomes.

The LIRG/SCONUL Impact Implementation Initiative was set up in 2003 (Payne and Conyers, 2005). Its aim was to develop a toolkit of impact research methodologies for HE libraries. The Initiative is based on action research principles that encourage reflection on the processes of investigation, and uses an established impact measurement methodology as the common model for all the participants (Markless and Streatfield, 2005). Working to this model the participants set objectives for their chosen impact theme, identify success criteria, specify the evidence required to assess whether those criteria have been met, and select appropriate data collection methods.

UWE Impact Study

UWE is the largest HE institution in southwest England, with approximately 26,000 students, 1000 academic staff and 10 faculties spread across seven campuses. Three years ago a virtual learning environment (VLE), Blackboard, was introduced. This has provided new ways of teaching and new learning opportunities for students, and has the potential to create new partnerships between the library and the teaching staff. It was within this context of change that the Impact study was carried out.

The study focused on the impact of our electronic information services (EIS), as we wished to discover whether the increasing costs of EIS represent value for money. EIS, for the purposes of this study, were defined as the electronic information services for which the library pays a subscription, e.g. Inspec, Science Direct, etc.

Our stated objectives were to measure the impact of EIS on students' learning, staff teaching, and research(ers) against our stated success criteria (Figure 11.1 on the next page). A mixture of quantitative and qualitative data collection methods were employed, including questionnaires, semi-structured interviews, participant observation, and annual relevant EIS usage statistics since 2000/01. Using multiple data collection strategies and a variety of data sources enables triangulation of results to give corroboration between the different sets of findings and increase the validity of the study.

Data collection

Online questionnaire

The student survey, consisting of 16 questions chosen for their perceived ability to measure impact against our stated success criteria, ran from mid-April to mid-June, a period when it was likely that all students would need to access electronic resources for their academic work. The respondents were self-selecting and anonymous.

Semi-structured interviews

This method was used with the academic staff. Interviewees were recruited through e-mails inviting them to participate. A direct approach was also made to some academics whose good rapport with the library or known familiarity with using the VLE would make them useful and co-operative participants.

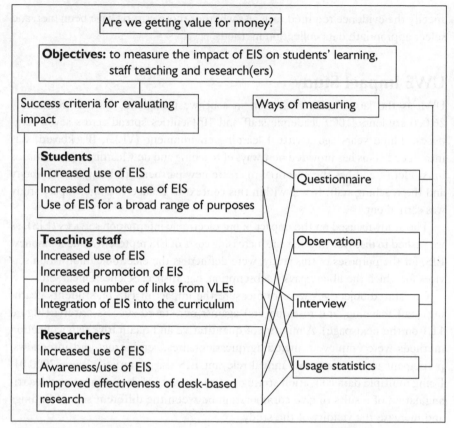

Figure 11.1   *Diagrammatic representation of the impact project*

Ultimately nine teaching staff were interviewed. Each interview lasted one hour and was conducted by a faculty librarian, with a note-taker present. The questions followed a predetermined open format, focusing on the academic's own use of EIS, their use of EIS in teaching, and their perception of the impact of EIS.

Questionnaires/participant observation

The method used with researchers involved participant observation as well as a questionnaire and interview. The format comprised a brief questionnaire to collect biographical data; observation of a set of tasks; and training on the basis of the observed behaviour. A short follow-up interview was carried out a month later to ascertain whether their desk-based research had improved as a result of the training.

Thirteen researchers from six faculties were recruited. Each interview, lasting about an hour, was conducted by a faculty librarian, with a note-taker present to record the actions and comments of the subject. In participant observation the observer takes an active role, in this case responding to the researcher's comments.

Key results

Objective 1 – impact on students' learning

Of the 387 student respondents 217 (56%) positively identified themselves as EIS users. These 217 responses were analysed further.

The respondents were evenly spread across the first (24%), second (30%) and third years (26%), but with fewer fourth-year and postgraduate students (9% and 11%, respectively). All faculties were represented except Art, Media and Design.

Students' awareness and use of EIS

Unsurprisingly, the respondents were IT literate, 89% having access to the internet at home; 96% with good to very good IT skills; and 98% claiming to have good to very good information-finding skills. In total, 30 different databases were identified as having been used.

Although just over half (53%) had received library training in using EIS, the majority of students discovered which EIS to use from faculty sources (teaching staff, module documentation and the VLE) in a ratio of 65:35 compared to library sources (librarian, library web pages and library publicity).

Impact of EIS as evidenced by the success criteria

- *Increased use of EIS.* In response to the question 'How has your use of EIS changed over the last year?', 72% said it had increased.
- *Increased remote use.* 63% of respondents mainly accessed EIS remotely, in most cases from home. However, with no baseline for comparison it is hard to say whether these figures represent an *increase* in remote use, except within the context of the general overall increase in use of EIS.
- *Use of EIS for a broad range of purposes, e.g. social, self-development.* It was felt that EIS could be judged to be truly embedded in the students' learning when they became aware of their wider applications, other than for course work. The purposes for which the students used EIS were as follows: finding their own reading for themselves or their coursework (35%); finding reading recommended for coursework (28%); finding primary data, e.g. statistics, financial data (14%); reference, e.g. maps, dictionaries, etc. (8%); career- or job-related information (6%); newspapers (5%); and hobby- or interest-related information (4%). This shows some broadening of use.

Objective 2 – impact on staff teaching

Academics' awareness and use of EIS

All nine academics interviewed had used library databases to a greater or lesser extent. Between them they identified 20 EIS that they regularly use. Eight of the nine used both the library and the library web pages as a guide to what is available and for information about, and training on, EIS. The library website was mentioned favourably several times. Nevertheless, overall awareness of what EIS the library provides could have been better.

There were as many references made to freely available websites as to library EIS, e.g. government websites, professional organizations' websites, blogs, discussion boards, etc. One respondent claimed to use Google instead of EIS, and another said they made links to these free websites from their VLE.

Impact of EIS as evidenced by the success criteria

- *Increased promotion of EIS.* All respondents claimed to promote EIS, especially the resources they were familiar with and confident in using.
- *Integration of EIS into the curriculum.* Seven academics had integrated EIS into the curriculum to varying degrees, by referring to them in module handbooks or assignment briefs, or by making their use a requirement when completing assignments. However, EIS are not yet as integrated as they might be. Two academics expressed their intention to integrate EIS further in the future, and both felt this would come about as a result of greater use of the VLE.
- *Increased number of links to EIS from VLEs.* Seven of the academics already provided links to EIS information from the VLE. Again, whether this represents an increase is uncertain, as we do not have a baseline.

It was generally felt that the use of a VLE would help to integrate EIS. However, one interviewee noted that by using the VLE to link to e-resources that are freely available over the web, there is a danger that library-provided EIS could be bypassed altogether. There was also an indication that VLEs are driving a preference for full-text resources, over, for example, bibliographic databases, as they enable linking at the article level.

Other factors that affect the impact of EIS on teaching

These could include academics' perception of the value of EIS to students' learning, and the barriers to their own use of EIS.

Perceived positive and negative impacts on students' learning

On balance there was a greater appreciation of the positive benefits, such as:

- Students retrieve large amounts of up-to-date information quickly and easily
- Improved student support by using EIS to provide links to learning resources
- Student dissertations now contain a wider range of references
- Students prefer electronic resources
- EIS can deliver resources that look more professional (more so than photo-copies), resulting in better course evaluation.

Anecdotal evidence suggested that there has been some improvement in the standard of student projects, which could be attributed to EIS, although the feeling was that 'good students will use EIS effectively and the weaker ones will not take the opportunity'.

On the negative side, six academics expressed concern that students were unable to adequately evaluate the large amount of information available to them, or assess its quality. As one respondent said, 'If we give them wide access, we also have to give them the skills to be discriminatory and know how to use information.'

The ease of plagiarism in an online environment was discussed, but as there was no evidence that it was increasing, most respondents did not seem unduly concerned.

There were also reservations about the possibility of 'spoon-feeding' students by simply giving them links to reading materials, rather than requiring them to search and retrieve information for themselves.

Barriers to academics' own use of EIS

- Lack of awareness of what EIS are available
- Behavioural – exploration vs exploitation – people tend to stick with what they are familiar with, rather than explore to find new resources
- Lack of time – a lot of extra work is involved in creating links from VLEs to EIS
- Lack of confidence with IT
- Password/access problems.

Objective 3 – impact on research(ers)

Impact of EIS on research(ers) as evidenced by the success criteria

- *Awareness/use of EIS within researchers' subject area.* All researchers were aware of the importance of EIS for their research, as illustrated by comments such as: 'EIS is essential'; 'Can't imagine how I managed without them.'

- *Improved effectiveness of desk-based research when using EIS.* The researcher's ability to navigate, know what EIS to use and what is available, their search strategies and knowledge of alerting services were judged on a scale of 1–4. There was a correlation between number of years of research experience and effective research using EIS. The impact of EIS on research(ers) could be further increased by one-to-one training.

Other factors affecting the impact of EIS on research(ers)

Access to multidisciplinary information provided by the wide range of EIS available, the high quality of the resources, and the support provided by library staff and by the library web pages were all positive influences.

Access problems and the slowness of the network, lack of knowledge about what EIS are available, and information overload were negative factors. A preference for full-text resources was frequently expressed, and for three researchers their information searching was exclusively restricted to the availability of full text.

Impact of EIS as evidenced by quantitative data

One of our success criteria for the impact of EIS was increased use across all user groups. The surveys generated a list of databases that the subjects used regularly and which in many cases could be compared with their usage statistics for 2000/01 and 2003/04 (Table 11.1).

For all titles where data were available, the increase in use has been considerable. This corroborates the evidence of increasing use of EIS obtained from the student survey. The reasons for this are expanded in the interviews with staff, i.e. that they themselves are using more sources in their research, they are recommending them to students (indeed, expecting students to use them), and are promoting EIS in a variety of ways that help to reach a wide cross-section of users.

Table 11.1 *Database usage statistics*

Databases	2000/1	2003/4	% increase
AMED	747	9688	1297
Business Source Premier (2001/02)	26464	84831	321
CINAHL	8410	40983	487
Compendex/EI Village	442	1279	289
Education Indexes	975	3619	371
Emerald	5159	6130	119
IBSS	1341	2385	178
LEXIS-NEXIS	9662	31990	331

Continued on next page

Table 11.1 *Continued*

Databases	2000/1	2003/4	% increase
Medline	9023	31790	352
Mintel	809	5943	735
PsycInfo	809	7793	963
Science Direct	14225	15927	112
SportDiscus	414	1860	449
Zetoc	315	1443	458

Discussion

To what extent do the outcomes confirm the aims/objectives and success criteria?

The success criteria for all the user groups appear to have been satisfied, thereby in theory proving the case for the impact of EIS at UWE. However, these results need to be viewed in context.

The definition of impact set out in the Introduction would dictate that we should be attempting to measure a change over time, but because a study of this scope has never been undertaken before by UWE Library Services this was impossible, as we had no baseline data. What we have is a snapshot in time, but one that will prove useful if we intend to carry out impact evaluation as a longitudinal study in the future.

Furthermore, could we, strictly speaking, say we were evaluating the impact of EIS, or were we in fact measuring the impact of training, the introduction of the VLE, or the increasingly widespread access to the internet from home? The truth is likely to be a complex combination of factors, as the interviews indicate. A closer consideration of the design of the research instruments could possibly identify ways of tackling this uncertainty. It is also important to be aware that other aspects of the methodologies, such as the sampling and interview techniques, could bias the results.

Interviews with teaching staff clearly revealed that the impact of library EIS on teaching was influenced by more than just the provision of EIS per se: their perception of the benefits for their students and the barriers that exist to their own use of EIS would also affect the extent of this impact.

However, as methods of delivery change through the e-learning culture attendant upon the introduction of UWE's VLE, so the impact of EIS will increase. The student survey would suggest that this is already happening, and it is likely to continue as more teaching staff become familiar with the technology and learn how to create links to the resources available.

That EIS are now firmly embedded as part of the research process was illustrated dramatically by the researchers' unanimous endorsement of EIS.

Conclusions

Are we having an impact?

The project has clearly demonstrated the value of EIS at UWE, with its potential to have an enormous impact on teaching and learning. However, what has also emerged is that the extent of this impact is dependent on a number of contextual factors. Whether the amount of money the library spends on EIS is worthwhile depends on whether we can maximize their impact by addressing some of the contextual issues. This study has highlighted some of the ways this can be achieved.

Promotion and training

The fact that only 54% of students identified themselves as users of EIS suggests there is a need for the library to make even greater efforts to promote their use.

All the academics, but especially researchers with years of experience, tended to use the resources that they were used to, and not to discover what new and possibly more useful resources might be available. It was felt that promotion of new EIS resources, and in particular face-to-face research-focused training aimed at established members of staff, would be welcomed.

Working with academics to help them identify relevant resources

This study indicates that academic staff are the main influence on students' decisions to use particular EIS (or not). Academic staff are therefore key to the impact of EIS on students' learning. Whereas in the past the focus of library training has been on the student population, this study highlights the importance of providing training for academics as well.

It is clear that, more than ever, there is a need for a team approach, with librarians working with academic staff to support use of EIS for learning. This would ideally lead to the convergence of library and teaching roles within the framework of e-learning support.

VLE training for teaching and library staff

VLEs are now considered an essential tool teaching tool, and some academic staff expressed the need to learn how to use them effectively before they could exploit them fully. Librarians will also require training if they are to offer advice on suitable EIS to be linked to from a VLE.

Experience gained

This ambitious project would not have been undertaken without the support and guidance of the Initiative. There have been enormous benefits: the relationships developed with the clients; the deepening of our understanding of the academic processes involved in teaching, learning and research; an opportunity to promote aspects of the library service in context; and the PR value of raising the profile of the library with academics and researchers.

There have also been staff development opportunities. Our project team was able to gain expertise in project management and research methods. Furthermore, we now have some useful baseline data and information with which to compare future evaluations.

Measuring impact is not something that will come to an end for us when our involvement in the Initiative finishes, but will be an ongoing process that will feed into our planning for the future.

References

Craven, J. and Brophy, P. (2004) Evaluating the Longitudinal Impact of Networked Services in UK Public Libraries: the Longitude II project. In *Proceedings of the 5th Northumbria International Conference on Performance Measurement in Libraries and Information Services, 28–31 July, Durham, UK.*

Everest, K. and Payne, P. (2001) *The Impact of Libraries on Learning, Teaching and Research. Report of the LIRG seminar held in Leeds, 30 October 2001, SCONUL Newsletter,* 24, Winter 2001, 60–3.

Markless, S. and Streatfield, D. (2005) Facilitating the Impact Implementation Programme, *Library and Information Research,* 29 (91), 10–15.

Payne, P. and Conyers, A. (2004) Are We Making a Difference? The LIRG/SCONUL Measuring Impact Initiative, *Library and Information Research,* 28 (88), 59–61.

Payne, P. and Conyers, A. (2005) Measuring the Impact of Higher Education Libraries: the LIRG/SCONUL Impact Implementation Initiative, *Library and Information Research,* 29 (91), 3–9.

12

Proving our worth? Measuring the impact of the public library service in the UK

Juliet Eve

Introduction

Are public libraries about books, or about meeting shared national and local government priorities? The obvious answer to this question is that they are about both, and that these things are not mutually exclusive. However, the public library sector in the UK seems to be suffering from an identity crisis, or perhaps more accurately, those with a significant stake in the service are divided as to its function and purpose. Consequently, what needs to be done to improve it, and how we should assess whether it is achieving its goals are matters of considerable discussion. If we are not sure who we are, or what our (main) purpose is, how can we establish and implement the best methods for assessing whether or not we are achieving our goals? Can we 'prove our worth' if there is significant disagreement about what the core nature of that 'worth' is? These might seem abstract distractions from the solid need to develop performance measures, and to devise methods for proving value and impact, but this paper argues that the issue of developing relevant measures of success is actually as much political as methodological.

Changing landscape of the public library service

The history of the public library displays a continuity of purpose and service provision (notably the provision of reference services and fiction, the promotion of reading, and attempting to meet the needs of all communities). In the last decade or so, however, there have been a number of trends that have significantly affected not only service provision, but also how the service perceives itself. The key question is one of purpose: what should a 21st-century library service look like and do? Allied to this are issues of how it should account for itself.

These trends can be summarized under three main headings, although the issues cannot be easily separated as they have developed concurrently and are closely interwoven:

1 Changing political landscape
2 Formalization of library roles
3 Technological developments.

Changing political landscape

There are two key factors at work here: changes in the way local government has to account for itself to central government, with a greater emphasis on value for money and meeting set targets that relate to central government goals; and the role of the public library service in delivering national agendas, such as equipping citizens with the necessary skills to participate in the 'information society'. This agenda has for the most part been taken up by libraries, keen to see themselves at centre-stage in delivering such a society. These changes have undoubtedly benefited public libraries, bringing unprecedented attention and increased funding for initiatives such as the national ICT infrastructure the People's Network. Greater, and tighter, inspection of local government services via the Comprehensive Performance Assessment has also given libraries the opportunity to prove their value by highlighting how they contribute to a range of policy agendas, established by central and local government as 'shared priorities'.

Formalization of library roles

Political shifts have led to a change in how the public service thinks and talks about itself, rather than a radical shift in what it does. For example, in the 1980s community librarianship sought to achieve similar goals to those in the current social inclusion agenda. The history of the 'Libraries Change Lives' award indicates how libraries have been committed to social inclusion for some time (e.g. projects working with prisoners, refugees and young people) (Community Services Group, 1992).

What has happened is a formalization of public library activities, as their goals become increasingly expressed in the language of central government social agendas. The policy statement of 1998, *Our Information Age*, sums up this trend, with its focus on lifelong learning, social inclusion and the expansion of ICT facilities and training (COI, 1998). Subsequent developments have given greater prominence to encouraging better literacy and numeracy skills in both adults and children (see, for example, the Moser report (DEE, 1999), the Skills for Life national strategy for improving adult literacy and numeracy (National Literacy Trust, 2005), the Green Paper *Every Child Matters* (DES, 2003), and related initiatives such as Surestart and Bookstart (see www.everychildmatters.gov.uk/).

Formalization of learning

Although libraries have always supported learning both formal and informal, they are now seen as centres for lifelong learning and are increasingly forming a key part of local authority education strategies. Birmingham's Central Library, for example, offers a Learning Shop and a Learning Centre, and is the city's hub for finding out about learning opportunities, as well as providing a range of courses supported by Learner Support Officers.

Partnerships

This formalization of roles has increased, and depended upon a huge growth in partnership working, which has expanded what libraries can offer and where, and has often been key in meeting the social inclusion agendas discussed. One aspect of these initiatives has been increased evaluation: all externally funded projects require evaluation, and continued funding is dependent on it.

Technological developments

These developments have taken place against a backdrop of rapidly developing ICTs: indeed, it is impossible to separate the strands into easy categories, given their interdependence. The central government drive to increase access to ICT facilities and training is, of course, inherently political. The possibilities opened up for libraries by this, and the attraction of delivering lifelong learning via ICTs, is best summed up by the People's Network (PN), a UK-wide ICT programme which has connected all UK public libraries to the internet and which provides PCs for learning and more. It has been suggested by the Tavistock Institute, which carried out a thorough evaluation of the PN, that this, among other factors, is leading to a paradigm shift in the service (Sommerlad et al., 2004). Importantly, this affects not just users, some of whom have been attracted into libraries perhaps for the first time in order to take an 'internet taster session' but also, crucially, politicians at national level, who see the networked public library as a key player in creating a suitably skilled 'information society'-ready populace, and the public library sector itself. Faced with a challenge of perceived irrelevance, the visionary *New Library: the People's Network* (Library and Information Commission, 1997) galvanized and inspired the sector and brought a perhaps much-needed sense of purpose to a service that had been underfunded for years and which lacked direction. Since then there has been something of a revival in the fortunes of the public library, and over the last 10 years national government has increasingly emphasized its importance in underpinning a number of key goals in its social agenda. This has been echoed across Europe in a number of 'information society' documents and initiatives, such as the recent Lisbon Strategy with its emphasis on lifelong learning (European Council, 2000). There is also a growing range of co-operation, sharing of good practice and research across libraries in Europe: for example, the PULMAN initiative (www.pulmanweb.org/) and the European-funded project Calimera (www.calimera.org).

What is a public library for in the 21st century?

Alongside these political and technological shifts, debate about the role of the library service has flourished. After the initial injection of enthusiasm supplied by the PN developments, tension has developed regarding the main purpose of the service, including something of a backlash against ICT provision from some quarters. The brief revival of fortunes has given way to a perception – much covered in the media – that the service is in a state of (terminal) decline, and there is fierce argument about how to reverse this trend. For every champion of the PN and its new content and services there is a voice of 'doom and gloom' predicting the closure of public libraries in the next 20 years if they fail to become more like bookshops (Coates, 2004; Libri, 2005). This is of course to simplify the debate. In the last five years, however, there has been an unprecedented number of reports addressing the state of the service (Audit Commission, 2003; Department for Culture, Media and Sport (DCMS), 2003; Leadbeater, 2003; Coates, 2004; Libri, 2005).

The argument can be simplified as follows: that the future of the service lies in delivering the range of activities that have burgeoned in the last few years, and that libraries should focus on what is perceived to be their key role, namely to provide fiction and reference books for borrowing, or 'having somewhere quiet to get on with homework or other research' (Libri, 2005, 2). These disputes are key, in that they dictate the nature and direction of evaluation: continued funding of the service depends on 'proof' of success, and on raising the profile of public libraries and demonstrating that they are good value for money. The government has made it clear that extra spending will only be considered when there is a clear strategy to deliver value for money, and when a track record of increased resources leading to improved results can be demonstrated (MLA, 2005c).

Evaluating the work of the public library

What are the questions we need to be asking, and how do we best measure results? How has the public library sector traditionally measured its success, and what might be the way forward in the light of all the current issues and obstacles outlined above?

Formal evaluation of the sector

Formal evaluation of public libraries falls to the Department for Culture, Media and Sport (DCMS), though it has no say in core funding, which is the responsibility of local government.

The measurement of public library success has long been seen as book issues and visitor numbers; for some time libraries have also carried out user satisfaction surveys (the PLUS surveys, co-ordinated by CIPFA, the Chartered Institute of Public Finance). These are limited in that they are usually carried out every three years with only library users, and supply quantitative information about library usage. Even so, particularly when libraries are also carrying out other surveys (e.g. of externally funded projects), 'questionnaire fatigue' can be an issue, 'and not just for the public' (Bundy, 2005, personal communication).

LISU, the Library and Information Statistics Unit, provides annual reports on library usage, including public libraries, and notes trends in spending on books, issue figures, etc. Their figures have been used in several of the controversial reports that have placed falling book issues and visitor numbers at the heart of the public library's problems (Coates, 2004).

Only in 2001 were library standards introduced; these were revised in 2004 in light of the document *Framework for the Future* (DCMS, 2003). The ten standards cover areas such as:

- distance from a library
- opening hours
- workstations with internet access
- number of library visits per thousand population (not including, or measuring, virtual visits)
- the rating of the service; the data to come from PLUS surveys
- items added annually per thousand of population.

Interestingly, given the controversy surrounding the subject, no standard is set for book issues. In terms of evaluating social effects, more sophisticated measures to include the kind of outreach work libraries are being encouraged by government to perform are also not included.

Changing nature of evaluation

Evaluation is vital if libraries are to know whether what they are doing is successful. Yet this may not be as straightforward as it appears: successful by whose standards? Public libraries have a very wide remit, in that they must attempt to serve the whole population, and what people want from them is likely to vary enormously. This has been evident in a number of studies evaluating the success of ICT programmes in libraries, which have highlighted many positive success stories and real benefits, but also picked up on the tensions between these new services and the more traditional library role (Eve and Brophy, 2000; Brophy, 2004).

From outputs to impacts

There has been a welcome move over the last few years towards an evaluation of the **outcome** of a particular service or initiative, and an interest in the **impact** the library can have; a study in 2002 provided an excellent overview of impact evaluation across the museums, libraries and archives sector (Wavell et al., 2002). This has replaced the input–output model which has for so long dominated measurement of library success: how much are we spending on books and how many people take them out? Of course, at a time when the promotion of literacy in adults is a key national priority these are still important indicators of a library's contribution, but evaluation and impact measures must go further than this if they are adequately to address the complexity of provision a modern library service can offer.

This trend is particularly notable in studies seeking to evaluate the PN and the role of libraries in supporting learning. Sommerlad et al. (2004) looked at the impact of the PN on library users, on developing library services, and on the impact on wider social objectives. The Museum, Library and Archives Council (MLA)'s *Inspiring Learning for All* (MLA, 2005b) set out a number of generic learning outcomes against which both formal and informal learning can be measured. MLA also funded a series of supporting work, the Learning Impact Research Project (Hooper-Greenhill, 2002; Moussouri, 2002; Hooper-Greenhill et al., 2003). Findings from the Calimera project suggest that similar work is being called for across Europe (MDR Partners, 2005), and work in the USA has been attempting to map the economic contribution libraries make (Barron et al., 2005).

These evaluations also seek to adopt new methods that move beyond the traditional gathering of statistics, with qualitative indicators of success increasingly being sought and used. As the Cultural Heritage Consortium (2002, 19) states:

> the existing system for collecting quantitative data ... is patchy, inconsistent and incomplete . . . [and] *also is failing to generate any useful information on the outcomes of the services or the impact they make* [emphasis added].

The use of qualitative data and narratives (often charting personal success stories) is increasing and makes for powerful, and often moving, representations of the more intangible aspects of the public library service. This type of data, however, is time-consuming to collect and requires staff expertise to analyse and exploit it if it is to prove valuable. As Wavell et al. (2002) note, project evaluations vary enormously in quality and are 'more to do with immediate outcomes than really getting to grip with longer-term impact', and their use by policy makers may distort the true picture.

In line with recent trends, the DCMS has launched impact measures that show the contribution libraries make to five of the seven 'shared priorities':

- Raising standards across schools
- Improving the quality of life for children, young people, families at risk and older people
- Promoting healthier communities
- Creating safer and stronger communities
- Promoting the economic vitality of localities (MLA, 2005a).

These measurements seek to provide evidence of the wider social impact of the service, although this is not an easy task, either methodologically (how can the specific impact the *library* made be proved?) or given the kind of short-term results usually demanded from funders.

Future directions

In 2004, the Laser Foundation commissioned research to devise a number of impact measures for public libraries. These seek specifically to prove worth to government, by focusing on four of the 'shared priorities' (health, older people, education, and children). The report's key message is that 'more complex measures and methodologies are needed to properly capture the social benefits of library services', and that this should extend to economic impacts (PriceWaterhouseCoopers, 2005, 4).

This is the kind of work that usefully counteracts the narrow focus of reports such as Coates (2004), which stresses falling book issues and visitor figures but not much else, as it provides significant quantitative and qualitative data to suggest that libraries really are contributing to policy agendas. It is highly timely, and a step forward that the report suggests:

> Books are not everything, and book-borrowing indicators should not be used as the prime measure of how libraries contribute to local and national priorities.
> (PriceWaterhouseCoopers, 2005, 4).

This is in sharp contrast to the position of the library charity Libri, which co-financed the Coates report and has followed this up with *From University to Village Hall* (Libri, 2005, 5). They claim that 'lack of investment ensures that the core function of libraries continues to erode, and that many librarians seem to believe that lending books is no longer the prime role of the public library'.

These two approaches sum up how the battle lines are drawn: those who suggest the decline in the service is to be reversed by a focus on the prime function of providing a high-quality book service, and those who feel that the relevance or otherwise of the service will be judged on how it contributes to policy agendas.

Evaluation of the service will depend on what is seen to be its central purpose and what impact it can make. Yet public libraries are being sent highly contradictory messages, which makes responding to the challenges a significant problem, particularly when resources (notably in the form of staff time and expertise) to carry out increasingly sophisticated evaluation and impact studies are scarce.

Acknowledgements

I am grateful to Clare Nankivell, Monitoring and Evaluation Manager, Sure Start Birmingham, for reading and commenting on this paper. Thanks also to David Bundy, Quality Services Manager at Sutton Libraries, for his input.

References

Audit Commission (2002) *Building Better Library Services. The Audit Commission Summary*, www.audit-commission.gov.uk/reports/NATIONAL-REPORT.asp?CategoryID= &ProdID=9D0A0DD1-3BF9-4c52-9112-67D520E7C0AB [accessed 9 March 2006].

Barron, D., Williams, R. V., Bajjaly, S., Arns, J. and Wilson, S. (2005) *The Economic Impact of Libraries on South Carolina*, www.libsci.sc.edu/SCEIS/home.htm [accessed 19 August 2005].

Brophy, P. (2004) *The People's Network: moving forward*, London, Resource, www.mla.gov.uk/documents/id1414rep.pdf [accessed 27 July 2005].

Central Office of Information (COI) (1998) *Our Information Age*, London, Central Office of Information.

Coates, T. (2004) *Who's in Charge?*, London, Libri, www.libri-forums.org/ Who%27s%20in%20char_e_(as%20printed.pdf [accessed 29 July 2005].

Community Services Group (1992) *Celebrating the 10th Anniversary of the Libraries Change Lives Award*, www.cilip.org.uk/NR/rdonlyres/4135A646-D5BE-483C-83E6-43B2F3E0E4D8/0/ LCLA10yearbooklet.pdf [accessed 14 August 2005].

Cultural Heritage Consortium (2002) *Impact Evaluation of Museums, Archives and Libraries: quantitative time series data identification exercise*, London, Resource, www.mla.gov.uk/ documents/id18rep.pdf [accessed 15 August 2005].

Department for Culture, Media and Sport (DCMS) (2003) *Framework for the Future*, London, Department for Culture, Media and Sport, www.culture.gov.uk/global/publications/ archive_2003/framework_future.htm [accessed 1 August 2005].

Department for Culture, Media and Sport (2004) *Public Library Service Standards*, London, Department for Culture, Media and Sport, www.culture.gov.uk/NR/rdonlyres/2374D642-E0E0-40BF-8BE4-F12047103DBE/0/PUBLICLIBRARYSERVICESTANDARDSFINAL 1OCTOBER.pdf [accessed 2 August 2005].

Department for Education and Employment (DfEE) (1999) *A Fresh Start – improving literacy and numeracy*, London, Department for Education and Employment. For overview and recommendations: www.literacytrust.org.uk/socialinclusion/adults/moser.html [accessed 19 August 2005].

Department for Education and Skills (DES) (2003) *Every Child Matters Green Paper*, London, Stationery Office, www.everychildmatters.gov.uk/_files/EBE7EEAC90382663E0D5BBF 24C99A7AC.pdf [accessed 27 July 2005].

European Council (2000) *Presidency Conclusions: Lisbon European Council, 23 & 24 March 2000*, http://ue.eu.int/ueDocs/cms_Data/docs/pressData/en/ec/00100-r1.en0.htm.

Eve, J. and Brophy, P. (2000) Vital Issues: the perception, and use, of ICT services in UK public libraries, *LIBRES: Library and Information Science Research*, **10** (2), http://libres.curtin.edu.au/libres10n2/vital.htm [accessed 29 July 2005].

Hooper-Greenhill, E. (2002) *Developing a Scheme for Finding Evidence of the Outcomes and Impact of Learning in Museums, Archives and Libraries: the conceptual framework*, London, Resource, www.mla.gov.uk/documents/lirpanalysis.pdf [accessed 13 August 2005].

Hooper-Greenhill, E. et al. (2003) *Measuring the Outcomes and Impact of Learning in Museums, Archives and Libraries*, London, Resource, www.mla.gov.uk/documents/insplearn_ wp20030501.pdf [accessed 13 August 2005].

Leadbeater, C. (2003) *Overdue: how to create a modern public library service*, London, Laser Foundation, www.demos.co.uk/catalogue/default.aspx?id=262 [accessed 3 August 2005].

Library and Information Commission (1997) *New Library: the People's Network*, London, Library and Information Commission.

Libri (2005) *From University to Village Hall*, London, Libri, www.libri-forums.org/From%20University%20to%20Village%20Hall%20FINAL.pdf [accessed 9 March 2006].

MDR Partners (2005) *Calimera: report and recommendations on impact measurement for local services*, www.calimera.org/Lists/Resources%20Library/The%20end%20user%20experience, %20a%20usable%20community%20memory/CALIMERA%20%20Report%20and%20Rec ommendations%20on%20impact%20measurement%20for%20local%20services%20-%20Final.pdf [accessed 17 August 2005].

Moussouri, T. (2002) *A Context for the Development of Learning Outcomes in Museums, Libraries and Archives*, London, Resource, www.mla.gov.uk/documents/moussouri01_ver2.pdf [accessed 13 August 2005].

Museums, Libraries and Archives Council (MLA)(2005a) *Public Library Service Impact Measures – Proposals for 2005/2006*, London, MLA.

Museums, Libraries and Archives Council (MLA)(2005b) *Inspiring Learning for All*, London, MLA, www.mla.gov.uk/documents /insplearn_il4a200005.pdf [accessed 6 August 2005].

Museums, Libraries and Archives Council (MLA) (2005c) *Impact Evaluation Programme*, www.mla.gov.uk/information/evidence/ ev_impev.asp [accessed 19 August 2005].

National Literacy Trust (2005) *Skills for Life*, www.literacytrust.org.uk/socialinclusion/ adults/skills.html#quality [accessed 19 August 2005].

PriceWaterhouseCoopers (2005) *Libraries Impact Project*, London, Laser Foundation, www.bl.uk/about/cooperation/pdf/laserfinal6.pdf [accessed 2 August 2005].

Sommerlad, E., Child, C., Ramsden, C. and Kelleher, J. (2004) *Books and Bytes: new service paradigms for the 21st century library*, London, Big Lottery Fund, www.nof.org.uk/ documents/live/674pC_Peoples_Network_evaluation2.pdf [accessed 9 March 2006].

Wavell, C., Baxter, G. and Johnson, I. (2002) *Impact Evaluation of Museums, Archives and Libraries: Available Evidence Project*, London, Resource, www.rgu.ac.uk/files/imreport.pdf [accessed 15 August 2005].

13
Outcomes and impacts, dollars and sense: are libraries measuring up?

José-Marie Griffiths

Introduction

The measurement of return on investment (ROI) has been applied to many different types of organization and community resource. Although this is common in the for-profit sector, the application of benefit/cost, cost-effectiveness, impact and ROI measures to libraries, museums, schools and colleges, parks etc. has lagged behind considerably. Part of the difficulty has been in quantifying benefits from non-priced goods and services that can differ from use to use, user to user, as well as from library to library (as their mix of service offerings varies). In today's climate of strained budgets and pressures for increased accountability and transparency, the need for clear and accurate statements of how public monies are allocated and used, and the resulting benefits or outcomes, is paramount in ensuring continued investment.

Overview of the study

In 2004 we undertook a landmark comprehensive study to assess taxpayer ROI from public libraries, specifically the public libraries in the state of Florida in the USA. Public libraries allow users to share knowledge and services at a cost to them as taxpayers and in the time they spend using the libraries; however, all taxpayers in Florida benefit from the public libraries through their considerable contribution to education, the economy, tourism, retirement, quality of life and so on. This study examined several economic approaches to considering returns on public library availability and use, and found that they all show substantial returns that exceed taxpayer investment.

The results: what we learned

Utilization

How much use?

Florida's public libraries are extensively used, by both individuals and organizations. In 2003/4 there were 68.3 million individual visits to public libraries in Florida, and at least 25.2 million remote internet connections to the public libraries (not including remote connections by children under 18 or tourists). Florida's public libraries are used an average of at least 5.24 times per Florida resident per year, or 7.74 times per year by the 54% of Florida residents who have visited a Florida public library in the past year. Adult Florida residents account for just over half of the total personal visits to public libraries, school-aged children account for over one-third of visits, and tourists account for about 5% of visits. School-aged children visit Florida public libraries most frequently, at almost twice per month.

Adult Florida residents who use Florida public libraries via remote internet connections do so much more frequently than those who visit the libraries in person. Adult users of the public libraries (excluding tourists) make 5.16 personal visits annually, but make more than 15 (15.77) internet connections during the same time. However, because more individuals make personal visits than those who use the internet, there are almost three such visits per capita per year, compared to almost two remote internet connections made per capita.

Florida's public libraries are also used by librarians in other libraries on behalf of their own user communities, including schools, college/universities, businesses, government offices and hospitals. The total number of documents obtained from the public libraries is estimated to be 271,000 per year. Organizations also used public library meeting rooms, participated in library-sponsored groups and training, and used the public libraries' access to licensed online databases and electronic publications, both from within the libraries and via remote access.

Who uses the libraries?

In 2003/4 an estimated 11.8 million people visited Florida public libraries in person. Adult Florida residents form the majority of visitors, but tourists form a surprising 29% of such visitors, although they account for only 5% of visits as they tend to visit just once.

Over half of Florida's adult resident population and over a third of all Florida children make personal visits to Florida's public libraries. Looking at the population of library users by various demographics shows that library users are very diverse, although not in proportion to the Florida population as a whole. Library users tend to be female, slightly older, somewhat more educated, employed or retired, and slightly more affluent than the overall population.

Organizational users of the public libraries generally use the service via their own libraries. In Florida, 71% of government and non-profit organizations, 66% of businesses, 88% of colleges and universities, and 83% of K-12 (Kindergarten to Level 12) schools make use of the public libraries.

What do people do at the library?

People use a wide range of services offered in the public libraries, although checking out materials for use outside the library still predominates, accounting for more than 70% of total uses. In addition to borrowing materials, however, personal visitors also use other services at the library: they draw on reference services, use materials in the library, access the internet from the library, use computer workstations for non-internet access, attend library programmes or receive technology instruction at the library. Those who access the internet from the library do so for a number of different reasons, including e-mail, using the online catalogue, to view or download articles, to access online bibliographic databases, play online games, visit chat rooms, explore virtual museum exhibits, and to view or download e-books.

There are more than 25 million remote internet uses of the Florida public libraries annually. Remote uses of public libraries are mainly for searching the library's online catalogue, reserving books and searching online databases, though uses also include viewing or downloading articles, 'ask a librarian' services, viewing or downloading e-books, accessing online reference services and ordering photocopies of materials.

People use public libraries for many purposes

Public libraries are used for many different purposes. These can be organized into four major categories: recreational, personal, educational, and work-related needs.

Recreational needs account for a total of 19.2 million uses, of which 65% were in person and 35% were remote internet connections.

Adults seek information from public libraries to support a wide variety of personal needs. Adult Florida residents make a total of 16 million uses per year of the public library for personal information needs. Of these, 54% are personal visits and 46% are through remote internet connections. These needs range from health/wellness and hobbies/work to learning about culture and supporting occasional problems.

Public libraries are used to support the educational needs of people, both students and teachers. Adult residents of Florida made a total of 18.4 million educational uses of public libraries in the past year. Of these visits, 50% were in person and 50% were through remote internet connections. The majority of the educational uses by Florida adults were in their role as students. The majority of adult students are engaged in undergraduate level study. Teachers' educational uses tended to be related to undergraduate and K-8 teaching. Students' educational uses of the libraries included work on assignments and as a place for study. Teachers use the public library to prepare lessons, presentations, papers, etc., and to keep up with the literature.

Public libraries are also used to support people's work-related needs. In the past year, Florida adults made 6.2 million uses of public libraries for such purposes. Of these uses, 70% were in person and 30% were through remote internet connections. The types of work-related need ranged from research to management to locating individuals. Organizational uses of public libraries cover a broad spectrum of services. The most common was for borrowing books (all types of library), photocopies of articles (government and non-profit libraries) and reference services (school, and government and non-profit libraries).

Florida adults indicate that public libraries are important for all purposes of use

Public libraries are important to their user communities in numerous ways, depending on the type of need/use. Overall, public libraries were considered more important for educational and work-related uses than for recreational and personal uses.

Public libraries are important in supporting the various types of use in many ways. Public library users consider the importance of the libraries in terms of the positive outcomes or benefits that result from their use. Some of these outcomes are quantifiable, such as time or money saved; others are more qualitative and relative in nature.

Financial impacts

Our analysis revealed that overall, Florida's public libraries return $6.54 for every $1.00 invested from all sources ($2,933.660 million ÷ $448.903 million = $6.54).

The total revenue investment in Florida's public libraries is $449 million. The total economic return attributable to the existence of the public libraries is $2.9 billion, based on an analysis of what would happen if the public libraries ceased to exist; this includes the net benefits (added costs to use alternatives), the benefits that would be lost because users would not bother to use alternatives, and revenues that would be lost by vendors, contractors, etc.

Using State Library and Archives of Florida data and data from the surveys we carried out, the Regional Economic Modeling Inc. (REMI) model looked at the initial public investment in public libraries ($443 million) and considered the implications of not funding them, but of redistributing the money to alternative government spending activities. Projecting forward over 32 years (2004–2035), the REMI model indicated that if funding for public libraries were to be reallocated across Florida's government sectors, the state economy would result in a net decline of $5.6 billion in wages and 68,700 jobs. Thus, for every $6,448 spent on public libraries from public funding sources (federal, state and local) in Florida, one job is created.

For every dollar of public support spent on public libraries in Florida, GRP increases by $9.08.

For every dollar of public support spent on public libraries in Florida, income (wages) increases by $12.66.

Benefit (B) to cost (C) ratios are estimated from the multiple approaches using survey data or REMI as follows:

The B/C (availability) of Florida's public libraries is 5.2:1. ($2,331.922 million ÷ $448.903 million = 5.2).
The benefit (B) to the state (in terms of availability of Florida's public libraries) is $2.3 billion, measured as the total cost to use alternatives, if the public libraries did not exist. The cost (C) is $449 million.

The B/C (use) of Florida's public libraries is 7.2:1.4 ($3,211.219 million ÷ $448.903 million = 7.2).
The benefit (B) to the state (in terms of time and money saved through use of Florida's public libraries) is $3.2 billion. The cost (C) is $449 million.

The B/C$_{REMI}$ (wages) is 5.0:1
The benefit (B) to the state (in terms of wages) is $9.2 billion. The cost (C) is $1.83 billion.

The B/C$_{REMI}$ (GRP) is 3.7:1
The benefit to the state (in terms of GRP or output) is $6.7 billion. The cost (C) is $1.83 billion.

It is clear that, regardless of the approach used, the Florida public library cost–benefit ratios are impressive.

Methodologies – how we performed the study

The study to measure taxpayers' return on investment in public libraries in Florida was conducted from December 2003 to August 2004. It consisted of several components, including:

- a literature review
- a workshop of key stakeholder groups
- data collection and analysis:
  - annual data reported to the state
  - household telephone interviews of adults 18 and over
  - in-library surveys of adults 18 and over
  - survey of school, university and college, industry, and non-profit librarians, media or information specialists
  - a follow-up survey of public libraries and/or systems.
- a special economic input/output model and analysis (REMI) was performed by the Center for Economic Forecasting and Analysis, Florida State University.

In the analysis stage, we considered and computed benefits as well as contingent valuation – that is, what would happen if the libraries were not available.

Literature review

We began with a literature review of relevant articles examining other ROI studies of libraries and other approaches to examining their usefulness and value. The review covered ROI and similar studies of a variety of information and public services, such as public, academic, school and special libraries; museums; hospitals; public parks; and so on. Much of this work involved special libraries, although there are exemplary studies on public libraries as well. The approach to the study of libraries began in the early 1980s and evolved over time. A bibliography of these studies is available in Part ii of the full published report.

A series of studies published by the author with King Research considered the costs (investment) of the libraries and their services, the outputs produced, the use of the outputs, and the outcomes resulting from that use. The ROI relate the costs to the outcomes from multiple perspectives: the user community, the community served (users and non-users), and the funding decision makers. Public library outcomes are organized into three broad categories:

- Improved quality of life
- Support for lifelong learning
- Support for the community's economy.

In the mid to late 1990s the concern for measuring ROI waned as the world wide web, electronic publishing and digital libraries evolved and demanded attention. It is only recently, in the wake of the dotcom collapse, the tragedy of 11 September 2001, and several high-profile scandals in all sectors, that ROI has re-emerged in response to a need to justify public expenditures.

Workshop

We conducted a two-day workshop on ROI approaches. Two economists, Tim Lynch, Florida State University, Center for Economic Forecasting and Analysis, and Steven Stewart, University of Arizona, joined our staff and representatives of the Division of Library and Information Services (DLIS), key stakeholder groups, and selected public library directors to discuss alternative approaches to taxpayer ROI and public libraries. It is through this interactive workshop that we crafted an ROI approach that was considered meaningful to the key stakeholder groups; that was feasible from the data collection perspective; and that could be implemented in a longitudinal manner by the libraries themselves or DLIS on their behalf. The workshop was held in March 2004, with several project team members in attendance.

Household telephone interviews with adults 18 and over

A telephone survey of Florida households was conducted from 10 May to 16 June 2004 by the University of Pittsburgh, University Center for Social and Urban Research (UCSUR). The list-assisted random digit dialling (RDD) methodology was used. Telephone numbers were randomly selected from all 100-banks of numbers (i.e. area code, exchange, and first two digits of the last four numbers – 123-456-78XX) within the state that included at least two (White Page) listed households. This method, commonly used in the survey industry, increases efficiency, resulting in more households reached without greatly increasing coverage error. RDD sampling is superior to samples of White Page-listed households in that they include unlisted numbers as well, making them theoretically representative of all telephone households in a particular geographic area. The adult in the household having the most recent birth date was selected for the interview. Computer-assisted telephone interviewing (CATI), in which interviewers read questions from a computer screen and key answers directly into the system, was used. A minimum of six calls was made to each number at varying times of the day and on different days of the week to maximize the likelihood of contact. The telephone questionnaire was designed by project staff and a telephone script version prepared by Janet Schlarb (UCSUR) and a Spanish version prepared by

UCSUR staff. A total of 7,294 telephone numbers were sampled, resulting in 764 completed interviews, including 55 conducted in Spanish.

In-library survey

Even though it was not initially proposed, following the workshop in February we felt that it would be helpful to conduct interviews in Florida public libraries to validate visit-related questions obtained from the household telephone interviews and, in some instances, to combine responses from the two surveys. Also, we asked some questions not asked in the telephone survey.

The survey consisted of two self-administered questionnaires having most questions in common, but with some questions unique to each. This method allowed us to keep the questionnaires relatively short (six pages) and yet provide all of the necessary questions. Questionnaires were sent to the participating public libraries in both English and Spanish. A total of 1,982 questionnaires were sent to the libraries.

Survey of organization libraries

Public libraries are used to support organizations such as businesses, schools and others in two ways: employees use the public libraries directly to obtain information for work-related purposes, students use them for class assignments, or employees will seek information from their organization's library, which in turn may have to use their public library or another source to obtain the information. This may typically involve interlibrary loans, reference services, access to government documents and so on.

The survey of organization libraries was designed to obtain information about the extent to which this takes place and the outcomes of the organizational use of public libraries, although it did not establish the outcomes of the original users' needs or uses of the information. The organizations surveyed came from lists of such organizations as schools, colleges and universities, businesses and non-profit organizations. The survey involved a self-administered questionnaire that was mailed by UCSUR in early June, along with a post-free return envelope.

REMI

The REMI is a widely accepted and used dynamic integrated input–output and econometric model. For this study, staff used REMI version 6.0, released in September 2004. REMI is used extensively to measure proposed legislative and other programme and policy economic impacts across the private and public sectors of the state. In addition, it is the most frequently chosen tool to measure the economic effects of business and government project impacts by a wide array of private research groups, federal, state and local agencies and major universities across the state and nation. Staff developed two scenarios: first, the associated rate of growth of government spending and individual user (time and resource) expenditure to use of the current Florida public library system. Scenario two examined the surveyed user systems benefits by quantifying value-based estimates of the 'alternative' cost of providing these same services in the private sector, presuming that public libraries did not exist in the state.

Conclusion

Throughout the study, a conservative approach of estimating benefits and returns was used, such that the results can be considered a lower bound. This means that the ROI and benefit–cost ratios are at least those reported, and might with further study be even higher.

Florida's public libraries are recognised as active community participants, offering a wide range of services to the public in their quest for knowledge, information and enlightenment. However, relatively little was known about how Florida's public libraries contribute economically to their users, the communities they serve and the state as a whole. This study provided information specific to the state of Florida and the value of its public libraries, as well as a model for similar assessments of library systems. Librarians worldwide can and should use similar assessments to increase public awareness about the important fiscal impact of their work, and thus provide governments and their citizens with assurance that funds spent on library programmes and services help to strengthen their local economies and communities.

The full reports of this work, including detailed tables and illustrative figures are available at http://sils.unc.edu/griffiths. The PowerPoint slides used in Dr Griffiths' presentation can be downloaded from http://sils.unc.edu/griffiths/documents/LWW6Griffiths.pdf.

14

Longitude II: assessing the value and impact of library services over time

Peter Brophy and Jenny Craven

Introduction

The Longitude II project, funded by the UK Museums, Libraries and Archives Council (MLA), was designed to develop and test a methodology for assessing how the impact of IT-based services in public libraries is achieved over time – in other words, to move from the more usual 'snapshot' views of impact towards assessing longer-term effects. We were concerned in this project both with situations where there was continuing engagement between the user and the library service, and where a single or short series of interactions led to effects later in life. We tested approaches suited to both these situations, although it is fair to say that the former predominated.

Fieldwork was carried out in two public library authorities in the UK: Cheshire County and Birmingham City Libraries. This enabled us to check that the methodologies were practical and economic to apply, as well as being sound and rigorous. As a subsidiary benefit of this approach, we gathered data on longitudinal impacts that shed light on the longer-term achievements of IT-based services in public libraries.

There is at present particular interest in the UK in securing evidence of the impact of investment in IT-based infrastructure and services in public libraries. The investment of more than £170 million (including the cost of a major training programme for library staff and the associated content digitization programme) by the People's Network (www.peoplesnetwork.gov.uk) has enabled a step-change in service delivery. However, it brings with it the need for both accountability for past investment and justification for continued expenditure.

Related studies

The project followed on from earlier work, notably the VITAL (Value and Impact of End-User IT Services in Public Libraries) project, which developed methodologies for assessing impacts on individuals and groups at particular points in time. VITAL has been described in detail elsewhere (Eve and Brophy, 2001).

During the Longitude II project we undertook a study of published research on the topic of longitudinal impact, and this has been published elsewhere (Craven, 2002). As that paper noted, 'Although much work has been undertaken in the field of library performance measurement, it tends to be of a more quantitative nature such as population and usage statistics, which only provide part of the picture and are not enough to enable assessment of impact on the users'.

Library profiles

Although our focus would be on collecting qualitative evidence, it was clear that there was a need to include in the methodology both quantitative and qualitative data that would describe the environment in which the research was taking place. Importantly, it would also highlight changes in that environment which might have driven, or otherwise influenced, changes in user behaviour. An obvious example would be where the library had upgraded its infrastructure and thus changed the possibilities and opportunities for its users.

Library profiles were thus defined, drawing as much as possible on data already available to the libraries. For example, one profile can be summarized as shown in Table 14.1.

Table 14.1 *Summary of library profile*

2003	2004
Library X offered 19 computers for public use.	Library X offered 19 computers for public use.
The number of PC hours available each week was 931 and the number of hours available each month was 3724.	The number of PC hours available each week was 884 and the number of hours available each month was 3538.
The number of PC hours booked weekly was 387 and the monthly figure was 1548. The number of PC users each week was 513, of which 377 were adults.	The number of PC hours booked weekly was 465 and the monthly figure was 1858. The number of PC users each week was 631, of which 582 were adults.

User profiling

The next part of the methodology involved collecting data on the profiles of the users who were being questioned. We wanted to know their employment status (interestingly, in our sample the largest group turned out to be those in full-time employment, followed by people not in employment and those who had retired); the frequency with which they used the library and the IT facilities ('once a week' appeared to predominate); whether they had access to IT facilities elsewhere (around 40% had a computer at home); and why they chose to use the facilities in the library. On this last point the following were the responses (in order of frequency, with the most frequent first):

- To contact other people
- Hobbies
- General use (unspecified)
- Helping to do work
- Helping to find work
- Learning a new skill
- Checking government services
- Shopping
- Local history.

We also checked with our respondents what they felt were the advantages of having internet access in the public library. They responded (again in frequency order):

- Convenience
- Free access
- Other resources available on the computers
- Better PCs than they had access to elsewhere
- Availability of staff help
- Information available on the computers
- The library environment
- Privacy
- Social aspects of use.

In both lists there were some changes over the period we surveyed, though these were not generally significant (and, we must repeat, the purpose of the exercise was to develop the methodology rather than to collect data; hence these are merely indicative findings).

We also asked our respondents about the value and importance they attached to having IT facilities in the library. Over 80% stated that they were 'of great value', and over 90% stated they were 'of great importance'. Again there were some small changes in percentages over time.

Methodologies

Although it is theoretically possible to use surrogate measures to assess impact, we determined early in the project that we would need to gather information primarily from the users themselves. Although quantitative measures are part of the picture (for example, increases in use of facilities are one indication that users are receiving some kind of value from them) we wanted to be able to assess the external impacts on individuals' lives – for example, had access to library computers enabled them to learn new skills which had changed their work or other achievements?

In consultation with the two library authorities we decided to test two different approaches. In Cheshire we conducted individual interviews with users immediately after they had used the library computers, and asked about the impacts that usage was having. We then contacted those same users again nine months later and asked about impacts attributable to their usage over that period of time.

In Birmingham we used a focus group approach instead. This had the advantage of enabling us to access some of the disadvantaged groups who were meeting in the libraries (as well as using the IT facilities) and who were targeted by the libraries' social inclusion policies. A disadvantage was that the groups tended to some extent to be self-renewing, so that rather than discussing how the experience of using library facilities had changed them over time, there could be a tendency for the later meeting (after nine months) to be another initial meeting with new users. In fact, this did not prove to be a major issue, although this is of course very dependent on the nature of the groups themselves.

Findings

Although we did not set out primarily to collect evidence of the impact of IT services in the two library authorities, we could not avoid actually collecting data. Without in any way claiming that these data are representative of the situation in the groups surveyed, it is interesting to note the kinds of developing impact our work helped to uncover. So, for example, one interview respondent said this in Phase 1:

> When I get experienced, the email is an enormous thing, that's the thing that will be of most use I think.

Nine months later, in Phase 2, the same respondent commented:

> We contacted people through Friends Reunited – all got together and had a party. Keep in touch via email.

Or take this comment from a participant in a focus group, talking in Phase 2 about their change in attitude after a period of using library IT:

> We know that eventually everything will be done (by) telephone and computer. . . . A couple of years ago I would not have been bothered, but now I am.

The Longitude toolkit

The major output from the project has been a toolkit, now freely available on the MLA website www.mla.gov.uk/action/pn/longitude.asp, containing the following sections:

1 Definitions
2 Planning Longitudinal impact assessment
   — quantitative methods
   — qualitative methods
   — issues for consideration
3 Collecting your data
   — statistical data
   — questionnaires
   — interviews
   — focus groups
   — diaries
   — observation
4 Sampling methods
5 Analysing your data
   — qualitative data analysis
   — quantitative data analysis
6 Using and presenting your data
7 Longitude in context.

The idea behind the toolkit is to make information on the design of surveys, on data collection, analysis and presentation, and on associated topics readily available to public library managers. It is too early yet to say how useful this will prove to be.

Conclusions

The Longitude II project successfully explored the development of methodologies for longitudinal evaluation of the impact of public library end-user IT services. We found that either individual semi-structured interviews or focus groups could be used, although the former appeared to give more reliable data (mainly because we could be sure we were re-interviewing the same people in Phase 2, whereas focus group membership often changes). The final report has been published and one of its comments is worth repeating here:

> By developing and applying rigorous assessment methodologies, the evidence demonstrating impact can be both comprehensive and robust. The evaluation of impact should then become a natural part of the whole process of performance measurement within an organisation (such as a library) rather than something to be evaluated in isolation.   (Brophy and Craven, 2004)

References

Brophy, P. and Craven, J. (2004) *Longitude II: a library networking impact toolkit for a user-driven environment*, London, Museums, Libraries and Archives Council, www.cerlim.ac.uk/projects/longitude/index.php.

Craven, J. (2002) A Review of Related Work in the Field of Longitudinal Assessment of Public Library IT Services, *New Review of Libraries and Lifelong Learning*, 3, 27–41.

Eve, J. and Brophy, P. (2001) *The Value and Impact of End-User IT Services in Public Libraries, Library and Information Commission Research Report 102*, CERLIM, Manchester Metropolitan University, www.cerlim.ac.uk/projects/vital/abs-pref.php.

15

The use of electronic journals in academic libraries in Castilla y León

Blanca Rodríguez Bravo and
María Luisa Alvite Díez

Introduction

This paper constitutes an initial approach to surveying the use of electronic journals in the state universities of the Spanish Autonomous Region of Castilla y León (the universities of Burgos, León, Salamanca and Valladolid). It is based on the samples provided by the smallest and most recently established universities, Burgos (UBU) and León (ULE).

The work focused on the use made by these two university communities of the journals included in the Emerald, ScienceDirect, SpringerLink and Wiley InterScience packages during the first few years of their joint subscription, between 2002 and 2004.

The literature on this topic has recently been revised and consolidated by Tenopir (2003) and in the papers of the seminar that the Ingenta Institute (2002) devoted to the subject of joint purchases and the extent to which they were worthwhile.

In the early days of the transition from paper to digital formats, consortial purchase served to expand collections in a way that suited publishers' interest in generating a fresh demand for their products. They did this by offering in an electronic form, at marginal cost, material that in principle would not have been acquired for printed collections. The journal packages considered were obtained by the Castilla y León consortium (BUCLE) following the pattern of what has been termed a 'big deal'. Such an arrangement was especially aimed at consortia, who were offered a spectacular increase in the accessibility of scientific information, breaking away from the former tendency towards continual cutbacks in library periodical collections. This approach has been the subject of debate

(Frazier, 2001a, b; Rowse, 2003; Sanville, 2001). The economies of scale represented by consortia are very well known and are borne out by the constant growth in the number of such arrangements.

The financial benefits of joint acquisition of journals and the spread of their use in large collections set up on the basis of big deals have been the topic of a number of studies. These give a framework of reference for the current work, particularly the works by Sanville (2001) and Urbano et al. (2004). It is in this context that the employment of usage statistics for electronic resources should be viewed, as also should be any evaluations of the return on investment and details of user satisfaction. Views on the usefulness of the data obtained were brought together and organized by Peters (2002). This distinguished between reasons of an academic nature, the purposes of planning and assessment of library services, financial reasons relating to the internal management of consortia and the libraries participating in them, and, finally, with motivations of a financial nature with respect to the renegotiation of licences.

Because this paper is limited to a partial analysis of usage statistics for electronic journals in two universities, the conclusions relate fundamentally to the academic use of the contents of the packages studied. As Sanville (2001) points out, in the early stages of introducing a computerized library users have not yet fully taken on board the possibilities of obtaining information from the electronic packages offered.

Objectives and methodology

The most general objective was to provide a first approximation of the consumption of electronic information by the university community in the Castilla y León region. This would yield the benefits of strengthening the hand of university libraries in negotiating with suppliers of electronic resources and guiding decision making on contracts and on how to invest limited budgets. In particular, the work would permit knowledge to be obtained about what is being used and who is using it.

UBU is a young university with 10,000 students, teaching 31 degrees and ten technical qualifications. ULE is an institution of middle size in the Spanish university context. It has 14,500 students, distributed over 54 programmes. Of particular note because of its long tradition is the degree in veterinary science, whose origins go back to 1852 and which brings together a major group of research staff.

The use made of digital packages acquired through consortial purchase was analysed, covering MCB Emerald, ScienceDirect from Elsevier, SpringerLink and Wiley InterScience. These are multidisciplinary suppliers, with the exception of Emerald, which is concerned exclusively with the distribution of material in social sciences, primarily economics and information science. The thematic range of ScienceDirect is noteworthy, as its chief orientation towards natural and health sciences is accompanied by a lesser but not negligible presence of pure and social sciences and technology. Springer has no material in the area of social sciences, but is strong in natural, pure and health sciences. Finally, Wiley shows a balanced spread over the various academic areas, although it is strongest in the fields of pure, natural and health sciences and technology. None of the packages has any real content in the area of humanities, even if there is a token presence in ScienceDirect (Rodríguez Bravo and Alvite Díez, 2005).

The period over which data were gathered ran from 2002 to 2004:

Phase 1: Data collection

Data on the use of journals from the various packages were gathered on the basis of information provided by publishers: files of total use over time of the entire set of publications available through the publishers' portals, and detailed files for each title.

Once the main standards for gathering information and setting up usage indicators for electronic information services had been reviewed, it was decided to formalize value indicators on two levels:

- Total downloads, broken down by packages and institutions for each year
- Downloads for each title, split up into institution and year.

Phase 2: Data processing and analysis

In this phase spreadsheets and graphs were produced as necessary. An in-depth study was undertaken of the body of data processed, with particular emphasis on the following:

- Individualized data for each institution:
  — articles downloaded by the institution in each year
  — titles used, broken down by institution and supplier
- Overall usage data for each of the packages of contents:
  — core titles by institution and supplier
  — spread of downloads of articles over the collections
  — usage concentration rate
- Analysis of the most frequently used titles, itemized by institution and supplier:
  — the accumulation of downloaded articles from core titles
  — the presence of newly subscribed titles among the core of most frequently used items

— the relevance of publications, taking into account the ISI Impact Factor
— comparative preferences for distributors and topic areas
• An evaluation of the adequacy of the relationship between resources and demand intended to determine the real use made of content (concentration and dispersion), with respect to the knowledge areas of the universities under consideration and the preferences of users for specific packages.

This phase turned out to be complex, given that the collection of data for the various publishers is not homogeneous or uniform over the full course of the years studied. Moreover, in the case of UBU the data put forward by title are less regular than those from its counterpart institution in León. Previous studies (Rodríguez Bravo and Alvite Díez, 2005) have also noted difficulties in identifying the titles covered by BUCLE licences, and likewise the lack of information on the use made of collections held in paper format is well known. In the case of ULE the data for downloads from Emerald for 2002 are not given, because the figures put forward by this publisher seem to reflect on-screen reading rather than downloading. Information on articles downloaded from Wiley in 2002 is also lacking for ULE.

Results

Total downloads broken down by packages and institutions for each year

With the limitations noted above taken into account, Tables 15.1 and 15.2 offer the data for downloads of articles made at each of the two institutions.

Table 15.1   Downloads of complete articles by UBU

	2002	2003	2004
Emerald	230	355	396
Science	9,222	15,201	17,340
Springer	838	505	840
Wiley	1,773	3,863	3,595

Table 15.2   Downloads of complete articles by ULE

	2002	2003	2004
Emerald	–	640	368
Science	20,642	46,018	46,210
Springer	2,023	989	2,494
Wiley	–	3,666	3,794

A general growth in the use of the packages at both institutions in 2003 is confirmed, the exception being Springer, use of which diminished in the year in question but recovered in 2004. In ULE it is also noteworthy how use of the Emerald package declined in 2004.

There is a very obvious disparity in the total figures for the use of ScienceDirect and for the rest of the distributors. ULE clearly makes much heavier use than UBU of the Elsevier and Springer packages, whereas the figures for Emerald and Wiley are roughly similar in the two universities.

It would appear that there was significant growth in the first year, but some deceleration and stabilization in later use.

Data on downloads of each title broken down by institution and year

The information on titles used takes into account only the downloads carried out, and not all possible accesses, such as articles read on screen or abstracts viewed. The threshold level employed to establish the core group involved journals that within the course of one year had been involved in ten or more downloads.

Table 15.3 *Use of packages in UBU*

	Titles subscribed to	Titles used	Core titles
Emerald	179	62	9
Science	1782	763	252
Springer	474	95	13
Wiley	551	205	42
Total	2986	1125	316

In UBU the use made of the electronic publications offered is rather limited. Not one of the packages achieved a 50% usage rate, with a good half of the journal runs available not being used at all.

Table 15.4 *Use of packages in ULE*

	Titles subscribed to	Titles used	Core titles
Emerald	179	71	13
Science	1800	1235	610
Springer	466	155	35
Wiley	491	240	108
Total	2936	1701	766

In ULE the rate of use of titles reached nearly 60%, outstripping levels recorded in similar studies elsewhere.

The ratio between titles actually used and titles subscribed to yields the spread for each of the distributors. In general, it can be noted that packages offering a larger number of titles are those that are most used. It may be observed that there is a striking spread for ScienceDirect, which in ULE exceeds 68% and in UBU 42%.

The ratio between core titles and titles actually used gives the concentration of use. The greatest concentration is to be seen with respect to the ScienceDirect package, where a high percentage of titles were used on more than ten occasions per year. The intensive use made of the Wiley package by ULE is worthy of note.

Most frequently used journals

Tables 15.5 and 15.6 show the most heavily used titles in decreasing order of use. The existence of previous paper holdings, or the fact that the title was new to the collection, are indicated, as are the publication's impact factor for 2004 according to ISI, and the topic area it covers.

Table 15.5 *Emerald in UBU*

Title	Paper version	Impact factor	Topic area
Accounting, Auditing, Accountability Journal	Yes	–	Social sciences
Library Hi Tech	Yes	–	Social sciences
European Journal of Marketing	No	–	Social sciences
Supply Chain Management: an international journal	No	–	Social sciences
Journal of Intellectual Capital	No	–	Social sciences
Journal of Consumer Marketing	No	–	Social sciences

Table 15.6 *Emerald in ULE*

Title	Paper version	Impact factor	Topic area
Journal of Intellectual Capital	No	–	Social sciences
Managerial Finance	No	–	Social sciences
European Journal of Marketing	No	–	Social sciences
Journal of Managerial Psychology	No	–	Social sciences
Journal of Documentation	Yes	1.542	Social sciences
Library Hi Tech	No	–	Social sciences

It can be noted that three of the most-used titles from this distributor are common to both universities. Two of these were previously taken in a printed format by UBU and one by ULE. Another (*Journal of Documentation*) was the only periodical in these lists with an impact factor in the *Journal Citation Report* (JCR). In the ranking for 2004 presented by Emerald, the most frequently used title is *European Journal of Marketing*, with *Journal of Consumer Marketing* coming in fifth place.

The data for this supplier appear to show use being made of titles not previously held, these representing 66.66% at UBU and 84% at ULE.

Table 15.7 *ScienceDirect in UBU*

Title	Paper version	Impact factor	Topic area
Tetrahedron Letters	Yes	2.484	Pure sciences
Analytica Chimica Acta	Yes	2.588	Pure sciences
Journal of Human Evolution	Yes	2.767	Natural sciences
Soil Biology and Biochemistry	Yes	2.234	Natural sciences
Tetrahedron	No	2.643	Pure sciences
Bioresource Technology	Yes	1.387	Natural sciences/ technology
Inorganica Chimica Acta	No	1.554	Pure sciences
Journal of Membrane Science	Yes	2.108	Natural sciences/ technology
Fluid Phase Equilibria	Yes	1.356	Pure sciences/ technology
Electrochimica Acta	Yes	2.341	Pure sciences / technology
Science of the Total Environment	No	1.925	Natural sciences
Talanta	Yes	2.532	Pure sciences
Applied Ergonomics	No	0.889	Technology
Journal of Electroanalytical Chemistry	Yes	2.228	Pure sciences
Journal of Chromatography – A	No	3.359	Pure sciences
Atmospheric Environment	Yes	2.562	Natural sciences
Chemometrics and Intelligent Laboratory Systems	Yes	1.899	Pure sciences
Applied Geochemistry	Yes	1.904	Natural/pure sciences

Table 15.8 *Science Direct in ULE*

Title	Paper version	Impact factor	Topic area
Theriogenology	Yes	1.640	Health sciences
International Journal of Food Microbiology	No	2.490	Health Sciences
Fertility and Sterility	Yes	3.170	Health sciences
FEMS Microbiology Letters	No	1.840	Natural sciences
Meat Science	Yes	1.656	Health sciences
Animal Reproduction Science	Yes	1.410	Health sciences
Biological Conservation	No	2.166	Natural sciences
Veterinary Microbiology	No	1.930	Health sciences
Veterinary Parasitology	No	1.445	Health sciences
FEBS Letters	No	3.843	Natural/pure sciences
Free Radical Biology and Medicine	No	5.625	Natural/health sciences
International Journal of Production Economics	No	0.879	Social sciences
Journal of Chromatography – A	No	3.359	Pure sciences
Aquaculture	No	1.627	Natural sciences
Animal Feed Science and Technology	Yes	0.895	Health sciences
Biochemical and Biophysical Research Communications	No	2.904	Natural/pure sciences
Neurobiology of Aging	No	5.516	Health sciences

The titles selected at ULE range between 3,200 and 700 downloads. In UBU, as data on downloads are available in individualized format by titles only for the year 2004, the selection of titles is only approximate. Nevertheless, it clearly shows the orientation of research towards the natural and pure sciences. There is good evidence for the weight attached to veterinary studies at ULE.

All of the serial publications included in Tables 15.7 and 15.8 have an ISI impact factor, with two in ULE's preferred group exceeding a five-point score. Of the selection shown, only *FEMS Microbiology Letters* appears in the ranking list of most heavily used titles for 2004 put forward by Elsevier.

There was wide acceptance of new titles in the Elsevier package on the part of ULE. In UBU there seems to be some preference for the electronic format of periodicals previously taken in paper versions. This feature might be explained by the large number of journals from the Elsevier stable already held there.

Table 15.9 *Springer in UBU*

Title	Paper version	Impact factor	Topic area
Biology and Fertility of Soils	Yes	1.276	Natural sciences
Analytical and Bioanalytical Chemistry	Yes	2.098	Natural/pure sciences
European Food Research and Technology	Yes	1.084	Health sciences
The Chemical Educator	No	–	Social sciences
Applied Microbiology and Biotechnology	Yes	2.358	Natural sciences
Bioprocess and Biosystems Engineering	Yes	0.916	Natural sciences/ technical
Fresenius' Journal of Analytical Chemistry	Yes	–	Pure sciences

Table 15.10 *Springer in ULE*

Title	Paper version	Impact factor	Topic area
European Journal of Applied Physiology	No	1.332	Health sciences
Applied Microbiology and Biotechnology	No	2.358	Natural sciences
TAG Theoretical and Applied Genetics	Yes	2.981	Health sciences
Current Genetics	No	2.495	Natural/health sciences
Parasitology Research	No	1.060	Health sciences
Molecular Genetics and Genomics	No	2.371	Natural/health sciences
Archives of Microbiology	No	2.374	Natural sciences
Planta	No	3.113	Natural sciences
Current Microbiology	No	1.075	Natural sciences
Oecologia	No	2.899	Natural sciences
Mammalian Genome	No	2.658	Natural/health sciences
Analytical and Bioanalytical Chemistry	No	2.098	Natural/pure sciences

At UBU the downloads over the three years studied vary between 348 and 61. At ULE the concentration of use was significantly greater, at between 670 and 109 downloads. It may be observed that two titles in the field of natural sciences occur in both lists (*Analytical and Bioanalytical Chemistry* and *Applied Microbiology and Biotechnology*). All the journals included in the selection for ULE and over 70% of those at UBU have an impact factor.

Of the titles in the SpringerLink package of which most use is made in UBU more than 85% are already subscribed to by the library in printed format. In ULE, by contrast, 91.7% are serial publications that were taken for the first time in the digital package.

Table 15.11   *Wiley in UBU*

Title	Paper version	Impact factor	Topic area
American Journal of Physical Anthropology	Yes	2.693	Natural sciences
Angewandte Chemie International Edition	Yes	9.161	Pure sciences
International Journal of Osteoarchaeology	No	–	Natural sciences
Evolutionary Anthropology: Issues, News, and Reviews	Yes	–	Natural sciences
Electroanalysis	Yes	2.038	Pure sciences/ technology
Chemistry – A European Journal	Yes	4.517	Pure sciences
European Journal of Organic Chemistry	Yes	2.426	Pure sciences
Science Education	Yes	1.312	Social sciences
European Journal of Inorganic Chemistry	Yes	2.336	Pure Sciences
Strategic Management Journal	Yes	1.980	Social sciences
Biotechnology and Bioengineering	Yes	2.216	Natural sciences/ technology
Journal of Research in Science Teaching	Yes	1.202	Social sciences
Journal of Chemometrics	Yes	2.385	Pure sciences
Journal of the Science of Food and Agriculture	Yes	0.871	Natural sciences

Table 15.12   *Wiley in ULE*

Title	Paper version	Impact factor	Topic area
Journal of Comparative Neurology	No	3.400	Health sciences
Hippocampus	No	4.516	Health sciences
Molecular Reproduction and Development	Yes	2.331	Health sciences
Permafrost and Periglacial Processes	No	0.984	Natural sciences
International Journal of Climatology	No	1.658	Natural sciences
BioEssays	No	6.430	Natural sciences
Journal of the Science of Food and Agriculture	Yes	0.871	Natural sciences
Biotechnology and Bioengineering	No	2.216	Natural sciences/ technology

Continued on next page

Table 15.12 *Continued*

Title	Paper version	Impact factor	Topic area
Journal of Research in Science Teaching	No	1.202	Social sciences
Strategic Management Journal	Yes	1.980	Social sciences
Journal of Quaternary Science	No	1.612	Natural sciences
Journal of the American Society for Information Science and Technology	Yes	2.086	Social sciences
Journal of Raman Spectroscopy	No	1.996	Pure sciences

The data by title for this distributor show considerable homogeneity for the two institutions. The title heading the list in both cases had over 1,300 downloads. The title at the end of the UBU list achieved 126 downloads.

Once again a majority use publications already subscribed to at UBU, where new titles from Wiley represent 7.14% of the total. At ULE, in contrast, the acceptance of new titles is striking, reaching 69.24%.

The overall quality of the publications that form the selection at the two universities is noteworthy, with the impact factor of the two titles *Angewandte Chemie International Edition* and *BioEssays* being particularly striking. Three of the titles most heavily used at UBU are in the top titles ranking established for 2004 by Wiley.

Discussion and conclusions

The thematic coverage of contents and technical and functional aspects of the distributors had already been undertaken (Rodríguez Bravo and Alvite Díez, 2005; Alvite Díez and Rodríguez Bravo, 2005). This was because, as Eason et al. (2000) point out, usage is affected by the influence of contents (coverage and relevance) and ease of use.

Similarly, Sanville (2001) states that additional titles in packages, bibliographic links and improved search options will lead to increased downloading of articles. Similarly, the overall breadth of coverage, range of topics and availability of back numbers in the Elsevier package are reflected in the more intensive use made of it by both university communities.

Although there are no precise data on the overall number of titles that constituted the periodicals holdings of the UBU and ULE libraries at the turn of the millennium, it is evident that they both gained considerably from the consortium arrangement. Although these conclusions are not definitive, it may be deduced that patterns of use are different in the two universities analysed: ULE got more out of the consortium agreement, whereas there was a better match of the previous paper-based collection to the needs of the academic community at UBU.

It may also be noted that there has been no stagnation in the number of articles downloaded. None the less, growth can be predicted to moderate in future years with contracts for new information products. Although data are not presented on a month-by-month basis, it is possible to observe that in the early days of operation of packages two phenomena occur that make it difficult to evaluate changing usage. These are curiosity on the part of researchers, and trial runs by librarians. There are also isolated peaks in use which may reflect work being done on assignments by students.

The core of most heavily used titles points to the greatest use being concentrated on titles that already have a reputation and impact factor. Nevertheless, it would seem that at the universities studied use is still likely to grow as libraries train users and personalize the organization of holdings.

The work by Urbano et al. (2004) looking at usage in Catalan universities of various suppliers' offerings, among them Emerald and Wiley, noted a greater spread for Emerald (around 45%) than for Wiley. This was corroborated by the company (Evans and Peter, 2005), but still does not correspond with what was found in the universities in Castilla y León.

This Catalan research pointed to a higher intensity of use of the Wiley package relative to that of Emerald. This trend was confirmed by Sanville (2001), who stated that the favoured package has periodicals with a larger number of articles, and that these are more up to date and fuller than those offered by Kluwer and Springer (who have recently merged into a single platform). This greater intensity of use for Wiley was likewise found at UBU, and especially at ULE.

The authors hope that this analysis provides useful knowledge of the consumption of electronic information at two universities at the time when Spain was in transition from paper to electronic formats.

References

Alvite Díez, M. L. and Rodríguez Bravo, B. (2005) Distribuidores de Contenidos Electrónicos: acceso, interfaz y funcionalidades. En 9as, *Jornadas Españolas de Documentación*, Madrid: Fesabid, 29–46.

Eason, K., Richardson, S. and Yu, L. (2000) Patterns of Use of Electronic Journals, *Journal of Documentation*, **56** (5), 477–504.

Evans, P. and Peter, J. (2005) Analysis of the Dispersal of Use for Journals in Emerald Management Xtra (EMX), Emerald Group Publishing Limited.

Frazier, K. (2001a) The Librarians' Dilemma: contemplating the costs of the 'big deal', *D-Lib Magazine*, **7** (3), www.dlib.org/dlib/march01/frazier/03frazier.html [accessed 11 August 2004].

Frazier, K. (2001b) To the Editor: letters in response to the opinion piece 'The Librarians' Dilemma: contemplating the costs of the "big deal"', *D-Lib Magazine*, **7** (4), www.dlib.org/dlib/april01/04letters.html [accessed 11 August 2004].

Ingenta Institute (2002) *The Consortium Site Licence: is it a sustainable model? Edited proceedings of a meeting held on 24 September 2002, London*, Oxford, Ingenta Institute.

Peters, T. A. (2002) What's the use? The value of e-resource usage statistics, *New Library World*, **103** (1172/1173), 39–47.

Rodríguez Bravo, B. and Alvite Díez, M. L. (2005) Survey of the Providers of Electronic Publications Holding Contracts with Spanish University Libraries, *D-Lib Magazine*, **11** (4), www.dlib.org/dlib/april05/alvite/04alvite.html [accessed 11 August 2004].

Rowse, M. (2003) The Consortium Site License: a sustainable model?, *Libri*, **53** (1), 1–10.

Sanville, T. (2001) A Method out of the Madness: OhioLink's collaborative response to the serial crisis: four years later progress report, *Serials*, **14** (2), 163–77.

Tenopir, C. (2003) Use and Users of Electronic Library Resources: an overview and analysis of recent research studies, Washington, D.C., Council on Library and Information Resources, www.clir.org/pubs/reports/pub120/pub120.pdf [accessed 11 August 2004].

Urbano, C., Anglada, L. and Borrego, A. (2004) The Use of Consortially Purchased Electronic Journals by the CBUC (2000–2003), *D-Lib Magazine*, **10** (6), www.dlib.org/dlib/june04/anglada/06anglada.html> [accessed 9 August 2004].

16

The integration of library activities in the academic world: a practitioner's view

Ursula Nielsen and Marie-Louise Axelsson

Introduction

Linköping University introduces itself on the web as follows:

> Exploring new fields, walking new paths. A non-traditional cooperation across subject and faculty borders defines the interdisciplinary approach that is the hallmark of Linköping University (LiU). An entrepreneurial spirit of education characterizes the university's history. Since its foundation in the 1960s, the university has established itself as an innovative and modern institution in both education and research. It was first founded as an independent college in 1970 and in 1975 it became Sweden's sixth university. Today LiU is organized in four faculties: Institute of Technology, Faculty of Arts and Sciences, Faculty of Health Sciences, and Educational Sciences. LiU has about 27,000 students.

Linköping University Library has about 100 employees, 42 of whom work full-time or part-time as subject librarians, as part of their job description. Many of them have been working with course-related web pages for five years. Together with teachers and researchers they have created library resource pages with internet links to course literature and reading lists; they have collected relevant web pages for courses; and have selected important journals and useful databases. Students can reach the pages from their course web. During the first two years of this project financial support was received from the Royal Swedish Library. Later extra funding was provided by the two faculties involved, the Institute of Science and the Faculty of Arts and Sciences.

The aim has been to create methods for:

- dealing with questions and problems that might arise when working with the integration and teaching of information retrieval in subject courses, modules and study programmes
- rendering teachers' information retrieval more effective in order to save time, get better results and increase the understanding of students' needs.

Background

The Swedish Parliament has decided on changes to the Higher Education Act (Högskolelagen, SFS 2001:1263, Chapter 1). The new statutes are more stringent than previous ones, saying that undergraduate education shall provide students with:

- the ability to make independent critical judgements
- the ability to independently distinguish, formulate and solve problems
- the ability to prepare for changes in working life.

Within the area of study encompassed by the educational programme, and in addition to gaining knowledge and competence, students should develop the ability to:

- search for and evaluate knowledge on a scientific level
- follow developments in their areas
- exchange knowledge with persons who do not possess any special knowledge in the area.

This statute concerns and has consequences for how the university works with students' information retrieval skills and the even wider concept of information literacy, which includes searching, quality assessment, and how to use the information critically. Furthermore, this is not only limited to current studies: the skills and abilities gained must work long-term as well. Higher education must equip students with information literacy that works throughout their life.

However, information retrieval is not something one can learn in isolation, out of the proper context. Training in how to use a library, searching for literature, finding relevant data, evaluating facts and making critical judgements about information found on the web only become relevant if they take place in the proper context, which is naturally linked to one's current studies or research project. It is in such circumstances that the student/researcher experiences the need for knowledge.

Knowledge of information handling is critical for the teachers and researchers of any university. The literature 'charts' change quickly, not least in terms of e-books, journals and reviews, but also in terms of e-text archives and bibliographic databases. Even people who have made extensive use of the library need to update their knowledge of how to retrieve information.

Information literacy

The American Library Association (ALA) defines information literacy as follows:

> Ultimately information literate people are those who have learned how to learn. They know how to learn because they know how information is organised, how to find information and how to use information in such a way that others can learn from them.
>
> (ALA, 1989)

Everyone knows that libraries look quite different today compared to five years ago. Development has moved very fast as regards the number of electronic resources, the speed of technological development and the availability of technology. It is still difficult, however, to integrate the library into core teaching and learning activities and to regard it as a partner in the teaching environment.

> Courses in information literacy for teachers are a first step. The quick changes, not least as regards e-books and journals make it necessary even for teachers who are seasoned information seekers to update their knowledge. One important aspect for them is to assume the role of student, thus appreciating the difficulties and the problems facing students working with information retrieval. A teacher who has a certain level of information competency has much better chances of supporting the students and contributes to improving the quality of teaching and the quality of their own research.
>
> (Hansson and Rimsten, 2003, 50).

It is quite common to commission libraries to 'make' students achieve information competency. Naturally, information literacy is an issue for librarians, but is not exclusively an issue for libraries. Information literacy must be 'owned' by the entire educational department/institution.

In their report *Paths for Knowledge* (SUHF, 2003), the Association of Swedish Higher Education said this:

> Universities and university colleges have tended to regard 'information literacy' as an issue solely concerning their libraries, thus disengaging it from other academic work. Each university and university college must rather ask itself how it best should co-ordinate different efforts in order to fulfil the new goals stated in the Higher Education Act. (p 15) In order to achieve a shared view regarding the learning processes, those responsible for undergraduate education, pedagogic development and library activities should co-operate to create integrated learning environments (p 16).

In the report *Strategic Crossroads* (Linköpings Universitet, 2003, 24), Helena Wedborn expresses this idea in the following way:

> The educational system at Linköping University should emphasize information literacy as a strategic part of its activities. The institution, through the faculties, the educational committees, the directors of studies for research, single subject courses and study programmes, and the library management, should initiate and support collaboration between teachers and librarians to integrate information retrieval as part of the teaching and education, as well as raising the level of information literacy. This in turn will lead to an increased and better use of the university library's information resources.

Some issues raised in the report *Education in Collaboration* (Hansson and Rimsten, 2003), a pedagogical development project at Örebro University, are valid for most educational institutions:

- The elements of information literacy that exist within the study programmes and subject courses are not always visible in a particular subject's framework (such as syllabi and curricula)
- Being constrained by reading lists/course literature lists gives less room for actively seeking information
- The opportunities provided through electronic media have not been taken advantage of and thus have not been given a chance to contribute to improved pedagogy
- Lack of knowledge of the choices available
- Students regularly need exercises where they see information retrieval as a meaningful process
- Courses in information retrieval are not sufficiently integrated into the course subjects
- There is no natural meeting place for the librarian and the teacher
- The students' experience from and knowledge of information retrieval and the evaluation of sources are not given enough attention. Exercises where students have searched for and processed information are too seldom discussed and/or examined.

The project

With the aid of extra funding for about five years the university library has been able to offer teachers and students courses in information handling. Together with teachers, the subject librarians have discussed and planned student information needs. Furthermore, each programme's director of studies and teachers have been invited to discuss the possibilities of helping teachers become more familiar with the library's information resources. The goal has been to integrate the information retrieval process into designated courses, and, together with the teachers, to create high-quality web pages to assist students' learning.

The eight subject librarians and teachers from the two faculties who have been working on the project have produced a great number of web pages. The project has been evaluated by interviewing participating teachers and librarians. Students have contributed by answering the course evaluation form.

Co-operation

In their article *Philosophical Shift: teach the faculty to teach information literacy*, Smith and Mundt (1997) discuss the different roles of departments and librarians regarding students' information literacy. The authors say that departments are in a much better position than the library when it comes to 'controlling' the learning environment and creating a situation where information retrieval can be a vital part of problem solving. Therefore, it is time for libraries to refocus their teaching resources and the way they convey information to departments and teachers. However, the possibility of integrating information literacy in syllabi is limited as long as the librarians themselves have to do all the work (p 4).

In the project we discussed the question of whether teachers might be in a better position than librarians to work with students' information literacy. Opinions differed. Many teachers feared a heavier workload. Others thought it was an interesting idea, and moreover the right way to go. A great deal of the problem naturally has to do with time and resources. However, having a clear policy from the University Board and a desire to see change – which both librarians and teachers want – the library can begin to co-operate in things such as course development.

Thoughts from librarians:

> The work with the project has been a big boost in our everyday work as subject librarians.

> What one wants to achieve as a subject librarian is co-operation with the teacher at the department – i.e. to become a natural part of the education and teaching process. And to be able to contribute with something the teacher sees as valuable. To be able to offer the teacher a course web page with information resources for his/her particular course, that is – once the teacher became interested – just such a service that made us become included in the education process in a way that we have never been before.

The teacher and the students have been pleasantly surprised by learning about all the resources available. In some cases this has led to a boosted interest for the library and its services. This way one can clearly say that this work has definitely improved the communication between us as subject librarians and the departments we work for. This is also true for issues not specifically related to the course web pages as such.

The tough part was to arouse the teachers' interest in the very beginning – before we even had a course web page to show. It's not that easy to come and present something new for a teacher who already feels the pressure of a heavy workload – there are always apprehensions as to this being something that will require a great effort by the teacher as well, and also costs in the future.'

Then you can always see flaws in the co-operation surrounding the design of a web page. There was general talk about the fact that other things apart from searching for literature were given priority in the education programme or subject course.

Örebro University has produced an outline of what the division of responsibility might look like when developing a course (Table 16.1).

Table 16.1   *Division of responsibility*

Teacher responsibility	Shared responsibility	Librarian responsibility
Course idea	Knowledge review	Media purchase
Syllabus, aim, content, etc.		
	Implementation of information literacy	
	Course literature/ reading list	
Lectures, group work, thesis, etc.	Support tasks, learning support, seminars	
Examination		

(Hansson and Rimsten, 2003, 10)

Course web pages

Linköping university library started working with targeted course web pages when one of its branch libraries was closed down.

Working with teachers to develop library web pages has turned out to be a very good way of collaborating. For example, on the 'E-business and Business

Development' course, where the literature used to be in the form of compendia, these have been removed and replaced by e-literature instead.

The subject librarians use these course-related pages to give students knowledge of information resources. What the project also aimed to do was to try 'teaching the Faculty to teach information literacy'. Many studies show that you cannot bring information literacy to anyone at the wrong time.

We wanted to integrate the library resources with the classroom and help the teachers understand the need for information literacy in the teaching situation. We also wanted to improve the quality of information retrieval carried out by teachers for their own purposes. This would save time for them as well as for the library staff, and also increase their understanding of students' information literacy needs. Faculties control the learning environment, and academic staff can create situations that force students to use information resources for problem solving to a much greater extent than is possible for librarians. Maybe it is time to let the teachers teach information literacy?

We started by offering teachers information about relevant sources for their courses. Some said they didn't need it, some didn't have the time, but some came to the library seminars. It was obvious that the mental climate in the department, and the attitudes of the teachers in the different departments, were affecting our chances of real integration. We found that it was much easier to involve teachers from the Faculty of Arts and Sciences than those from the Institute of Science, a phenomenon also discussed in some Swedish publications.

The fact that co-operation between teachers and librarians has begun and that the web pages are beginning to take shape does not mean the work is complete. The evaluation clearly showed that students need incentives and a great deal of information in order to discover and find the pages useful. It is not enough just having a link on the course page. Something more is needed; for example:

- Students are given exercises that require them to seek information, perhaps when preparing a report or an examination paper.
- Teachers must be interested in and know the web pages well enough to actively refer students to them when appropriate questions arise.
- Pages are combined with a lecture/information session where the librarian informs about and demonstrates the pages.

Results

What was achieved by the project? First, closer co-operation with teachers. The library has now become a partner in the teaching process, much appreciated by many of the teachers. Their understanding of the librarian's professional role is improving, and this gives us the opportunity to market library resources and skills to the university academic environment.

The project also influenced the work of the librarians. If librarians wish to carry out their role successfully they must understand learning theories and teaching methods. The evaluation showed us that these competencies increased among the library staff.

An effect of co-operation is that subject librarians are more familiar with course content and that teachers have become more active and interested in the information retrieval process. In this way the teacher/student will gain a long-term understanding of the importance of making the right choice from the vast information flow, of critically judging and assessing information, and of paying attention to the scholarly level of different texts.

One of the real obstacles in this project was time. Few teachers or library staff thought they had the time to really become involved. The teachers were afraid that we would give them more work. When we discussed the idea of asking teachers to deal with their students' information literacy, most of them did not want to be involved. Comments such as 'The librarians can do it much better' were common, but the librarians also did not have time! This project was just a part of their ordinary work, and a lot of 'normal' work also had to be done.

The evaluation shows that the project has led to better knowledge among the teachers of library information resources and how to use them. Heavy workloads, however, have meant that the project has not reached all teachers. Better and more effective marketing from the librarians is also desirable.

Project participants have dedicated much time and effort to the course web pages. One of the directors of study suggested that every teachers' meeting should set aside time to discuss literature and library resources. The point of this is to raise awareness of how one's own library web pages are used, and to have a discussion on course literature/reading lists. We are aware that this type of course-related web page may not be useful in all subject courses or study programmes, but they can often be a meaningful tool for getting students more interested in the flow of information.

The strategic plan

In May 2005 the University Board approved a strategic plan for information supply at Linköping University. This is very satisfying. In the directive it says that 'The university board commissions the rector to set up a permanent group, consisting mainly of the university's academic management, to discuss and draw up strategic proposals – the scope of which being 3–5 years – that are relevant to activities at the institution relating to the supply of information for the university and thus also relevant for the development of the university library.' The report summarizes the strategic goals in the following way:

- Information supply will be a clear and natural part of the core activities of the university.
- The University Library (UL) will participate in the realization of our university's student focused pedagogy.
- The UL will take an active part to help develop information literacy in students, and if the need arises also help teachers/researchers and other staff.
- The UL will secure good access to scholarly and scientific information, based on the needs of undergraduate, graduate and research education.
- The UL will participate in activities that strengthen the Linköping University brand.
- The UL will promote and develop its services by:
  — participating in active dialogue with faculties and departments
  — making clear the role of subject librarians to students, researchers, teachers and other staff in the department.
- The UL will contribute to the integration of information literacy in all undergraduate education through:
  — offering to help teachers responsible for subject and programme courses to produce information resources on course web pages and learning platforms
  — working towards becoming involved in the pedagogy courses for future teachers given by CKU (Centre for Competence Development).

How to move on

Many studies show that instruction in information retrieval must be integrated and given at the right time.

> Individual teachers and librarians can surely make a difference. However, it is only the board/management that can achieve the structural and strategic changes that permeate the whole campus/institution. A policy document is needed that emphasizes the need for integrating information resources and information technology into syllabi. This way, the students can get a chance to become effective lifelong learners.
>
> (Hansson and Rimsten, 2003)

Students' information paths are quite set and limited, not least at the Institutes of Technology, according to a study from Lund University:

> In education where the literature is set beforehand, the students are fairly independent of the library. Undergraduate students do not seek a great deal of information

on their own, compared to graduate students. Nor do they discover literature in other more informal ways, such as teachers/researchers do. Hence, the libraries also have the role of supporting, widening and supplementing students' narrow paths of information. For the students, the library becomes the arena where the learning perspective can be opened and own discoveries can be made. The library plays a significant role as a supporting environment for the development of students' information paths.   (Lund University, 2000, 28)

Biblioteksbarometern also shows that some 25% of all students do not use any electronic library services at all. Most of these are young students of technology. According to the study, the way students use the library reflects well-established learning patterns in their undergraduate education, where very set teaching, a strong focus on course literature/reading lists and compendia correlate to poor use of the library.

The work to raise students' information literacy levels leads to a wider task for the university library. This in turn calls for librarians to be good teachers/instructors. It is therefore important that librarians undertake further training, above all within the field of teaching, but also as regards critical thinking and better subject knowledge. In the USA they have coined the phrase 'teaching librarians', to emphasize that the library profession is entering a new phase.

Conclusions

Thanks to the funding, Linköping University Library has been given an opportunity to work actively towards integration in teaching, and in many courses with successful results. The evaluation showed that all the parties involved would like to see greater co-operation, and that they are positive about the continuation of the subject course web pages. This is most gratifying.

The project has also meant that new contacts between departments and the librarians have been created. This has been appreciated by teachers, students and librarians alike.

Link to a course web page in the project

Library page for the course Theory of Relativity:
www.bibl.liu.se/kvartersbibl/KB/IFM/Kurs/TFYY57/Start.htm.

Links to the resource web pages can also be found on each subject course or study programme home page.

References

Note: Swedish law referred to in the text is not referenced.

American Library Association (1989) *Presidential Committee on Information Literacy: final report*, American Library Association (ALA), www.ala.org/ala/acrl/acrlpubs/whitepapers/presidential.htm.

Hansson, B. and Rimsten, O. (2003) *Utbildning i Samverkan, Information literacy vid Örebro universitet*, Örebro Universitet.

Linköpings Universitet (2003) *Strategiska Vägval: en utredning om vetenskaplig informationsförsörjning vid Linköpings universitet (2003)* Electronic articles on academic policies and trends no 5, Linköping University Electronic Press, www.ep.liu.se/ea/apt/2003/005/apt03005.pdf.

Lund University (2000) *Biblioteksbarometern 2000 Lund: Lund universitet, utvärderingsenhetens rapport 2001:210*, www.evaluat.lu.se/publ/Bibl.baro/Biblioteksbarometer.pdf.

Smith, R. and Mundt, K. (1997) *Philosophical Shift: teach the faculty to teach information literacy*, www.ala.org/ala/acrlbucket/nashville1997pap/smith.htm.

SUHF – Sveriges Universitets och Högskoleförbund (2003) *Vägar för Kunskap – behov av en gemensam strategisk nyorientering för högskolorna och deras bibliotek*, Stockholm, SUHF – Sveriges universitets- & högskoleförbund, www.suhf.se/BinaryLoader.aspx?ObjectID=108&PropertyName=FileList&PropertyValueIndex=2&CollID=File.

17
Monitoring PULMAN's Oeiras Manifesto Action Plan

Robert Davies

Introduction

The European Union's Lisbon Agenda and subsequent versions of its eEurope Action Plan set out the ambition for Europe to have 'the most competitive economy in the world' by the year 2010, by moving rapidly toward an economy based on knowledge and a digitally inclusive society. In accordance with this, the Lund Principles for e-Europe digitization of cultural heritage (European Commission, 2004), agreed in April 2001, set out an approach ranging from bottom-up involvement of the cultural institutions themselves, for example in determining cases of best practice, to top-down initiatives on policies. During 2005, in response to a high-level initiative from European heads of government, plans were announced for the creation of a European Digital Library (European Commission, 2005).

Throughout this period and before it, the European Union's Information Society Technologies (IST) research and development programme acted as an important focus for policy co-ordination and monitoring activities in the cultural heritage area. For example, the MINERVA Network of ministerial agencies, funded under this programme, developed a benchmarking framework (Minerva, 2003) as a tool for co-ordinating and harmonizing national activities, as well as for developing measures to show progress, improvement and good practice.

A key aspect of this question is the contribution of local cultural institutions (libraries, museums and archives), and a sequence of actions has been funded to co-ordinate their activity, each building on the last, over several years and covering three IST research framework programmes (FP):

- FP4 – PubliCA: accompanying measure (1998–2000)
- FP5 – PULMAN: concerted action (2001–3) (www.pulmanweb.org)
- FP6 – CALIMERA: co-ordination action (2004–5) (www.calimera.org).

Perhaps the key policy outcome of PULMAN was its Manifesto and linked Oeiras Action Plan, issued as a result of its policy conference held in Portugal in March 2003 (see Appendix, page 166). The monitoring of progress against this action plan is the subject of this paper.

The CALIMERA (Cultural Applications: Local Institutions Mediating Electronic Resource Access) Action, which concluded its work in May 2005, brought together a consortium representing more than 40 countries. Partners included local cultural institutions, national authorities, research centres and Eblida, the European sectoral association.

A major thrust of CALIMERA was work in the policy arena, designed to sensitize decision makers, professionals and solution providers at the European, national, regional and local levels to the existing and potential contribution of local cultural institutions, including the way in which they can support broader policy agendas, such as those for e-government, social inclusion, e-learning, skills for employment, regional local economic development, etc. To this end, a range of European co-ordination and benchmarking activities was envisaged for CALIMERA.

Monitoring the Manifesto and Action Plan

Following the publication of the PULMAN Manifesto and Oeiras Action Plan, it was agreed that a process of monitoring its implementation was required. An instrument was designed for this purpose by the CALIMERA consortium and circulated to PULMAN Country Co-ordinators with a request that they complete it in consultation with other national experts, as appropriate. Responses were received in the period October 2003 to March 2004.

Replies were received from all 36 countries involved in the extended PULMAN Network (including Europe's neighbouring countries involved in the PULMAN-XT network). However, the Belgian assessment applies to the situation in the Flemish-speaking region of the country only.

It should be emphasized that this monitoring exercise represents a process of self-assessment. Although every attempt was made to provide unambiguous descriptions of the options underlying the scores for each Action Point, inevitably subjectivity is involved. In a few cases, querying of initial responses led to some 'normalization' in the interests of a result that compares actual situations across Europe as accurately as possible.

The scores for each Action Point were analysed according to a variety of types of average and by range (lowest to highest). It is a matter for discussion as to whether each of these average types reveals usefully distinct information. However, the intention in using different average types was as follows:

- **Range:** to illustrate the gap between the lowest and highest scores across Europe
- **Mean:** to provide the most accurate illustration of the overall performance of local cultural institutions, compared between the ten different Action Points
- **Median:** to enable comparison of individual country performances: are they above or below the average of the country in the 'middle of the table'?
- **Mode:** to enable comparison of individual country performance with the largest group of other countries having one single score: that is, the most common situation
- **Top quartile:** this is, cautiously, treated in this assessment as providing a benchmark score for current practice in Europe, illustrating a level to which all countries should be aspiring now if they wish to implement the PULMAN Manifesto.

Overview of results

The scores indicate huge disparities in the performance of Europe's local cultural institutions against the criteria offered by the Oeiras Action Plan: for each Action Point, individual country scores cover the full range 0–5. The overall total (714 from a possible 1750) also demonstrates that Europe's local cultural institutions are only a comparatively short distance along the road to achieving the goals made explicit by the PULMAN Manifesto. That being said, it appears that advancement is gathering speed, with increasingly visible benchmarks to aspire to, under most of the Oeiras Action Points. These are the overall averages for the ten Action Points:

- Range   2–47 (maximum total 50)
- Mean   20.2
- Median   20
- Mode   24
- Top quartile   26.

The textual narratives requested from respondents in the form of 'Evidence' and 'Comments' have been analysed by the author to establish, as far as possible as additional 'metrics' and indicators, to illustrate and draw meaning from the scores returned for each of the Action Points.

The data show Denmark with the highest score (47 out of 50) and Turkey with the lowest (2 out of 50), with a large number of countries clustered in the 16–26 range. Table 17.1 provides the full results, the Action Points being:

1 Strategies
2 Funding priorities
3 Policy co-ordination
4 Partnerships
5 Interactive access
6 Centres of excellence
7 Staff
8 User needs
9 Benchmark
10 Research/take-up

Table 17.1 *Countries in order of total self-assessment score (with scores for each Action Point)*

Oeiras Action Point	1	2	3	4	5	6	7	8	9	10	Total
1 Denmark	5	5	4	4	5	4	5	5	5	5	47
2 Finland	4	4	3	5	4	4	4	4	5	2	39
3 UK	4	5	5	4	4	5	3	4	2	2	38
4 Netherlands	4	4	4	4	4	4	3	2	3	3	35
5 Norway	4	4	5	3	2	2	4	4	3	2	33
6 Ireland	3	5	4	3	3	2	3	3	4	2	32
7 Luxembourg	4	4	4	3	2	1	3	3	3	3	30
8 Belgium	2	5	1	3	3	0	3	3	3	3	26
8 Russia	0	3	4	2	3	3	2	2	4	3	26
10 Latvia	3	3	4	2	2	2	3	2	3	1	25
11 Italy	1	4	5	1	4	1	2	2	3	1	24
11 Austria	1	3	3	2	4	2	3	2	2	2	24
11 France	4	4	2	3	4	1	2	1	1	2	24
11 Sweden	1	5	3	3	2	2	2	2	2	2	24
15 Lithuania	5	3	4	2	2	2	2	1	1	1	23
15 Belarus	4	3	1	3	1	1	1	2	4	3	23
15 Hungary	3	3	1	1	1	1	3	4	3	3	23
18 Slovenia	3	4	1	1	0	2	2	3	3	1	20
19 Romania	1	1	2	2	1	2	3	2	3	2	19
20 Moldova	1	4	1	1	1	4	2	1	3	0	18
21 Portugal	1	2	1	2	2	1	3	2	1	2	17
22 Czech Republic	3	3	0	1	1	0	2	3	3	0	16
22 Spain	3	4	1	0	1	2	2	1	2	0	16
22 Greece	1	2	1	2	2	1	3	2	0	2	16
25 Ukraine	0	1	0	3	2	2	3	0	2	1	14
25 Estonia	0	4	3	1	0	1	0	1	3	1	14
27 Croatia	2	1	1	1	1	1	1	2	1	1	12

Continued on next page

Table 17.1 *Continued*

Oeiras Action Point	1	2	3	4	5	6	7	8	9	10	Total
27 Slovak Republic	3	0	1	1	3	1	0	1	0	2	12
29 Macedonia	2	3	3	0	0	0	3	0	0	0	11
29 Germany	0	3	0	0	1	2	2	0	1	2	11
31 Albania	1	1	1	0	0	2	2	0	2	0	9
31 Poland	1	2	1	0	1	0	1	0	2	1	9
33 Serbia and Montenegro	1	2	2	1	0	0	1	0	0	0	7
34 Bosnia and Herzegovina	1	1	0	1	0	0	0	1	0	2	6
35 Bulgaria	0	0	1	1	1	0	0	0	0	0	3
36 Turkey	0	0	0	0	0	0	1	0	1	0	2
TOTAL	76	105	77	66	67	58	79	65	78	57	728

Analysis of responses on Action Points 1–10

In this section the detailed results for each of the Action Points are analysed.

Action Point 1

Establish *strategies* that utilize and develop the skills and infrastructure of Europe's comprehensive physical network of public libraries, archives and museums in order to develop their full social, cultural and economic potential.

0	There is no published national strategy for local cultural services, nor any evident planning for one.
1	A draft national strategy covering at least one domain (public libraries, museums or archives) is in preparation.
2	A national strategy covering at least one domain has been published recently, but did not fully address key areas of national economic and social policy or information society issues.
3	A comprehensive national strategy covering at least one domain has been published.
4	A national strategy linking and co-ordinating two or more domains and addressing key areas of national social and economic policy, including information society issues, has been published.
5	One or more recently published national strategies has had a visibly beneficial impact on the way in which cultural services are developed and delivered at the local level.

The results were as follows:

- Range   0–5
- Mean   2.1
- Median   2
- Mode   1
- Top quartile   4.

Most countries now have at least a draft strategy covering at least one domain, either in preparation or already published, but the extent to which information society issues are addressed is sometimes limited. Cross-domain strategies are still not the norm.

In some countries with more 'federal' systems of administration, local libraries, archives and museums are managed and co-ordinated by regions or states. In Italy, for example, strategy is local by nature, with the regions issuing their own bye-laws and regulations but co-operating through a co-ordinating body that liaises with the national bodies, e.g. on library policy guidelines. In Germany, the legal structure can make it difficult for action to be taken on any federal-level support initiatives: responsibility for all aspects of culture is a state/local responsibility.

Action Point 2

Identify national and local *funding priorities* in support of key activities such as providing access to electronic resources and the internet, digitization, piloting new services, ensuring an adequate technical infrastructure, including broadband connectivity where feasible, and the adoption of common standards.

0	There is little or no evident new discussion or planning of funding priorities for public libraries, museums and archives at national or local level.
1	There is discussion of funding priorities, but it does not recognize the need for spending on these key activities.
2	Some local authorities have taken a decision to direct more funding to the key activities listed.
3	There is advocacy or guidance from national government on the allocation of funds to the key activities.
4	Many local authorities are already spending significant sums of money in these activity areas, or there has been major central government spending on them.
5	A visible difference in services is becoming evident as a result of increased spending on the key activities.

The results were as follows:

- Range   0–5
- Mean   2.9
- Median   3
- Mode   4
- Top quartile   4.

This is the Action Point with the highest overall score. Most countries have reached at least Level 3, and Level 4 – a decision to allocate extra money at local authority level – appears to be the benchmark. Five countries, Ireland, Belgium, Denmark, Sweden and the UK, said that they are seeing a visible difference in service provision as a result of extra spending. Extending internet use, developing e-government, and digitization are three evident strategic funding 'drivers'.

However, wide disparities remain. At the other end of the scale, in Albania in 2001 only 2% of the total budget, for public libraries – 0% for local museums and archives – was planned for spending on information technologies; similarly, in the Slovak Republic 'the funding of the cultural sector has no priority, both at the national and local levels'.

Funding by foundation, such as local Soros Foundations, is still of key significance in developing automation, creating portals and training staff in many of the 'neighbouring' countries (e.g. Ukraine).

Action Point 3

Consider the establishment of cross-domain agencies and inter-ministerial co-operation for *co-ordinated policy making* within the cultural heritage sector (public libraries, museums and archives).

0	The idea of cross-domain agencies or inter-ministerial co-operation does not appear to be on the national agenda.
1	Cross-domain policy co-ordination has been discussed but no decision to act has been taken.
2	A decision to set up co-ordination mechanisms has been agreed but no visible action has yet been taken.
3	There are national or regional co-ordination forums or agencies but they have had little significant impact yet.
4	The first steps in policy co-ordination have been taken and are beginning to have an impact.
5	There is a substantial cross-domain co-ordination activity which is showing real results.

The results were as follows:

- Range   0–5
- Mean   2.1
- Median   2
- Mode   1
- Top quartile   4.

In most cases cross-domain policy co-ordination has not moved beyond the discussion stage. In several instances (e.g. Belarus, Czech Republic, France, Slovak Republic, Slovenia), this discussion has so far been between professional communities rather than at the political level. One risk identified (both where cross-domain agencies have been established and where they have not) is the perception of one domain that it might be being ignored at the expense of the other(s).

However, there are examples of strong progress which provide a clear benchmark for countries wishing to travel in that direction, although Norway (NALMA) and the UK (MLA) are currently the only countries with cross-domain strategic agencies for libraries, museums and archives.

Action Point 4

Develop effective *partnerships* between the local cultural heritage sector and other key economic and social sectors (e.g. education, employment, tourism, community organizations, etc.) to facilitate re-engineering of local services, as well as cost-effective provision and management.

0	There is little or no partnership activity at national or local government level that affects the services offered by public libraries, museums and archives.
1	In some individual localities, partnerships between local authority services or with other agencies are beginning to be discussed.
2	Discussion is leading to the formation of some national partnerships which will affect the delivery of services to the public at local level.
3	There is a clear national commitment and government support to encourage partnerships in local services, which is leading to action at local level.
4	A range of partnership-based services involving public libraries, museums and archives is now available to the public in a substantial number of localities.
5	Local services, including public libraries, museums and archives, are being fundamentally re-engineered to provide new-style services for an e-Europe.

The results were as follows:

- Range   0–5
- Mean   1.8
- Median   2
- Mode   1
- Top quartile   3.

The extent of this development remains uncertain in many countries, with only one country (Finland) claiming the top level and only two (Denmark, UK) claiming Level 4. However, government-encouraged commitment to put partnership working into action (Level 3) may be seen as the current benchmark, perhaps especially in the area of education/lifelong learning (e.g. Netherlands, Sweden, UK).

It is difficult to judge how far this commitment has yet translated into services in a substantial number of localities. It seems clear that much progress remains to be made in exploiting the power of effective partnerships in support of strategic objectives such as e-government, e-learning and social inclusion, where local institutions have a role to play but cannot succeed alone. Competition for limited funding is seen by some as a deterrent to partnership (e.g. Germany).

Action Point 5

Provide *interactive access* to content through state-of-the-art multimedia digital resources documenting local history, literature, art, music and community interests, packaged where appropriate as learning resources.

0	There is no evident planning or delivery of services to the public at local level that uses digitized multimedia resources.
1	In some individual localities, projects exist to develop such services.
2	In some individual localities, prototype services are being tested with the public.
3	There is a major national initiative or policy which is intended to lead to the widespread provision of multimedia services based on digitization at local level.
4	Services of this type are already available to the public in a significant number of localities.
5	The delivery of interactive services based on multimedia digital resources through local cultural institutions is pervasive throughout most or all of the country.

The results were as follows:

- Range   0–5
- Mean   1.9
- Median   2
- Mode   1
- Top quartile   3.

In most countries (e.g. Norway), interactive access remains at the local project or prototyping stage, for example for chat-based services, interactive publishing and information literacy programmes. National policies (Level 3) represent the top quartile benchmark, but barely. It is not always clear from the responses that the concept of interactivity has been consistently interpreted as involving two-way communication. Many appear to refer to the process of creating and providing access to digital resources without clear reference to the interactive mode.

Only one country (Denmark) claims to have established national pervasiveness of services (Level 5): many digital services documenting local history, literature, art, film and music are offered. In the UK, the NOF Digitization Programme and e-government targets for local authorities are leading to the development of interactive services.

Action Point 6

Support the development of *centres of excellence* to stimulate the up-take of good practice, where necessary as a starting point for wider implementation of innovative services.

0	There are no designated or effective centres of excellence among local cultural institutions.
1	A small number of services with the potential to be centres of excellence are starting to emerge.
2	Some local services are starting to act as centres of excellence, for example by disseminating news of their innovative activities and offering training to other services in these areas.
3	A national strategy for designating centres of excellence among local cultural institutions (public libraries, museums and archives) has been or is being developed.
4	A significant number of new centres of excellence have been established in one or more of the domains and are offering support, guidance and inspiration to other localities.
5	A widespread network of centres of excellence has been established and is playing a key role in the development of local services throughout the country.

The results were as follows:

- Range   0–5
- Mean   1.6
- Median   2
- Mode   2
- Top quartile   2.

The development of centres of excellence is apparently the least further progressed of all ten Action Points. Only the UK considers itself to have achieved Level 5, especially through regional hubs in the museums sector. More countries consider themselves to be at Level 0 than at any other. The top quartile benchmark is only Level 2, and only one country (Russia) considers itself to have a national strategy for centres of excellence.

In some countries the concept of centres of excellence as a means of development has little direct currency, for example Denmark, where 'In the national context, we don't use the expression "Centre of Excellence"', and Finland. Elsewhere (e.g. the UK) the response suggested that the idea of centres of excellence was potentially at odds with any policies emphasizing entitlements to level provision of services.

Yet the need for inspiring examples of digital service provision and overall management practice is elsewhere well recognized (Albania, Germany, Latvia, Italy, Sweden), and the creation of a desire to emulate individually excellent services is seen as a potentially important way of leveraging progress that might otherwise be hard to achieve.

This approach can extend to the cross-domain level (e.g. Ireland, Norway). Sometimes the area of excellence is confined to a single aspect of service.

Sometimes (e.g. Belarus, Czech Republic, Luxembourg, Norway, Slovak Republic) large central institutions such as the National Library, Museum or Archive are considered centres of excellence and offer education, training and dissemination services from which local services benefit.

In other cases, a structured approach to 'excellence' is handled at a regional level, for example in Lithuania, where the government has approved a programme of cultural development in the regions and decided to establish ten county libraries, which will serve also as centres for the development of library services. A similar structure has recently been established in Slovenia.

Action Point 7

Implement *staff recruitment and training* policies, including adequate salaries and conditions, to provide the capacity and skills to deal effectively with user needs, e.g. learning support and the use of information society technologies.

0	Staff in local cultural public institutions are paid at a level which makes it almost impossible for them to recruit and retain staff with these skills, and little systematic training is available to assist their development.
1	Some self-motivated staff in a few of the more ambitious localities have acquired the necessary skills, but poor pay and conditions make it difficult to establish a 'critical mass'.
2	Some individual local services have set out and been able to recruit or train staff with these new skills, but pay, conditions and the availability of training remain a serious barrier.
3	A national programme or initiative is being planned or under way, designed to ensure that staff receive training and operate under employment conditions that make it possible for them to deliver services of an appropriate quality.
4	A large number of institutions have recognizably modified their recruitment and training policies in order to deliver a new range of services to users.
5	Most local cultural institutions have achieved a new balance of staff skills and capacities that effectively supports the delivery of this new range of services and are able to retain key staff.

The results were as follows:

- Range   0–5
- Mean   2.2
- Median   2
- Mode   3
- Top quartile   3.

This is the Action Point with the second-highest overall score. The top quartile benchmark and the most commonly achieved level are both Level 3, indicating that a national programme or initiative exists or is planned. But few countries have yet seen a far-reaching impact through changed practices. Only one country (Denmark) claims Level 5, and only two more (Finland, Norway) Level 4.

In Denmark and the UK, national and regional training and continuing education programmes involving ICT have reached all libraries. Elsewhere (e.g. Hungary), training and re-training requirements for library staff are regulated by the government. In Belgium, the 2002 Library Legislation requires that public libraries evolve by 2007 to a 50/50 balance between librarians and technical staff in order to be able to meet the new challenges of the information society and changing user needs.

The recruitment and retention of staff with ICT skills is a more immediately intractable issue for many countries, perhaps especially for the 'accession' (negotiating for membership) and neighbouring countries with lower GDP. Uncompetitive salaries and inflexibility of pay are a frequently cited issue (e.g. Belarus, Czech Republic, Italy, Lithuania, Romania). Sometimes (e.g. Ukraine) libraries try to get round this by using grants to cover the salaries of technical staff.

Action Point 8

Monitor the changing *needs of users* as a part of evidence-based policy development and investment planning.

0	There is little or no systematic attempt to match the services provided at local level with changes in user needs.
1	Some individual local services have conducted research to establish user needs, but this has not fed through into widespread national changes in spending or service provision.
2	There is significant interest in the assessment of user needs, but a lack of commonly agreed mechanisms or methodologies restricts the effective use of data to establish useful findings.
3	Comprehensive systems for user-needs research (including the use of IST) have been or are being developed for national comparative purposes, but await implementation at local level.
4	Relevant reports on user needs are produced and made available to local cultural services on a regular basis and are having an impact on service development, although some areas of uncertainty are not addressed.
5	A culture of user needs research and testing, feeding the cyclical development of services, is widely established and has a visible and acknowledged impact on what local cultural institutions do.

The results were as follows:

- Range   0–5
- Mean   1.8
- Median   2
- Mode   2
- Top quartile   3.

Driving service development according to changing user needs is still not a well established practice in Europe's local cultural institutions. Only one country (Denmark) claims Level 5, and four others (Finland, Hungary, Norway and UK)

Level 4. The majority come no higher than the pre-implementation Level 2.

Furthermore, the response from the UK (a country with standardized mechanisms for user-needs research in pubic libraries) suggests that 'if we are talking specifically about use of digital services, we may be at Level 2, and only just climbing out of 1'. There is little or no reference to work on the usability of digital services and/or IT solutions in any of the responses.

It is common practice for national or local questionnaire surveys to be conducted to establish user and/or non-user attitudes to library services, cultural practices such as reading, museum visits and other leisure activities.

Action Point 9

Measure and evaluate services on a regular basis, especially those involving new technologies, and establish *benchmark* criteria to assess the impact and outcome of investment.

0	There is little or no culture of monitoring or evaluation of cultural services at local level.
1	Some individual local services monitor the outcomes, e.g. by statistics or surveys.
2	There are attempts to compare evaluation data between local authorities, but these are limited in scope and exclude some areas of investment (e.g. new technologies).
3	A national initiative to establish evaluative criteria, data collection and/or benchmarking procedures for local cultural services in one or more domains has been established or is planned.
4	Most local cultural services are accustomed to carrying out systematic monitoring and evaluation and to the idea of benchmarking their services.
5	The use of evaluation is widespread and has been developed into effective processes that support the understanding of the impact of services on the daily lives of users, and this is having a visible effect on patterns of expenditure.

The results were as follows:

- Range   0–5
- Mean   2.2
- Median   3
- Mode   3
- Top quartile   3.

The current benchmark appears well established at Level 3, national initiatives, and has been attained by many countries, although it is not always clear from these responses. Only two countries (Finland and Denmark) claim Level 5.

Overall, the monitoring and evaluation of local museums and archives appears less developed than for public libraries. There is little specific reference in the responses to issues relating to the evaluation of digitally delivered services.

Some countries have well established traditions of using user surveys and statistics in the evaluation and/or benchmarking of library services. In the better cases these have been collated on a standardized basis and fed into the Europe-wide LIB-ECON survey, supported by the EC IST programme, supporting the development of some Europe-wide performance indicators. This has often involved the adoption of the ISO standards 2789: *Information and documentation. International library statistics*, and 11620: *Library performance indicators*, as in Latvia and Norway, for example. A danger identified is that these sometimes extensive statistics can be used only to justify the presence of a service, rather than to re-evaluate and modify the services offered.

More qualitative evaluation procedures have been developed and implemented, for example in Denmark and the Netherlands. In the UK, benchmarking clubs are run for public libraries, but the focus on digital services is currently limited. All local authority services are required to be evaluated according to the Audit Commission's Best Value regime, which assesses their contribution to specific national policy goals. Some projects have also piloted impact evaluation and beneficiary monitoring at the individual user level.

Action Point 10

Propose *research and take-up activities* at national or European level, based, where appropriate, on partnerships with support organizations and private sector companies, including those skilled in information access, content building and digitization.

0	There is no programme or context in which local cultural institutions can participate or benefit from the results of relevant research.
1	Some individual localities have conducted research or shown an interest in its results, but there are serious constraints (e.g. lack of access to technology, funding or skills) in putting such research into practice.
2	There is relatively wide recognition that research has an important role to play in the development of local cultural services and some organized attempt to identify and exploit the results of R&D at national and European level, but resources restrict widespread exploitation and take-up.
3	One or more research programmes is funded or planned nationally, with clear potential for local cultural institutions to participate and exploit the results.

Continued on next page

4   A significant proportion of local cultural institutions has participated in research activity and benefits actively from a flow of information on relevant national and European research.

5   A well established research culture, in which local cultural organizations are involved in a range of partnerships with public and private sector partnerships, is having a clearly visible impact in the shape of services provided, including those involving the exploitation of technology.

The results were as follows:

- Range   0–5
- Mean   1.6
- Median   2
- Mode   2
- Top quartile   2.

This Action Point returned the second-lowest total score of all. Only one country (Denmark) claimed Level 5, and one other (Ireland) Level 4. The current benchmark is merely recognition that research has an important role to play for local institutions, but lack of resources to support this are restrictive. Nine countries responded with a Level 0. There is little evidence of the take-up of research conducted in other sectors, e.g. by universities. These indications and the responses from most countries seem to underline the continuing importance of the European Union's IST research programme for local cultural services.

In a few countries government-supported agencies conduct basic as well as applied research in the cultural sector, and (e.g. Denmark) operate as a driving force behind technological development in research, concentrating on IT solutions. Others (e.g. Belgium, Czech Republic, Norway) have the establishment of such support as a goal or under consideration. In the UK, previous programmes for the library sector have been discontinued and the focus switched to commissioning strategic short-term research. Funding for more basic research must be obtained in competition with other fields through the academic research councils.

Conclusion

It appears that, taken as a whole, Europe's local cultural institutions are only a comparatively short distance along the road to achieving the goals made explicit by the PULMAN Manifesto, but that advancement is gathering speed. It is hoped that the work described in this paper has contributed to the provision of increasingly visible benchmarks to which Member States and others may aspire. The latest updated country reports on the CALIMERA website, written in 2004/5, provide further indications.

The re-formulation of European policy following the mid-term review of the Lisbon Agenda has led to the announcement of a forthcoming new initiative: iEurope 2010, with somewhat revised goals. Any attempt to benchmark continued progress among local cultural institutions will need to take account of these modified objectives.

Any such work would also require consideration of the reliability of data, the role of self-assessment and any possibilities for improving validity through the interpolation of more 'objective' metrics and data collection mechanisms.

Appendix

The Oeiras Action Plan

The PULMAN conference calls upon ministers, policy makers and practitioners at national and local level, within a specified timeframe, to:

1 Establish strategies that utilize and develop the skills and infrastructure of Europe's comprehensive physical network of public libraries, archives and museums in order to develop their full social, cultural and economic potential.

2 Identify national and local funding priorities in support of key activities such as providing access to electronic resources and the internet, digitization, piloting new services, ensuring an adequate technical infrastructure, including broadband connectivity where feasible, and the adoption of common standards.

3 Consider the establishment of cross-domain agencies and inter-ministerial co-operation for co-ordinated policy making within the cultural heritage sector (public libraries, museums and archives).

4 Develop effective partnerships between the local cultural heritage sector and other key economic and social sectors (e.g. education, employment, tourism, community organizations, etc.) to facilitate re-engineering of local services, as well as cost-effective provision and management.

5 Provide interactive access to content through state-of-the-art multimedia digital resources documenting local history, literature, art, music and community interests, packaged where appropriate as learning resources.

6 Support the development of centres of excellence to stimulate take-up of good practice, where necessary as a starting point for wider implementation of innovative services.

7 Implement staff recruitment and training policies, including adequate salary and conditions, to provide the capacity and skills to deal effectively with user needs, e.g. learning support and the use of information society technologies.

8 Monitor the changing needs of users as a part of evidence-based policy development and investment planning.

9 Measure and evaluate services on a regular basis, especially those involving new technologies, and establish benchmark criteria to assess the impact and outcome of investment.

10 Propose research and take-up activities at national or European level, based, where appropriate, on partnerships with support organizations and private sector companies, including those skilled in information access, content building and digitization.

Oeiras, March 2003

References

European Commission (2004) eEurope Digitisation: the Lund principles, www.cordis.lu/ist/digicult/lund_principles.htm [accessed 31 January 2006].

European Commission (2005) Commission unveils plans for European digital libraries, http://europa.eu.int/rapid/pressReleasesAction.do?reference=IP/05/1202&format=HTML&aged=0&language=en&guiLanguage=en [accessed 31 January 2006].

Minerva (2003) Benchmarking Framework Working Group, www.minervaeurope.org/structure/workinggroups/benchmarking.htm [accessed 31 January 2006].

18

Enabling the library in university systems: trial and evaluation in the use of library services away from the library

Chris Awre, Ralph Quarles and Steven Smail

Introduction

Universities today operate numerous computer systems to serve the different activities within them. Among other things, administrative systems help to manage enrolment, student records, exams, staff employment and finance. Teaching and learning are often supported through course management systems or virtual learning environments, enabling interaction between staff and students. Research departments use a range of tools to facilitate collaboration and research itself. Libraries have also built up an array of systems over the years to manage the information and knowledge they hold, and to provide access to such collections for users.

Most of these systems have been established independently, with overlap only being established where essential, such as feeding student module choices from student records to course management. Library systems have been particularly independent, with limited interaction or integration with other systems within the institution. Yet, information provided by the library is integral to the learning, teaching and research activities of the institution and, arguably, success in these areas. Providing simpler access to library resources within alternative university systems will enable these to be used more effectively and directly. But is this valuable? Is it what users want?

This paper focuses on two approaches to testing access to the library within non-library university systems and contexts. The Contextual Resource Evaluation Environment (CREE) project sought to gather user requirements to inform technical development. The Twin Peaks project, in contrast, followed a rapid prototyping approach, allowing users to see what functionality might be provided before refining this on the basis of feedback. Jointly, what follows are the comparative stories of how each approach worked out via consideration, in turn, of our respective projects' origins, background, stakeholders, development processes, evaluative processes and outcomes.

Genesis
The CREE project
As the range and number of search tools available has developed it has become apparent that, despite being beneficial in its own right, each is adding to the number of user interfaces a user needs to know about and understand when searching for information. In parallel, many institutions are creating web environments that seek to provide all the information and application requirements for their staff and students through a local common interface, or are implementing systems through which learning, teaching, research and administrative activity is being channelled; how can external search services feed into these and provide more streamlined access for users?

To investigate this issue more closely the CREE project was funded by the UK's Joint Information Systems Committee (JISC) in early 2004. The project was tasked with two main areas of activity:

- The investigation of user requirements for access to search tools within a range of different institutional contexts.
- The investigation and testing of standards (SR 168 (http://developers.sun.com/ prodtech/portalserver/reference/techart/jsr168/) and WSRP (www.oasis-open. org/committees/tc_home.php?wg_abbrev=wsrp) to enable the surfacing of search tools within portal and other conformant environments.

The Twin Peaks project
Since 2001 academic computing services and the libraries at Indiana University (IU) had worked to integrate their respective services so that teaching and learning sites might access library resources from within the Course Management System (CMS) with a single user logon. There had been some success with course reserves for seamless linking, and a basic library tool wizard was created in CMS that allowed users to pick from a list of library online subscriptions. This tool only provided outside links for searching via the vendor's site. Yet a new course management system planned for complete adoption by spring 2006 will eliminate even this basic tool for default access from within local CMS. IU's University Information Technology Services (UITS) and IU libraries recognized

that each had a virtual mountain of resources, yet they forced users to jump between them. In 2003 the Twin Peaks project thus began to build bridges between these separate peaks of library resources and course management. The intention is to meet course authors at the point of need by replicating a path a user might choose naturally during the creation of course content (https://twin-peaks.dev.java.net/).

Background
The CREE project

The introduction of an institutional portal at the University of Hull in September 2003 was preceded by a number of sessions where users were invited to contribute their views as to the type of service it would be beneficial to see within the portal. This involvement has led to usage by up to 15,000 users per week, and the establishment of the portal as a recognized place for access to institutional services and information.

The basis for introducing the portal was to enable the streamlining of institutional processes, thereby saving resources, time and money. The resources dedicated to the portal thus had to reflect this and not increase the resources being used overall across the university. Gathering user requirements in advance and in parallel with technical implementation allowed these needs to be met from the start.

Notwithstanding, the library has remained relatively under-represented, both within the portal and outside of its home website (www.hull.ac.uk/lib/).

The Twin Peaks project

IU libraries provide subscribed or local access to over 46,000 digital collections of images or text. IU libraries also maintain an online catalogue of over six million items, many with links to some web-based information even if the original artefact is in print format. The database-driven website for the libraries at www.libraries.iub.edu/ provides a central portal for all resources from anywhere, with authentication for remote users. Logs show that about 165,000 visitors per month sought library resources here in spring 2005.

IU adopted CMS technology in 1999 via a local system called OnCourse (https://oncourse.iu.edu/). OnCourse provides space for lessons, group work and communications from anywhere, with authentication. It is currently in transition to be replaced by OnCourse Collaboration and Learning (OnCourseCL), a local instantiation of the Sakai project, of which IU is a principal partner (www.sakaiproject.org/).

Goals

The CREE project

The institutional background to establishing user requirements as part of technical development and implementation at the University of Hull fed into the work of the CREE project. CREE sought to investigate a more detailed and focused use of individual services rather than informing the implementation of a major piece of infrastructure. But the same principles applied. User involvement in the process would allow services to be developed that addressed current needs, thereby providing a base upon which future services could be developed, both at Hull and elsewhere. This, in turn, would aim to save resources and prevent users feeling frustrated by systems that do not do what they need them to do. CREE also hoped to show the feasibility of using the JSR 168 and WSRP standards in presenting search tools within a portal environment.

The Twin Peaks project

The goals of the Twin Peaks project stem from empirical observations in public library service and campus technology support of a desire by users for extended possibilities to search at the 'point of need' within CMS. Essential to expectations is library expertise that understands which subscribed and local resources offer persistently usable links, quality in content and the availability of rights for use.

The project provides a simple keyword search of the library resources that can be tapped to add links to articles and images to assignments, resource lists, calendar items, or anywhere else in the teaching, learning and collaboration environment. The intention from the start has been to experiment with any suggested possibilities so that stakeholders on campus may see what is possible via both electronic subscriptions and local collections. Deliberately evolutionary in design and the scope of its goals, this is a 'moving target' using feedback from faculty, students and maintainers of infrastructure in OnCourseCL in an ever-improving tool that can be offered for adaptation by all institutions using the Sakai software.

Stakeholders

The CREE project

The following user groups assisted with analysing the results of the user requirements gathering, and in helping focus the development of services to these groups:

- Teaching staff
- Research staff
- Clerical staff
- Support staff
- Library staff
- Postgraduate students taught
- Postgraduate students research
- Undergraduates.

CREE was a partnership project and was able to carry out specific user requirements gathering at two higher education institutions (University of Hull and University of Oxford) and one further education institution (Newark and Sherwood College) to help identify any apparent differences across institutions.

A particular interest in the work of CREE came from the library staff. The search tools CREE was testing within different contexts provided access to a number of services they already advertised and offered through external links and websites. The outcome of the project would assist the library particularly in planning how it would provide search services to staff and students, and where these needed to be delivered. The technical partners were also key stakeholders in their investigation of the two standards and how these might be used to enable the delivery of services via alternative routes and in alternative contexts.

The Twin Peaks project

The LibQUAL+ 2004 survey of over 25,000 students, faculty and staff at 40 large university research libraries such as Indiana University library offers a useful profile (www.arl.org/newsltr/236/lqaccess.html). Over 60% of the undergraduates surveyed used the library premises at least weekly, and 75% use it monthly. Yet access to the library's electronic resources from home or office was rated at 8.39 out of nine points by undergraduates, graduate students and faculty alike; 40% of faculty reported using the library website daily, but over 90% said they used search engines on a daily or weekly basis. Only 11% of undergraduates said they used the library website daily, and 5.5% said they never used the library website. So, the patrons for whom the library exist value remote services and the libraries, yet choose to access them via the central portal provided by the libraries significantly less often than they use search engines such as Google.

In contrast, IU's Course Management System has enjoyed use comparable to that of search engines by stakeholders. Statistics from the spring 2005 semester's server logs at https://oncourse.iu.edu/statistics/ show that 89% of students and 82% of faculty were active users, with 75,517 of the 89,600 registered students logging into the system at least five times or more during the semester. Thus,

OnCourse is a preferred 'meeting point' in virtual space for the library's stake-holders.

Faculty and library staff have expressed concern regarding the lack of a default library tool in the new CMS. The patterns of use noted above would indicate that patrons prefer to use resources online but away from the libraries' web portal. Yet even new bridging possibilities such as Google Scholar (www.scholar.google.com/) do not remove barriers from hidden stakeholders who publish and market resources. Librarians provide knowledge of barriers such as a lack of persistent arti-cle links and difficulty with customizing searches for local subscriptions and digital rights. So, publishers insist on sustained branding and proper rights management; the librarians are concerned that patrons obtain useful, authoritative sources and take advantage of local subscriptions; and the patrons just want an easy, quick consolidated search for information. Meanwhile, those who provide network infrastructure naïvely wonder why the libraries cannot easily facilitate 'drag and drop' from all 46,000 subscribed databases in a common interface from inside course pages, and figure it must be the libraries' fault!

Process

The CREE project

A three-pronged approach to gathering user requirements was adopted by the CREE project.

1 In September and October 2004 a national survey was used to kick-start the CREE project. The survey sought to gather information on two levels. First, it gathered information on existing circumstances: what search tools are cur-rently used and what they are used for. It then requested opinions on potential uses of search tools: searching more than one resource at the same time, how results should be displayed, and use of search tools in different contexts such as a CMS.

2 Focus groups were then held and covered the same topics as in the survey. Whereas the survey provided individual views, the focus groups allowed the opinions expressed to be validated or contradicted within the group. This led to a better understanding of the reasoning behind certain views, and why dif-ferent views were held. All opinions on the potential for using search tools in different contexts were, however, based largely on a theoretical understanding of what might be possible without prior experience.

3 In parallel with the first two activities, technical investigation of the JSR 168 and WSRP standards had been carried out to enable the presentation of search tools within an institutional portal. This enabled a proof-of-concept demonstrator to

be built highlighting how search tools might be integrated into such an environment. Two further demonstrators were built to show how library search tools might be embedded within local web pages and within a course management system. All three demonstrators were fully functional and allowed users to carry out test searches before responding to a questionnaire based on the findings of the survey and focus groups. These responses, based on seeing actual functionality, helped to refine the users' requirements and offered a greater depth to them.

The Twin Peaks project

The libraries' development model has been one of rapid prototyping followed by formative testing with a small group of users which informs refinement of the tool. User requirements were not gathered via formal research instruments, but directly from those who daily provide service to faculty and students. Thus, the process is literally one of 'try it and see what develops' to allow quick functional development, evaluative feedback via tryouts and exhibits of the evolving tool for stakeholders, then iterative revisions for continuous improvement. Suggestions are actively solicited from formal libraries committee of public service librarians and staff; faculty organizations; and individual faculties. Twin Peaks is intended as a local tool that will eventually become part of the Sakai project (https://twinpeaks. dev.java.net/), so there are also meetings with both IU and Sakai system development teams to discuss current and future directions. Thus, establishing what users want has been inescapably bound up in the actual development of the tool itself. Figure 18.1 reflects the contrast of process between the CREE project and Twin Peaks.

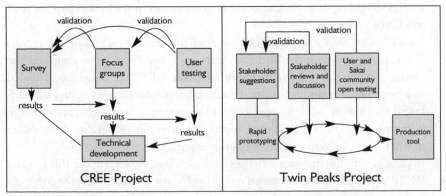

Figure 18.1   *Contrasting processes for establishing user requirements*

Testing and evaluation

The CREE project

The CREE survey received over 2000 responses for analysis, providing a wealth of data upon which to build. The results in many ways reflected the LibQUAL+ findings. It produced no major shocks in terms of understanding how and why users used search tools and what they used, but did provide solid evidence to back up accepted wisdom. It also provided some valuable insights into how open users were to using library search services in different contexts. This indicated open-mindedness towards the concept, albeit with a lot of doubt about what exactly it might mean.

The CREE focus groups did indeed validate the findings of the survey, but also provided valuable insights that only discussion can bring out. The focus groups also gave the users a chance to reflect on their own search behaviours, where before they had had no cause to do so.

The user testing with demonstrators provided a far more definite and positive view of library search services in different contexts. The presentation of predominantly subject-specific search tools within a CMS context was considered particularly useful, although access via local web pages and through an institutional portal also received good support.

Full results from all three user requirements activities within CREE can be found via the project website at www.hull.ac.uk/esig/cree/.

The Twin Peaks project

The testing focused on formative analysis of the prototype tools by all stakeholders. The key component is a functional demonstration site located at http://129.79.35.230:8080/portal/. It is open to the world with a username of 'demonstration' and password of 'demo@iu', and has been presented to a broad spectrum of potential users with encouragement that they try it on their own. Testers are encouraged to incorporate the Twin Peaks search tool into their usual workflow for crafting new authoring instances. Detailed feedback is then requested via the site or by separate e-mail. Other than adding Twin Peaks to the authoring tool, the demonstration is a fully functional generic installation of Sakai v2.0 to reflect the intended environment. The site receives visits at least daily, with a few IU faculty and staff being frequent participants. Key personnel in the Sakai project, IU faculty, IU information technology services, IU libraries staff, and staff from other libraries at campuses implementing Sakai have participated in the tests to inform development. We also posted the code and encouraged other developers involved in the Sakai project to try it out and suggest revisions.

Outcomes

The CREE project

It was not the aim of the CREE project to produce a final set of services by the end of the project. The aim of gathering user requirements was to inform technical development. CREE has enabled this in two ways. First, the technical partners have now been informed as to the value of their proof-of-concept investigations. Looking ahead, they can now develop services based on a knowledge of what users find valuable and what they do not like. Second, the University of Hull and others have been informed to the extent that they can now focus their resources on services they know users will find useful.

The user requirements work has had two further institutional benefits. Users taking part in the various activities have felt involved in the development process and have welcomed the opportunity to express their opinions. The library itself has also picked up on the value of gathering user requirements and is investigating ways in which it might do this on an ongoing basis.

The Twin Peaks project

It has always been a primary goal to produce operationally useful services, then to continue their development. The project is now operational and ready for production in its current state. Functionality encompasses direct searching within Sakai and choice among resulting links from sources, including those subscribed electronic resources that offer native persistent links; public-domain image collections; IU library catalogue items with online components; IU's electronic reserves system; IU libraries' custom course resource pages prepared at faculty request; and beta-level federated searching engines. Plans are under way to place Twin Peaks in local production of IU's OnCourseCL, and for the inclusion in v2.1 of Sakai to make it available to over 75 institutions in that project. Future developments include consideration of changes in infrastructure to seek a more common application interface layer, permitting more standard processes in adding search sources.

Twin Peaks was borne of stakeholder frustration yet succeeded through our common interests and a lack of any alternative tool for library resources in Sakai. As Sakai emphasized individual developers' initiative over one tightly controlled central development environment, there was an opportunity for libraries to become involved via evolutionary design in direct response to stakeholders, rather than by statistical justification. The basic result is at least the first few strands of a successful bridge between the rich mountain of resources offered by the libraries and the lofty peak of Sakai/OnCourseCL erected at IU as a learning and collaborative environment. In the libraries, we will use this project as a springboard to develop even tighter integration of libraries and our online course environment through a more federated searching and default tools customized by course for the student researcher's use.

19

Towards an integrated theory of digital library success from the users' perspective

Li-Hsiang Lai, Ming-der Wu and Yeu-Sheng Hsieh

Introduction

Since the early 1990s, with the rapid development of information and communications technology (ICT) and global attention to the conservation and preservation of cultural heritage, thousands of varieties of digital libraries (DLs) have been created all over the world for different applications. They are increasing in number and evolving in nature. Much effort has been made in the design and implementation of DLs, but their evaluation has not received as much attention in research and practice. Evaluation should be an integral part of the research and development (R&D) process. Although it has been seldom addressed in the literature, much work has been done, focusing on system-centred or objective evaluation. User-centred or subjective evaluation, using different approaches and methodologies, has increasingly attracted attention (Saracevic, 2004; Borgman, 2003; Marchionini et al., 2003). Nevertheless, DL evaluation is facing a conceptual and pragmatic challenge (Saracevic, 2000, 2004). For the conceptual challenge, a theoretical basis for evaluation is urgently needed.

The major purpose of this paper is to propose a multidimensional and multilevel integrated theoretical framework of DL success from the users' perspective. Based on the components and nature of DLs, the challenges of evaluation and the problems of existing assessment frameworks, the proposed framework mainly adopts DeLone and McLean's (2003) Model of Information System Success (D&M Model) as a theoretical base, with refinement for answering the questions: How do users evaluate DL success? How do individual differences and DL contexts influence users' assessment of DL success?

The components and nature of digital libraries

Scholars define a DL in different ways, but no matter how it is defined and evolves, a DL is an information system by nature. Borgman et al. (1996) and Borgman's (2000, 2003) two-part definition gives more insights into the components and nature of a DL. The first part of the definition emphasizes using information technology to organize electronic resources 'for creating, searching, and using information' (Borgman, 2000, 42). The second stresses the provision of user-centred services that are extended from physical to digital contexts. Through the information system (IS), users interact virtually with the DL to use services and to share ideas with other users. The two-part definition of a DL is not separated but inter-related, and it should be integrated as a whole both in research and in practice.

According to the definitions of a DL provided by Borgman et al. and other researchers (e.g., Saracevic, 2000, 2004; Van House et al., 2003, 1; Marchionini et al., 2003), we identify three major components of DLs as follows:

1 Users: as the centre of the DL, including local and remote users
   — use: users' use of the DL
2 Contexts: physical contexts as physical institutions or virtual contexts as an information service system on the internet or a combination of these two
   — content: physical/digital resources with information embedded
   — services: all kinds of service, including system, content, and support services, provided either physically or virtually
   — technology: a single or multiple/integrated information system(s) in networked environments, with emphasis on its/their communication, functionality and interface
3 Practice: the application and impact of a DL on users, institutions and societies.

It is clear that a DL has its multifaceted nature in its information system, interdisciplinarity, dynamism, integration, evolution and complexity.

The challenges of digital library evaluation

Evaluation is essential in order to 'understand the consequences of developing and interacting with digital libraries' (Dalton et al., 2004, 113), to 'assess how far they meet their stated objectives, and provide insights for further improvements' (Chowdhury and Chowdhury, 2003, 267), and to determine how they are ultimately transforming research, education, learning and living (Saracevic, 2000, 368). However, evaluation is facing conceptual and pragmatic challenges owing to the nature of DLs. Regarding the conceptual challenge, Cullen (2001, 668) pointed out that 'the theoretical framework and conceptual approach to evaluation within which the survey will be applied is rarely addressed'. In other words, there is currently no properly defined theoretical framework of DL evaluation from the users' point of view. Thus, the lack of a theoretical basis for evaluation is the most challenging issue.

A well defined theoretical framework is the foundation of DL evaluation, though this is still in the development stage. Current practice is based largely on a traditional system-oriented approach, i.e. objective evaluation. Furthermore, much evaluation in research and practice, especially for user surveys, lacks an explicit definition of dependent variables or of the relationships between the various factors or of DL evaluation. This is because different researchers have addressed different aspects, such as usability, system features, usage and impacts (Saracevic, 2004), and have seldom explored the relationships between the dimensions measured. For example, Saracevic (2004) identified several factors of DL evaluation from previous studies, but did not establish the relationships between them to provide a more integrated view, not did he define the dependent variables. If there is no well defined dependent variable, much DL evaluation will be speculative (DeLone and McLean, 1992, 61).

The problems in existing assessment frameworks

Although the evaluation of DLs has been less focused on R&D, a few empirical studies of user surveys from fields other than library and information science (LIS), such as management information systems (MIS), applied a well developed conceptual model to evaluation: the Information System Success model (e.g. DeLone and McLean 1992, 2003), the Technology Acceptance model (e.g. Davis et al., 1989), and the User Satisfaction and Loyalty model (e.g. Martensen and Grønoldt, 2003), for example. However, some problems in existing assessment frameworks and studies have been identified and must be taken into consideration.

Neglecting context effects on users

As users are the heart of the DL they and the digital contexts may affect each other (Bishop et al., 2003, 167). Accordingly, evaluation should not overlook context effects on users because individual and context observations are generally not completely independent. Rather, evaluation should consider combining both subjective (individual level) and context objective evaluation (context level) simultaneously to balance the research results. None the less, most empirical studies of DL evaluation utilized either the context level or the individual level separately to assess the effectiveness or performance of the DL or the users' perception of service quality. It has been found that empirical studies employing a user-centred approach rarely investigate context effects on users.

Confusing terminology of different study levels

Some previous studies on information system (IS) success (e.g. DeLone and McLean, 1992, 2003; Hong et al., 2002; Martensen and Grønoldt, 2003; Nelson et al., 2005) have tried to integrate individual and context level evaluation in a single framework to emphasize the effect of context on users, but this integration is confusing because of the terminology of 'study level' used in the framework. For example, in the D&M Model, 'system quality,' 'information quality' and 'service quality' are three dimensions of quality, all of which are used for the context level. If they are used for the individual level, they should be conceptualized as 'perceived system quality,' 'perceived information quality' and 'perceived service quality'. Otherwise, this may result in confusion with the study levels and measures used.

Ignoring influential individual differences

Although subjective measurement is considered, influential individual differences between users, which may affect their usage and perception of service quality, have sometimes been neglected in previous studies. For example, the assertion that 'a "good" information system perceived by its users as a "poor" system is a poor system' (Ives, 1983, 788) may be unfair or biased. Therefore, if users' perceptions of the service quality of DLs are different, it is necessary to examine how individual user differences, such as demographic characteristics, self-efficacy for information literacy and information needs, etc., affect their valuations of success.

Bewildering time sequence

In a theoretical evaluation research framework, it is also critical to distinguish the proper time sequence of causal relationships between the factors or dimensions of DL evaluation or IS success. The purpose is to avoid misleading results. Taking the individual level as an example, we argue that if users do not have experience of using a DL, how can they perceive its quality? The D&M Model hypothesizes that 'system quality', 'information quality' and 'service quality' affect the users' intention to use and their actual use of a DL. This sounds reasonable, but may not be true from the individual level point of view and may lead to biased research results if the time order of the constructs of DL evaluation is confusing.

A theoretical framework of digital library success

It is imperative to have a coherent theoretical framework for evaluating DLs which is responsive to their nature, to the challenges of evaluation, and to the problems of existing assessment frameworks for DL evaluation and IS success. The new framework should provide a comprehensive view of DL evaluation to ensure that it can be conducted effectively and that meaningful and purposeful data are collected.

An integrated theoretical framework of DL success from the user perspective is shown in Figure 19.1. This is based on the components and nature of DLs and uses the D&M Model as a basis. DeLone and McLean (1992) synthesize previous conceptual and empirical studies and incorporate different categories of IS into a multidimensional and interdependent integrated model of IS success, emphasizing the dependent variables. The model has been tested with various applications (Briggs et al., 2003). In 2003, DeLone and McLean revised their original model to define IS success according to four major dimensions: 'IS quality, 'intention to use/use', 'user satisfaction' and 'net benefits'. 'IS quality' is separated into 'information quality, 'system quality' and 'service quality'. Between dimensions, the hypothesized relationships are presented. Based on a refined D&M Model, we define DL success from the users' perspective by self-reported use, perceived service quality, satisfaction and perceived net benefits, but perceived net benefits is our major indicator of success.

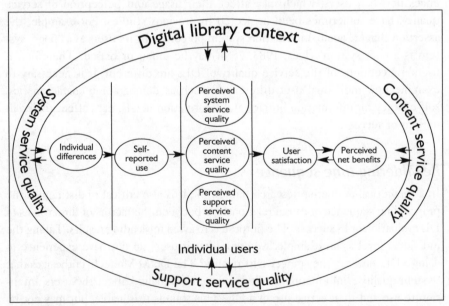

Figure 19.1   *An integrated theoretical framework of DL success from the users' perspective*

Because our theory centres on users, we focus on how they perceive DL success and how their perceptions are influenced by their characteristics and the DL context. Figure 19.1 shows that two study levels of success, in two-layered circles, i.e. individual users and DL context, are proposed. The DL context refers to a digital library website or a combination of a physical library extended into a virtual environment. Two-way arrows between the inner and outer layers of Figure 19.1 indicate how users within a DL context interact with it. Thus, we hypothesize that the service quality of a DL and the users' perception of DL success have reciprocal effects. In other words, the users' perception of DL success is based on its service quality on the one hand, and the improvement in service quality of the DL is reflected by the users' subjective perception on the other. The remainder of this section explains the framework in more detail.

DL context level

At the context level, emphasis is placed on the objective evaluation of service quality that is adopted from the quality construct of the D&M Model and modified as system service quality, content service quality and support service quality. System service is the technology-related aspect of an information system, such as its functionality, interface and communication to deliver services. Because content is king in the DL field (Fox and Urs, 2002, 523), content service refers to the digital resources in which information is embedded. Therefore, we use 'content service quality' instead of 'information quality' as used in the D&M Model as one dimension of service quality. The support service is another key service, supporting user interactions with the DL through the user's guide, online tutorials, online reference service, etc.

Individual level

From an individual level, the inner circle of Figure 19.1 indicates that DL success is reflected by users' perceived net benefits, satisfaction, perceived service quality and self-reported use. Their evaluations may be affected by their individual differences. Figure 19.1 also displays the relationships between dimensions and factors with a proper time sequence and causal relationships. We suggest that perceived net benefits and user satisfaction have a reciprocal effect.

Perceived net benefits

'User satisfaction is related to the benefit that is perceived to be gained in using the [digital] library service' (Miller, 2004, 125). Thus 'net benefits' in the D&M Model is employed and refined as the users' 'Perceived net benefits' to be the final dependent variable of DL success in Figure 19.1. Obviously, at an individual level, the user who perceives the benefits he or she gained from using a DL defines net benefits. These could be economic or academic, or in the form of a daily impact on the individual user.

User satisfaction

User satisfaction has been most often used as a factor to describe IS success or effectiveness (DeLone and McLean, 1992). However, it is frequently measured with overall satisfaction in a number of empirical studies (e.g. McGill and Hobbs, 2003; Livari, 2005). In order to distinguish differences in user satisfaction with different aspects of service quality, so as to feed back into the DL's decision making, planning and strategy developments (Bertot, 2004, 20), we suggest that user satisfaction be measured by the degree to which users are satisfied with system service quality, content service quality and support service quality separately, and with overall user satisfaction as a whole. It is hypothesized that user satisfaction is affected by the perceived net benefits and the users' perception of service quality.

Perceived digital library service quality

In order to have consistent terminology at the individual level and service quality at the context level, the three dimensions of quality in the D&M Model, i.e. 'system quality', 'information quality' and 'service quality', are modified according to the users' perception of service quality. In order to distinguish between differences in user perceptions of different aspects of the service quality of a DL, their perceived quality is divided into three dimensions, perceived system service quality, perceived content service quality and perceived support service quality. These three dimensions may affect user satisfaction, and in turn perceived net benefits. From a broader view of causal relationships, it is hypothesized that perceived DL service quality is influenced by users' self-reported use, individual differences and the DL context.

Self-reported use

DeLone and McLean (2003, 16) believe that system usage is an appropriate measure of success in most cases. However, as Seddon (1997) claims, 'use' is a behaviour, not a subjective perception. We contend that usage is a critical measure of DL success, but to be an important objective indicator it should be at the context level. It could be examined against users' self-reported use at the individual level to identify the relationships between the two indicators. Therefore, we use 'self-reported use' as an antecedent success construct at the individual level, and suggest that users' self-reported use has an impact on their own perception of service quality, of satisfaction with and benefits from using DL services. In other words, before a user perceives DL service quality, he or she should have experience in the use of DL services.

Individual differences

Individual user differences are relevant to IS success (Hong et al., 2002). Thus, at the individual level, we use 'individual differences' as a factor and suggest that it may have effects on the users' reported or actual use of a DL, and in turn on their perceived service quality, satisfaction and net benefits. Individual difference variables could be demographic characteristics, such as gender, age, education and status; or non-individual demographic characteristics, such as computer self-efficacy, information literacy self-efficacy, etc. The individual difference variables that should be included depend on researchers' interests and the DL context being evaluated.

Conclusion and future research

This study reviews the existing theories of evaluation and incorporates the traditional approach to (digital) library evaluation to propose an integrated theoretical framework for evaluating all types of DLs from the users' perspective. The framework gives a comprehensive view and provides a better understanding of issues regarding how individual users perceive DL success, and how individual differences and DL contexts affect their perceptions. We conclude that DL success should be defined by combining users' perception of success and the service quality of digital library-specific contexts in order to comprehensively reflect the quality of a DL and to minimize research bias. Users' perception of success should also integrate various aspects of perceptions of DLs. As a DL can be defined as an information system and may consist of several such systems, it should integrate subsystems as a whole to be evaluated. Therefore, DL success from the users' perspective is a system-, users' perception- and context and individual integrated evaluation.

The proposed framework is intended to be applicable to any type of DL. Thus, we suggest that measures of DL success be developed based on the proposed framework and DL context referred to for future research. In addition, empirical surveys should be conducted in different DL contexts to test the external validity of the proposed framework.

References

Bertot, J. C. (2004) Network Service and Resource Evaluation Planning. In Bertot, J. C. and Davis, D. M. (eds), *Planning and Evaluating Library Networked Services and Resources*, Westport, CT, Libraries Unlimited, 1–22.

Bishop, A. P. et al. (2003) Participatory Action Research and Digital Libraries: reframing evaluation. In Bishop, A. P., Van House, N. A. and Buttenfield, B. P. (eds), *Digital Library Use: social practice in design and evaluation*, Cambridge, MA, MIT, 161–89.

Borgman, C. L. (2000) *From Gutenberg to the Global Information Infrastructure: access to information in the networked world*, Cambridge, MA, MIT Press.

Borgman, C. L. (2003) Designing Digital Libraries for Usability. In Bishop, A. P., Van House, N. A. and Buttenfield, B. P. (eds), *Digital Library Use: social practice in design and evaluation*, Cambridge, MA, MIT, 85–118.

Borgman, C. L. et al. (1996) *Social Aspects of Digital Libraries: UCAL-NSF social aspects of digital libraries workshop*, invitational workshop held at UCLA, 15–17 February, 1996, Final Report to the National Science Foundation, is.gseis.ucla.edu/research/dl/UCLA_DL_Report.html.

Briggs, A. O. et al. (2003) Special Issue: Information Systems Success, *Journal of Management Information Systems*, **19** (4), 5–8.

Chowdhury, G. G. and Chowdhury, S. (2003) Digital Library Evaluation. In Chowdhury, G. G. and Chowdhury, S. (eds), *Introduction to Digital Libraries*, London, Facet Publishing, 267–83.

Cullen, R. (2001) Perspectives on User Satisfaction Surveys, *Library Trends*, **49** (4), 662–86.

Dalton, P., Tehbridge, S. and Hartland-Fox, R. (2004) Evaluating Electronic Information Services. In Andrews, J. and Law, D. (eds), *Digital Libraries: policy, planning and practice*, Burlington, VT, Ashgate, 113–27.

Davis, F. D., Bagozz, R. P. and Warshaw, P. R. (1989) User Acceptance of Computer Technology: a comparison of two theoretical models, *Management Science*, **35** (8), 982–1003.

DeLone, W. H. and McLean, E. R. (1992) Information System Success: the quest for the dependent variable, *Information Systems Research*, **3** (1), 60–95.

DeLone, W. H. and McLean, E. R. (2003) The DeLone and McLean Model of Information Systems Success: a ten-year update, *Journal of Management Information Systems*, **19** (4), 9–30.

Fox, E. A. and Urs, S. R. (2002) Digital Libraries. In Cronin, B. (ed.), *Annual Review of Information Science and Technology*, Volume 36, Medford, NJ, Information Today, 503–89.

Hong, W. et al. (2002) Determinants of User Acceptance of Digital Libraries: an empirical examination of individual differences and system characteristics, *Journal of Management Information Systems*, **18** (3), 97–124.

Ives, B. (1983) The Measurement of User Information Satisfaction, *Communications of the*

ACM, **26** (10), 785–93.

Livari, J. (2005) An Empirical Test of the DeLone–McLean Model of Information System Success, *The DATA BASE for Advances in Information Systems*, **36** (2), 8–24.

Marchionini, G., Plaisant, C. and Komlodi, A. (2003) The People in Digital Libraries: multifaceted approaches to assessing needs and impact. In Bishop, A. P., Van House, N. A. and Buttenfield, B. P. (eds), *Digital Library Use: social practice in design and evaluation*, Cambridge, MA, MIT, 119–60.

Martensen, A. and Grønoldt, L. (2003) Improving Library Users' Perceived Quality, Satisfaction and Loyalty: an integrated measurement and management system, *Journal of Academic Librarianship*, **29** (3), 140–7.

McGill, T. and Hobbs, V. (2003) User-Developed Applications and Information Systems Success: a test of DeLone and McLean's Model, *Information Resources Management Journal*, **16** (1), 24–45.

Miller, L. (2004) User Satisfaction Surveys, *Australasian Public Libraries and Information Services*, **17** (3), 125–33.

Nelson, R., Todd, P. A. and Barbarah, W. (2005) Antecedents of Information and System Quality: an empirical examination within the context of data warehousing, *Journal of Management Information Systems*, **21** (4), 199–235.

Saracevic, T. (2000) Digital Library Evaluation: toward an evolution of concepts, *Library Trends*, **49** (2), 350–69.

Saracevic, T. (2004) Evaluation of Digital Libraries: an overview, www.scils.rutgers.edu/~tefko/DL_evaluation_Delos.pdf.

Seddon, P. B. (1997) A Respecification and Extension of the DeLone and McLean Model of IS Success, *Information Systems Research*, **8** (3), 240–52.

Van House, N. A., Bishop, A. P. and Buttenfield, B. P. (2003) Introduction: digital libraries as sociotechnical systems. In Bishop, A. P., Van House, N. A. and Buttenfield, B. P. (eds), *Digital Library Use: social practice in design and evaluation*, Cambridge, MA, MIT, 1.

20
The role of digital libraries in helping students attend to source information

Steve Cohen, Susan Eales, Mike Fegan and Dean Rehberger

Introduction

This paper introduces the Digital Libraries in the Classroom programme and then details the particular approach to evaluation undertaken by Michigan State University as part of the Spoken Word project, which is exploring the role of digital libraries in helping students attend to source information.

Digital Libraries in the Classroom

Digital Libraries in the Classroom is jointly funded by the Joint Information Systems Committee (JISC) (www.jisc.ac.uk) and the National Science Foundation (NSF) (www.nsf.gov/) and is running from 2003 to 2006, with embedding activities within the host institutions in the UK continuing to 2008. The programme has been developed to bring about significant improvements in the learning and teaching process by bringing emerging technologies and readily available digital content into mainstream educational use. Projects are examining some or all of the following issues:

- The innovative use of distributed, multimedia multisource digital content and advanced network technologies and capabilities in education.
- Radically improving and extending the way teachers and students approach knowledge in a given subject area; this might involve re-examination of the foundations of a topical area and the methods by which topical knowledge is accumulated, understood and legitimized.

- Examining how the classroom experience can be enriched for both teachers and students through the use of innovative applications and access to digital resources.
- A better understanding of students' requirements for effective use of information and communication technology (ICT), virtual learning environments (VLE) and electronic information resources.
- How teachers can be assisted to incorporate ICT, VLE and electronic information resources appropriately, to provide balanced courses for students.
- The institutional information infrastructure required to deliver courses in these innovative ways, including the provision of suitable networks, resources, applications, and the development of strategies to manage all of these effectively.
- The organizational changes that will be required to deliver courses in this way and support the staff and students involved, and how these can best be managed by the institutions.
- The development needs of the teaching staff, the information service support teams and administrators, and consideration of the reward mechanisms for staff engaged in innovative activities.
- Economic models for the development, delivery and long-term support and development of ICT-based learning.

Four projects have been funded under this programme, as follows:

- **DART:** A partnership between the London School of Economics and Columbia University in the discipline of anthropology. This project aims to develop new digitized resources for the teaching of anthropology and to bring about meaningful and sustainable transformation of undergraduate education and professional practices in the field.
- **DialogPlus:** A partnership between the University of Southampton, the University of Leeds, Penn State University and the University of California, Santa Barbara, working in the geography discipline. This project aims to embed a wealth of existing digital resources developed in the USA and UK into the curricula of four US and UK higher education institutions in four different sub-areas of geography, which is a recognized subject of teaching and research excellence in the four participating institutions.
- **DIDET:** A partnership between the University of Strathclyde and Stanford University working in the design engineering discipline. The project combines the use of digital libraries with virtual design studios.
- **The Spoken Word:** Led by Michigan State University, Northwestern University and Glasgow Caledonian University in partnership with the British Broadcasting Corporation (BBC), exploring the use of digital audio in the humanities.

The programme is overseen by an international peer review panel, members of which are very keen to ensure that the projects undertake robust and broad evaluation of all their activities so that lessons learned can be disseminated widely across the international education community.

Enhancing the understanding and use of source information by students at Michigan State University

The learning experience is being revolutionized by information and communications technology (ICT), and the internet in particular. Students increasingly turn to the web for educational and scholarly material. This has resulted in increasingly better integration of the different technologies and applications in the development of digital libraries. However, although more and more rich source materials are being made available in digital libraries, educators and students do not always take advantage of them. Whereas some blame the distrust of online information and others the poor usability rating garnered by digital library interfaces, we tend only to focus on improving searching and usability and pay little attention to how students use and understand materials found in digital libraries. To this end, the Spoken Word project team has created a suite of tools that helps evaluate use and understanding while enhancing students' ability to attend to the key features of digital objects.

Framing the learning problem

Since the cognitive revolution took place in the 1950s (Gardner, 1985) a good deal of research on learning has used a novice–expert framework. According to this, many learning problems (i.e. learning chess, diagnostic radiology, mapmaking, etc.) can best be described by first defining the knowledge and thinking skills of a novice, and then considering what changes occur as the novice gains competence and ultimately achieves expertise. Changes in knowledge, knowledge organization, thinking skills, perception may all play a role in the development of expertise. Defining the changes needed to acquire expertise in a field is key for assessment: it offers a systematic way to assess how teaching and learning methods facilitate the development of expertise in a particular area or domain, and suggests opportunities to measure that development.

In 1991, Wineburg used an expert–novice framework to describe how novices (i.e. secondary and college students in history classes) and experts (i.e. practising historians) attend to source information. This work accentuated the cognitive challenges involved in helping students choose and interpret sources, rather than simply citing them correctly at the end of a paper. Wineburg suggested that expert historians use 'heuristics' when assessing the value of a particular source. In particular, he suggested that three cognitive heuristics come into play when experts think about a source. Wineburg (1991) found that, unlike high school students, historians sought out and evaluated the source of a document and used this to influence their interpretation of its content (referred to by Wineburg as a **sourcing heuristic**). Historians also attempted to situate the events in an accurate spatial–temporal context (referred to by Wineburg as a **contextualization heuristic**). Finally, Wineburg noted that experts directly compared content across documents systematically, and were therefore able to identify discrepancies (referred to by Wineburg as a **corroboration heuristic**).

Wineburg's description offers a target for instruction, assessment and further research. Building on his seminal work, other research teams both challenged and confirmed what Wineburg (1991; 1994; 1998; 2000; 2001) proposed, and in the process created a more detailed description of what it means for novices and experts to exercise these heuristics when evaluating potential sources. Research by Britt and Aglinskas (2002) identified particular features of documents that experts attend to and which novices often ignore, making it possible to assess in more detail what novices needed to learn. For instance, document type, author's motivation and position, and document date are some of the features that might or might not be taken into account when evaluating a source. These more specific features add measurability and instructional goals for assessment.

This research on sourcing has resulted in new methods of teaching students to attend to key source information, as well as a method for assessing how libraries without walls can be used to evaluate, assess and teach these skills. Out of this research came the first new approach to teaching sourcing: the Sourcer's Apprentice simulation. Designed to teach students to think carefully about the sources they cite (Figure 20.1 overleaf), it requires them to record key source information as they select resources from a virtual library.

The learning theory behind the simulation is that teaching students thinking skills in environments similar to the one where they will be used will lead to better education and more active minds. Situated cognition, as advanced by Brown et al. (1989), also suggests that apprenticeship is key to learning. The virtual library in the Sourcer's Apprentice offers a meaningful 'situated environment' for learning, and interactively tutors students to attend to key features of documents. The features accentuated come from research by Britt and Aglinskas (2002). The integration of research and instruction helps make assessing students' sourcing abilities relatively simple.

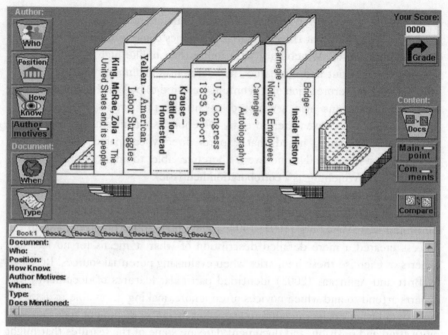

Figure 20.1   *Sourcer's Apprentice main screen with source information categories*

Using digital libraries to address sourcing education

As part of the Spoken Word project we are building on the research behind the Sourcer's Apprentice, and developing two new technologies to teach and assess sourcing skills. These new technologies are integrated into the web for good reason: digital libraries offer a tremendous opportunity to situate learning and teach students to attend to source information and create better essays. Digital libraries **are the ultimate in virtual libraries** and ideal for utilizing situated cognition. Here, rather than a simulated world, the instruction uses real sources and requires students to attend to source features as they integrate sources into papers and assignments. It is a learning world anticipated by proponents of situated cognition.

Digital libraries for acquiring sources and teaching sourcing

The potential improvement comes from two technologies working together. The first is MediaMatrix, a technology for collecting and annotating objects from Digital Libraries and websites. MediaMatrix (version 1.0) is an online server-side tool that helps users to find, segment, annotate, organize and publish streaming media found on the internet. MediaMatrix works within a user's browser, using the browser's bookmark feature. When users find a digital object at a digital library or while surfing the internet, they simply click the MediaMatrix bookmark and it searches through the page, finds the digital medium and loads it into an editor. The editor allows users to segment sound and video (isolate any size portion of a whole clip), resize and crop images, save text, and add their own annotations to that medium. They then submit that information to MediaMatrix and it is stored on the user's personal portal page. This page keeps all their annotations as well as providing direct links to the portions of the streaming media that were segmented. Users can organize their thoughts on the portal page and create either a paper with embedded media or a multimedia presentation using the media they find through easy-to-use templates. MediaMatrix allows teachers to gather and present media for the classroom, students to integrate media into their assignments, and scholars to perform the kinds of tasks carried out in traditional libraries with analogue objects (gather resources, take notes, publish findings).

Teachers can create a group for each of their classes and invite students to join that group, allowing both teacher and students to preview the work of and collaborate with other members of the class. MediaMatrix does not require any special downloads or plug-ins, a feature that makes the tool more accessible to teachers, students and researchers, who may be working in computer laboratories and at library workstations that often do not easily allow for the downloading of additional software. MediaMatrix identifies the universal resource indicators (URIs) of media found on a specific web page. The streaming media are then loaded into the appropriate media player (Real Player, Quicktime, Windows Media) and embedded into the MediaMatrix online editor. MediaMatrix does not actually record or save the audio, but instead stores the URI and the time offsets for the selected clip. When the user replays the clip, those offsets and the URI are then passed back to the player, and thus only the selected portion of the streamed audio is replayed.

Users can then add their own thoughts or analysis to the clip in the form of annotations (Figure 20.2). The user then titles the clip/annotation and submits it to his or her personal portal page. The annotations can then be easily saved, accessed, combined, exported, organized, edited, shared and published. The suite of tools developed for MediaMatrix not only allows users to work with and analyse digital objects, but also affords them the ability to locate new digital objects. MediaMatrix uses the information users submit when creating their profiles and groups to create browsable and searchable access points to portal pages created by other users. Users can also perform keyword searches over the annotations created by all users or specific groups of users. A teacher, for instance, can choose to search through only the information in 11th-grade Civics groups in the hope of finding information that speaks directly to his or her needs. Because users have gathered content from across the internet and from a variety of digital repositories, searching MediaMatrix is equivalent to searching multiple repositories at once. Once users find an object from a particular digital library, they can jump to that repository to find what other objects are available.

The second technology is MM/Cite. Cite, built on sourcing research, is a layer built into MediaMatrix that users can turn on and off. When it is turned on, students are required to answer a series of questions about the object that capture information that is often missed when collecting resources (Figure 20.3).

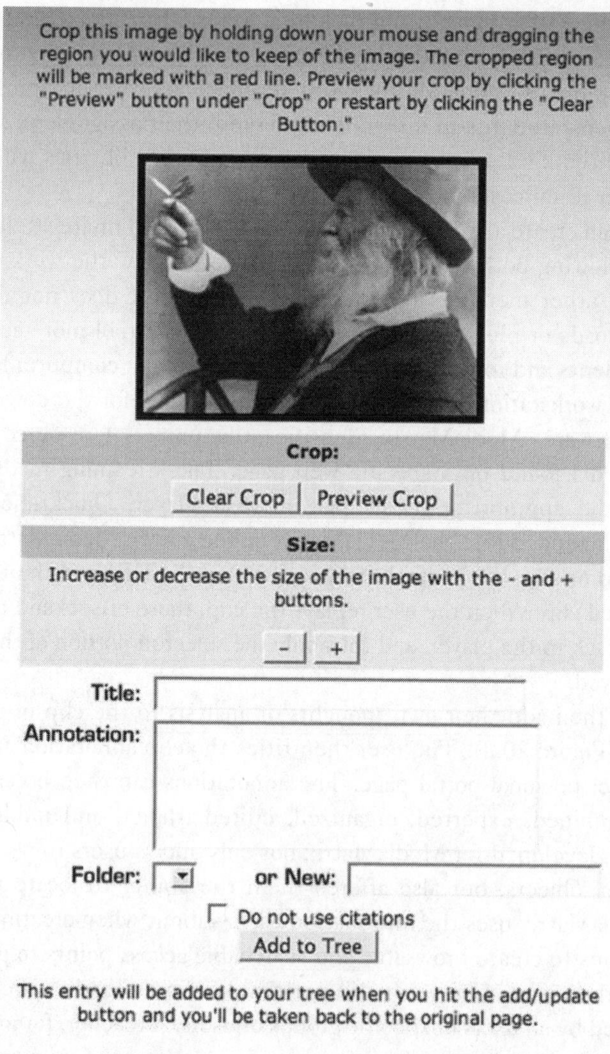

Figure 20.2 *An object collected with MediaMatrix is ready for annotation*

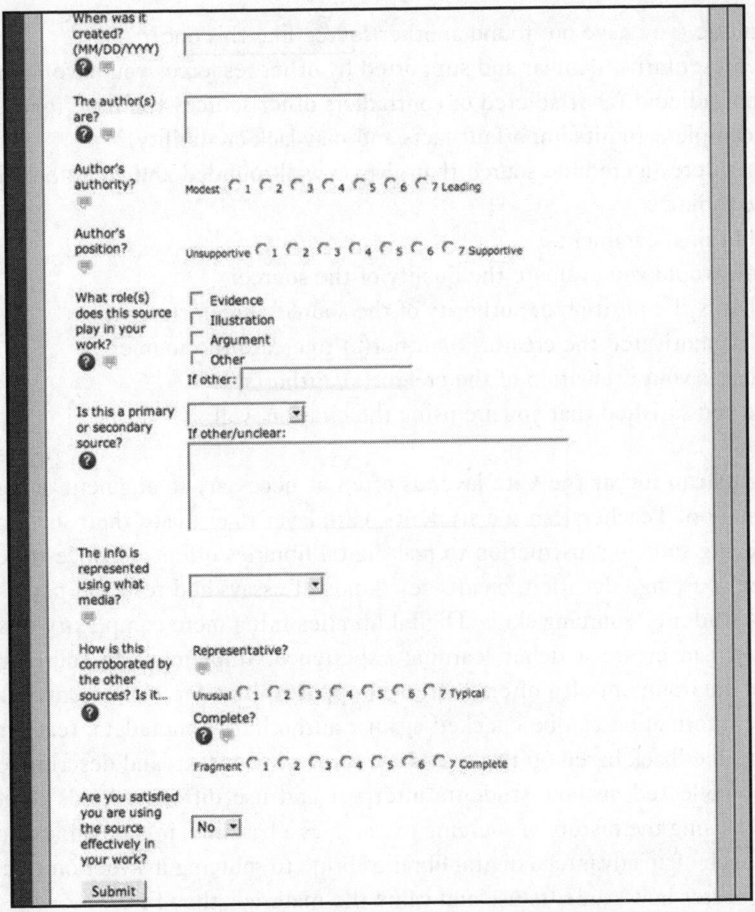

Figure 20.3 *Students answer sourcing questions for an image of WWII propaganda*

When a student saves an audio clip, for example, to his or her portal page, a series of questions is asked that help them to cite and evaluate the source, as well as giving space to make additional comments:

- When was it created? Be as specific as you can using '?' for any part of the date you don't know. Use MM/DD/YYYY as the format.
- Who created/authored the source? (Last Name, First Name)
- What kind of source/citation is this?
- Additional comments?
- Is this a primary source or secondary source?
- What medium is primarily used?
- How is this corroborated by the other sources for your project?

- Unique (you have not found another source like this one)?
- Representative (similar and supported by other resources you have found)?
- Contradicted (contradicted or contradicts other sources you have found)?
- Incomplete (omits important facts and may lack credibility)?
- Complete (a credible source that gives a well-rounded and complete view of the topic)?
- Additional comments?
- How would you evaluate the quality of the source?
- What is the position or authority of the source's creator(s)?
- What motivated the creator(s)/author(s) to create the source?
- What is your evaluation of the creator(s)/author(s)?
- Are you satisfied that you are using the citation well?

Students can revisit the Cite layer as often as necessary to augment or retrieve information. Teachers can see students' Cite layer to evaluate their sourcing.

Moving sourcing instruction to real digital libraries offers a chance to revolutionize sourcing education, create new kinds of essays and research papers, and assess students' sourcing skills. Digital libraries bring more complexity to sourcing and can create a richer learning experience. Implementing sourcing in a digital environment also offers increased opportunities for assessment. Student source information can be checked against authoritative metadata, teachers can provide feedback based on the use of the source in context, and descriptive data can be collected on how students interpret and use different kinds of object. Finally, using the history of sourcing research as a baseline, it is possible to assess how much of an advantage digital libraries bring to sourcing instruction to understand better how students use and value the materials they find.

The sum of the parts

Carefully integrating the learning theory, the citation layer and MediaMatrix makes a meaningful assessment possible. The learning theory, and related empirical validation by Britt and Aglinskas (2002), suggests a measurable learning problem: using a range of materials about some historical topic or incident, the goal is to measure the key features of source information to which students actively attend. As part of their research, Britt and Aglinskas have created a measurement rubric to address this problem. Secondly, there is the citation layer, a tool that requires students to identify key features of source materials, as well as defining the role those materials will play in their essay. The citation layer is based on the established rubric for attending to source information. Consequently, the technology tools students use to actively identify key features of source information is formally and conceptually linked to this rubric. This link preserves the bridge between the learning theory and the research activity students perform. Finally, MediaMatrix implements the citation layer in a way that allows students to do more than learn via a lecture or simulation (i.e. they are learning by integrating source information directly into assignments they need to create and complete). Students are required to use source information to justify why and how a source contributes to the virtue of their argument(s).

Ultimately we expect this system to improve students' ability to attend to and use source information for two reasons, both of which rest on students having access to digital libraries and related secondary repositories. Students are required to explicitly attend to source information when they evaluate and collect sources. The information metadata students have access to when using digital libraries bolsters the kinds of sourcing they can perform. Secondly, their sourcing work will be integrated directly into their essays, where staff can grade it, offer feedback, and compare students' sourcing acumen to the metadata available with the object. We believe this represents a major step forward in the way students use source materials and construct essays, and hope to demonstrate gains next spring (2006) via a rigorous outcomes assessment.

Acknowledgement

Support for the project comes in large part from the JISC/NSF Digital Libraries Initiative II: Digital Libraries in the Classroom Program–National Science Foundation, award no. IIS-0229808. The Digital Libraries in the Classroom programme website which links to each project website is at www.jisc.ac.uk/index.cfm?name=programme_dlitc. Further information on the National Science Foundation can be found at www.dli2.nsf.gov.

References

Britt, M. A. and Aglinskas, C. (2002) Improving Students' Ability to Identify and Use Source Information, *Cognition and Instruction*, **20** (4), 485–522.

Brown, J. S., Collins, A. and Duguid, P. (1989) Situated Cognition and the Culture of Learning, *Educational Researcher*, **18** (1), 32–42.

Gardner, H. (1985) *The Mind's New Science: a history of the cognitive revolution*, New York, Basic Books.

Wineburg, S. S. (1991) Historical Problem Solving: a study of the cognitive processes used in the evaluation of documentary and pictorial evidence, *Journal of Educational Psychology*, **83**, 73–87.

Wineburg, S. S. (1994) The Cognitive Representation of Historical Texts. In Castellan, J., Pisoni, D. B. and Potts, G. (eds), *Teaching and Learning in History*, Hillsdale, NJ, Lawrence Erlbaum Associates, Inc., 85–135.

Wineburg, S. S. (1998) Reading Abraham Lincoln: an expert/expert study in the interpretation of historical texts, *Cognitive Science*, **22** (3), 319–46.

Wineburg, S. S. (2000) Making Historical Sense. In Stearns, P., Seixas, P. and Wineburg, S. (eds), *Knowing, Teaching and Learning History: national and international perspectives*, New York, NYU Press, 306–25.

Wineburg, S. (2001) *Historical Thinking and Other Unnatural Acts: charting the future of teaching the past*, Philadelphia, Temple University Press.

21

A DiVA for every audience: lessons learned from the evaluation of an online digital video library

Elizabeth Mallett, Agnes Kukulska-Hulme,
Anne Jelfs and Chetz Colwell

Introduction

The Open University (OU) has been in existence in the UK for more than 30 years, specializing in creating and delivering course materials in all formats for students at a distance. As a result there is a large archive of learning resources, managed by the OU library, which could potentially be reused in the making of new courses. The Digital Video Applications (DiVA) project was set up in 2000 to investigate the potential reuse of OU video footage when digitized and made searchable. What would the benefits be to staff, and possibly students, of an online digital video library?

The project's aims included the following:

- Creating an online library of digitized OU video footage.
- Rendering the footage searchable by content through the use of cutting edge video-indexing technology.
- Evaluating the system in a number of different user contexts.
- Making recommendations for the use and future of such a system within the university.

The DiVA system and its applications

The operational specification for the DiVA digital video library system was written in consultation with a user group and project board from across the university, using the recommendations from the Informedia project evaluation (Kukulska-Hulme et al., 1999) as a starting point. We could not locate any open source solutions at that time, so a European tendering exercise was undertaken. This resulted in the purchase of the Virage suite of products.

Adding content to the video library

A 'video logging' station was employed to encode (digitize) the videos as Windows Media files at three different streaming bit rates (56K, 512K and MPEG2) to suit all users, while simultaneously creating automatic metadata using artificial intelligence to recognize words, sounds, faces and voices. However, the system needed to be 'trained' to recognize all of these except the words, which was time consuming. For this reason, we focused on word recognition, which created a transcript of each video using voice-to-text technology. Because of inaccuracies with this method (approximately 30% accuracy), original transcripts held by the library were also imported into the system. Additional metadata were also added manually. We chose IMS Learning Resource Metadata (IMS, 2001), and created our own extensions for video material.

As we were digitizing a small selection of programmes within the remit of the project (approximately 245 hours' worth of material) key stakeholders recommended the kind of footage they would like to see in the database. We used the resulting selection criteria as an aid to extracting short video clips or chunks from whole programmes, which we thought would be of interest as entities in their own right.

Search interface

The search interface (Figure 21.1) allows users to search or browse the video database by OU course code, Library of Congress subject heading or keyword using either a quick search/browse or a detailed search.

When searching by keyword the system searches in the metadata about the programme, plus the transcript. Videos can be played from the point at which the search term appears in the transcript, effectively allowing users to 'jump' into the video at the relevant point (Figure 21.2).

While a video is being viewed on screen the transcript plays alongside it, scrolling upwards in synch with the sound (Figure 21.3 on page 202).

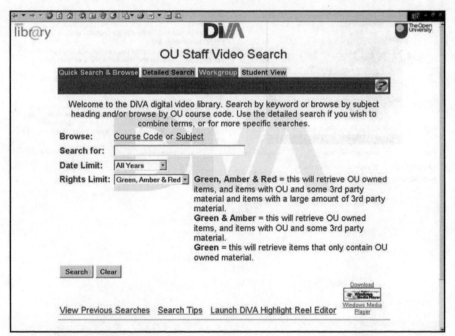

Figure 21.1   *The search interface*

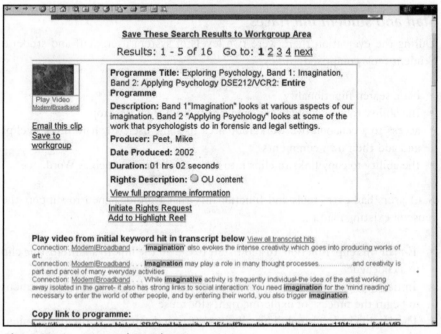

Figure 21.2   *Keyword searching*

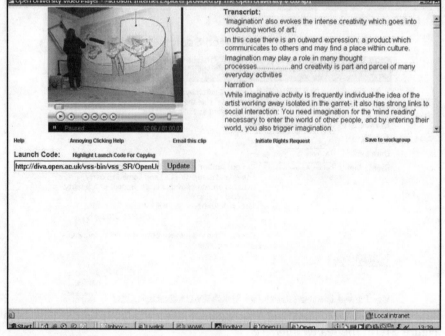

Figure 21.3   *Viewing a video on screen*

Staff and student interfaces

During the evaluation there were two levels of system user: staff and student. Student tools comprised:

- basic search functionality
- the ability to view footage and transcripts from their desktop
- access to a collaborative workgroup area to allow users to share links to clips and add their own comments
- the ability to copy links to clips into other applications, such as Word.

Staff users had extra tools and functionality that were designed to support the reuse of existing materials:

- 'E-mail this clip' function, to allow staff to e-mail the link to an interesting clip to a colleague
- 'Initiate rights request' form, which can be sent to the OU Rights Department to begin the process of exploring rights for reuse
- The Highlight Reel tool. This allows staff to indicate the particular segment of a programme they are interested in, marking the exact 'in' and 'out' points.

The evaluation programme

We wanted to find out whether the DiVA system would encourage reuse by help-ing academic teams find relevant footage. We were also interested in the potential impact on learning and teaching, and the extent to which the DiVA sys-tem could improve access to audiovisual material for hearing-impaired users and users with dyslexia.

The two-year qualitative evaluation was led by the OU's Institute of Educational Technology (IET) and comprised:

- an initial user study to test functionality
- experience of using the system for producing courses
- use by Master's level students accessing the system remotely
- use at a residential school in France
- an evaluation by students with disabilities.

A range of methods were used:

- Observations
- Questionnaires circulated to users following use of the system
- Interviews with selected users
- Examination of usage data from the DiVA system.

The initial usability study

The first evaluation of the system was an observation study, to examine its usabil-ity and gather some initial feedback with respect to potential use.

Twelve participants agreed to take part, representing all relevant stakeholders in course production and presentation, i.e. students, course team staff (those who write and produce the course content) and associate lecturers (tutors).

The study was carried out in the IET's Data Capture Suite (Open University, 2005). This facility can be used to capture video records of human–computer interaction which can be displayed in a four-way matrix, capturing up to four simultaneous 'views' of the user, the computer they are working at, and interac-tions with the application on the screen (Joiner et al., 2001). Participants were interviewed immediately after the observations.

Participants were able to navigate around the DiVA system and to find and use video clips. The ability to search and choose clips of video from across the uni-versity course materials (i.e. from different faculties) was felt to be extremely valuable. Areas where users needed clarification included terminology, descrip-tion of results, what exactly was being searched, and the transcript display (which was scrolling off screen too quickly). Following this study, the user interface was amended to take the feedback into account. For those areas where it was not possible to change the interface, it was decided that the comments would be used to provide help pages and instructions.

Experience with using the system for producing courses

Four interviews were conducted with course team chairs (the persons providing academic leadership in the creation of a new course). The ability to 're-version' or reuse material was very attractive to this group. It was felt that it was a much quicker system and much easier than the existing practice of expecting each course manager (the person responsible for administrative arrangements of course production) to find videos. DiVA would allow the course team chair to compare clips more easily and to make appropriate decisions on the content. DiVA also enabled the course team staff to write the activities at the same time as searching the system. This approach was identified as a cost-effective benefit for course development, as less time would be spent finding appropriate materials and there would be less wear and tear on video equipment. For instance, one academic estimated he had spent eight hours using DiVA to identify pertinent clips and share them with colleagues; and that it would have taken him at least three times as long if he had done the same thing the traditional way. This was for a course entitled 'Ways of Knowing: Language, Mathematics and Science in the Early Years'. There was a tight deadline to find reusable footage for the course CD-ROM. The academic in this case was the author of two of the language sections. He was looking for footage of the following, with a view to using it in activities that would require students to analyse what was taking place: assessment; bilingual children; children playing; standard dialogues; and conversations. He viewed 24 different clips, some of them several times, then saved 13 to the course workgroup for sharing with colleagues. He chose to use four of the clips found on DiVA in the final CD (depending on rights clearance).

A wish list emerged from the production use strand of the evaluation:

• The need to alert other appropriate staff to DiVA, e.g. editors, audiovisual producers
• The continuing need for dedicated library staff to assist with DiVA searches and training support
• A glossary of key search terms
• Titles for clips and whole videos to be slightly altered, to alert the user to the difference, particularly the length of the clip
• E-mail alerts of new content.

Opportunities and issues

Staff who used the system for course production purposes were positive about its potential. However, it was difficult to bring many course teams on board for the evaluation: initial interest was not easily converted to actual use within course production schedules. This was partly due to course team workloads at particular stages, and to DiVA's project status. The production use evaluation was affected by project staff resource and staff changes, and by various technical problems during the life of the project. The cost-cutting argument behind reuse of OU materials was well understood by course team members, but it was felt that if DiVA were to become a library service it would need to be strategically supported and involve a range of staff from different parts of the course production lifecycle (such as media producers early on).

Student evaluations

Master's level students accessing the system remotely

DiVA was trialled in June 2003 with a group of volunteer students who had recently completed an online Master's course, and between March and September 2004 with current students on the same course (H802: Applications of Information Technology in Open and Distance Education). Those who were studying H802 were professionally involved in online and distance education and had some experience in evaluating technologies and giving their insights. Both groups were accessing the system remotely.

The 2003 trial with alumni was with a group of 26 volunteers who had recently completed H802, and who were accessing the system remotely from home or work. They were divided into two groups, one using the student interface and one using the staff interface to see whether the functionality of the Highlight Reel tool (video mark-up tool) could be of value to students. They used DiVA as part of an online group activity, being asked to identify clips and discuss them in an asynchronous conference, and then paste a link to the clips into a web page.

The following year, DiVA was made available to current students on the same online course. Students were told that this was an opportunity to use DiVA as a resource on an optional, experimental basis throughout the year. The DiVA system was potentially relevant to several blocks of the course; however in 2004 it was not possible to use DiVA in a more integrated way on H802 because of concerns over student workloads and support issues.

Tutors were given an introduction to DiVA in their online tutor briefing just before the start of the course. The library was present online from the outset, to welcome students and answer any queries via a part-time helpdesk. A number of frequently asked questions (FAQs) and help sheets were posted in the forum.

Findings from the remote access students

There were a number of positive findings from the remote student use trial. It was found that participants who used the Highlight Reel tool were able to envisage constructing knowledge, taking a hands-on active role, and being stimulated to add commentary to their reels to aid their reflection. Others were positive about combining a repository of learning resources with a shared virtual space in which predefined or self-selected groups can work collaboratively (although DiVA's workgroup facilities are quite limited). They liked being able to home in on a section of a clip, building up their own library of clips and using them in assignments, and they appreciated the system catering to students who prefer information in auditory and visual formats rather than text.

However, on the whole the participants found it difficult to complete the activity in the time allocated, and there were some negative comments focusing on the quality of the video, including the small screen size and buffering. Much of the content used in the evaluation had the system-generated transcript, and its poor quality rendered it unusable in the opinion of some students (this has since been addressed). What was particularly interesting was a debate about the value of taking clips from a complete programme out of context. One student commented:

> Is it perhaps the case that advanced and deep learning requires sustained engagement with learning resources and that there is a danger of losing this if we rely on short clips?

In the second year on H802, given that access was optional, there was a good degree of interest in the system. Access statistics indicate that 21 students (out of 45 registered students) accessed the system at some point in the course. Seven different videos were accessed. Nine video clips were saved by students in the designated workgroup area within the DiVA system. However, end-of-course questionnaire comments suggest that students did not use the system to any significant degree for their actual coursework. It is possible that, had the online tutors engaged with DiVA, they might have modelled it for the students and this could have resulted in more extensive use.

Use at a French language residential school

The DiVA system was tested with students at a French-language residential school at Caen University during August 2003. To assist the students with their research for the oral and written tests that are part of the course, 7.5 hours of content had been added to the DiVA system. Students were asked to volunteer to use the system, and nine eventually took part in the evaluation (out of a total of 56). They were observed and filled in questionnaires. DiVA seemed to attract those students who were IT literate and confident in using computers.

Findings from the residential school

The residential school in France brought up a number of challenges. Extremely hot weather (38°C) plus the location of the computer room for the evaluation (separate from the other rooms, on the top floor) both contributed to the low take-up of volunteers. Of those that did use it, a high percentage did not find the content they wanted. However, they were mostly very satisfied with the quality of playback of video clips, which were accessed over a broadband connection.

The system appeared to work best when students knew exactly what they were looking for. Some people tried very complex and detailed searches, with expectations that the system would behave like the search engine Google, and unfortunately they were disappointed. For instance, the system did not rank results in the same way as Google, and some programmes appeared more than once in the list, which confused the students.

The automatically generated transcripts proved very problematic, producing many 'false positive' results. However, interestingly, when relevant programmes were found the transcripts seemed to be more useful than the programmes themselves, with students copying down phrases for their oral or written assignments. Students also thought it was useful to be able to use the transcript to jump to specific parts of the clip or programme.

Use by students with disabilities

The aim of this part of the evaluation was to examine the use of DiVA, in particular the use of transcripts alongside video, by deaf and dyslexic students, and students with other conditions affecting their use of video materials.

The production of transcripts is now particularly relevant in the light of the recent Disability Discrimination Act, Part IV (HMSO, 1995) which requires universities to make 'reasonable adjustments' to enable disabled students to participate fully in their courses.

Ten students were selected to take part in this section of the evaluation. Of these, five were deaf, three were dyslexic, and two had other medical conditions that affected their use of video material. Nine video clips were chosen for the students to watch, selected to represent the range of different types of content, styles of presentation and techniques commonly used in documentary programmes. Some of these techniques used were thought to be potentially problematic for disabled students, such as dialogue between people, narration over visuals, people talking to camera, subtitles for translation, and onscreen text, and were selected so these aspects could also be evaluated. Six of the clips had verbatim (or near verbatim) transcripts and three had software-generated transcripts.

The students were given a demonstration of the DiVA interface, including a search, and were informed about the two different types of transcript. The students searched for and watched the clips. They were asked to describe any problems they encountered, or improvements they would like to suggest. Two evaluators conducted the evaluations in the Data Capture Suite, as mentioned previously. After the students had watched the clips they were interviewed with closed and open-ended questions regarding their opinions of the specific features of the system described above that had not been discussed while they watched the clips. The data collected from the video recordings, the interviews and evaluators' notes were then analysed.

Findings from the use by disabled students

In general the disabled students found the verbatim transcripts useful, although some experienced difficulties with them. In particular, the students found it difficult to read the transcript at the same time as watching the videos, and to find the 'current' point in the transcript. The students did not find the software-generated transcripts useful because they were not accurate. Based on this evaluation several recommendations were made for improvements, as follows:

- Video material should be subtitled in addition to the provision of transcripts
- All transcripts of video material should include indication of background music, indication of sound effects, the names of people speaking, any on-screen text such as subtitles or explanatory information
- Transcripts that are delivered on-screen should provide an indication of the 'current' place in the transcript as the video plays.

All features should be optional where possible.

Since this evaluation was conducted the developers of the DiVA software have incorporated a facility to indicate the current point in the transcript. This takes the form of a highlight on each word as it is spoken. This new facility has not been evaluated with students.

Positive outcomes from the evaluations

Staff involved in course production have stressed how the system can facilitate collaboration and decision making among course developers. It has been proved (on a small scale) to save time and resources in locating footage for reuse.

Tutors could see possibilities for guiding students back to material to clarify information, and for accessing clips that were not used in course materials to further explore particular aspects of the course.

Students considered it useful to be able to jump to specific parts of a programme, and they made several suggestions for use of the system, such as adding commentaries, building up a library of clips to use in assignments, and learning collaboratively and in line with one's preferences.

Disabled students made recommendations on the interface and for the optional use of specified features.

Complementary to the qualitative user evaluations of DiVA described above was the library's quantitative evaluation of other aspects of the system, namely:

* 'process costing' of library cataloguing and video indexing processes
* technical monitoring: the impact of the DiVA system on the OU network. This was minimal owing to the small scale of use during the pilot.

Future evaluations

The evaluation did not cover all aspects that would be needed for an in-depth investigation of some issues. It did not gather evidence on specific effective pedagogical uses of DiVA, or the role of DiVA in 'bridging theory and practice', which was suggested by Zenios (2002) as a value of using streaming video in higher education. In the timescale of the evaluation there was no opportunity to undertake detailed work on staff and student workload impact. The evaluation raised some questions about the user interface to DiVA which could not be explored in detail. Finally, to assess issues of video quality and bandwidth access, specific trials would be needed. If DiVA is rolled out as a library service, more users will be available to participate in evaluating the system more extensively.

References

HMSO (1995) *Disability Discrimination Act*, London, HMSO, www.opsi.gov.uk/acts/acts1995/1995050.htm [accessed August 2005].

IMS (2001) *Learning Resource Meta-data Specification v.1.2, IMS*, www.imsproject.org/metadata/#version1.2 [accessed November 2004].

Joiner, R., Scanlon, E., O'Shea, T. and Smith, R. B. (2001) Technological Mediation for Supporting Synchronous Collaboration in Science and Statistics. In *First European Conference on Computer-Supported Collaborative Learning*, Maastricht, Maastricht University.

Kukulska-Hulme, A., van der Zwan, R. and Dipaolo, T. (1999) An Evaluation of the Informedia Digital Video Library System at the Open University, *Journal of Educational Media*, **24** (2), 131–6.

Open University (2005) *Data Capture Suite*, http://iet.open.ac.uk [accessed 28 June 2005].

Zenios, M. K. (2002) *The Use of Video Streaming in Higher Education: a report on the evaluation of the Click and Go Video case studies and the educational benefits for learners*, Lancaster, University of Lancaster, www.clickandgovideo.ac.uk/evaluation_casestudies.htm [accessed February 2005].

22
Usability evaluation of *ebrary* and *OverDrive* e-book online systems

Anne Morris and Panos Balatsoukas

Introduction

The publishing industry's largest growing sector is e-book sales (Macworld, 2004). For example, e-book sales for the first quarter of 2004 in the USA were up 46%, and e-book revenues were up 28% compared to the same quarter in 2003, according to the Open e-book Forum (2004). One sector likely to benefit from this growth is higher education, because the provision of e-books can be seen as a core feature of integrated e-learning strategies and synergies such as managed learning environments (MLEs) and virtual learning environments (JISC, 2003). Although many problems surround the provision of e-books, such as pricing and licensing ambiguity, budget constraints, and content bias towards the American market (Armstrong et al., 2002), e-books are making inroads into academia. E-books are being purchased from individual publishers, and aggregators of e-books, such as *ebrary*, *OverDrive* and *NetLibrary*, already established in the USA, are starting to penetrate the UK market. The latter provide integrated solutions for libraries based on remote-access servers that accumulate collections of e-books provided by different publishers. Although some research has been undertaken investigating the use of aggregators in public libraries (Dearnley et al., 2005) little has been done in the academic sector, particularly with respect to the usability of such services.

Some usability research has been undertaken on e-books in general, however. The Visual book experiment, for example, was one of the early attempts to define particular issues concerning the design of usable e-books (Landoni et al., 2000). The experiment revealed the positive implications of visual rhetoric and the book metaphor in e-book design. In addition, the Web project that followed the Visual experiment revealed that 'scannability' further improves the reading and overall usability of e-books (Landoni et al., 2000). The EBONI project followed. As part of this project a series of experiments was conducted, for example the Web Book II and the Psychology e-book projects, which confirmed the need for scannability and the book metaphor in the design and usability of e-books (Wilson et al., 2003), and a usability assessment of three online encyclopaedias that revealed the need to integrate web interaction features with the book metaphor (Wilson et al., 2004).

The usability of portable e-books in both academic and public libraries has also been investigated (Dearnley et al., 2004; McKnight and Dearnley, 2003; Wilson and Landoni, 2003).

In terms of general guidelines for design, researchers are divided on whether e-books should be based on the 'book metaphor' or not. Lee et al. (2002, 236) and Henke (2002, 10–13), for example, recommend a conventional approach to e-book design based on balancing the dynamic features of web technology with the traditional book metaphor, whereas others, such as Su (2005) and McFall (2005), advocate a more radical approach. Nielsen (1998), in a critical approach to the usability of e-books, asserts that the electronic book should not mimic its printed counterpart. Nielsen identifies the nature of the e-book as dynamic and evolution-ary, far from merely replicating the paper book. Furthermore, features such as hyperlinking, searching, connecting to other sources and updating of the content have been identified as significant factors for facilitating a more non-linear read-ing that matches the nature and use of the web.

The outcome of the research described above has resulted in usability guide-lines (e.g. The EBONI guidelines). However, Bennett and Landoni (2005) claim that e-book aggregators are still ignoring users' needs. The research detailed here aimed in part to investigate this claim. More specifically, the aim was to evaluate the user interface and assess the usability of *ebrary* and *OverDrive*, online e-book provision systems.

Usability test methodology

The systems under evaluation

The *OverDrive* and *ebrary* online systems were chosen for the purpose of this study. They differ in terms of website structure and interface design, e-book readers' for-mat (Adobe Reader for the *OverDrive* service and *ebrary* Reader for the *ebrary* service) and access models (download of the whole document in the *OverDrive* system and 'one page per time download' in the *ebrary* system). Such elements of differentiation, among many others, can provide useful criteria for comparison between the two systems.

Usability subjects' profile

Because this research intended to investigate and analyse usability issues in higher education, the 16 testers of the systems were students. They were divided into two groups: expert and novice users of e-books and the web, and were recruited by means of e-mails and announcements on university notice boards. Information provided by the students, in the form of a background questionnaire, was used to categorize them as expert or novice users.

Usability test design method

Task list analysis and scenarios

The main objective of the usability task testing was to evaluate users' interaction with the particular systems' basic functionality and usability. A set of nine tasks was developed that reflected the performance of simple and typical procedures:

1 Logging on to the system
2 Browsing by subject
3 Using the system's search facility
4 Borrowing, downloading or accessing an e-book
5 Finding a part of an e-book
6 Copying text
7 Highlighting text
8 Adjusting the screen display
9 Using the online help facility.

Data collection research methods

From the tasks specified a number of 'performance' and 'preference' data, analysed within a qualitative and quantitative framework, were collected.

A variety of data collection instruments were developed and used for the purpose of the research. These included observation through 'manual data collection forms', 'tape recording devices' (as a think-aloud technique was applied), 'screen recording software' (Camtasia, Version 2), and the use of questionnaires (background and post-test questionnaires). The post-test questionnaires were a modified version of the Questionnaire for User Interaction Satisfaction developed by the University of Maryland. They used a semantic differential nine-point scale following the structure of the QUIS.

Table 22.1 summarizes the data collected/measures (left-hand side of the table), the data collection techniques involved (top horizontal series of the table) and the criteria evaluated as prescribed by Nielsen (1993, 26).

Table 22.1 *Summary of the data collection types, methods and criteria (idea adopted from Wilson et al., 2004, 1688–92)*

Data Collection	Task testing	Satisfaction questionnaire
Time needed for the completion of each task	Learnability	
Successful or unsuccessful completion of each task	Learnability	
Number of errors per task	Errors	
	Memorability	
Nature of errors encountered	Errors	
Negative or positive comments	Satisfaction	
Ranking or rating of the systems' particular tasks/tools		Satisfaction

The research implements were piloted, and testing took place during the first half of July 2005 at the Multimedia Laboratory of the Department of Information Science of Loughborough University.

Hypotheses

It was assumed that there was no difference between the *ebrary* and *OverDrive* systems in terms of:

- the total time taken to complete all the tasks
- the time needed to complete each task
- learnability
- the total number of errors performed to complete all tasks
- the errors performed in each task
- memorability
- expert and novice users regarding time taken and errors produced.

Results of the study and discussion

Differences between the systems in terms of time and learnability

Users needed significantly more time to perform the tasks in the *OverDrive* system (82.97 seconds) than in the *ebrary* system (49.07 seconds) with a mean difference between the two systems of 33.90 seconds. However, this difference was not significant when the effects of the sign-in process of Task 7 of the *ebrary* system are taken into account. The user had to sign in or create a new account (different from the one used for logging on to the system) in order to create a personal bookshelf and be able to use added-value features such as annotating and highlighting text. In this particular case the highlighting feature in the *ebrary* system is not totally independent of the process of creating an account and log in the personal bookshelf where the user can save highlighted parts of the text.

Figure 22.1 illustrates the time taken to complete the individual tasks with both systems. It shows that tasks 4 (accessing the e-books), 5 (finding specific information within e-books), and 9 (using the help system) represent the most significant differences in time between the two systems. In particular, the inclusion of the download function within the 'add to basket feature' of the *OverDrive* system (Task 4), the insensitivity of the search feature of the Adobe Reader

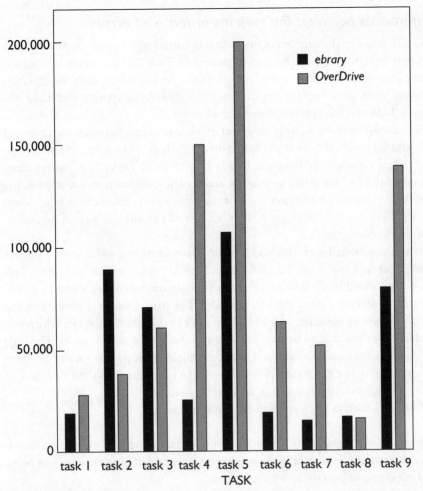

Figure 22.1 *Estimated marginal means of time between the two systems and across tasks*

system which resulted in a high retrieval rate (Task 5), and the verbose 'online help' provided (Task 9) were identified as the basic causes of slow performance in that system.

The estimation of the learnability factor is based on the time needed for users to complete a certain task successfully using the two systems under evaluation. According to the results of the time analysis it would appear that the *ebrary* system is easier to learn than the *OverDrive* system. However, the difference in learnability between the two systems is not significant if the extra time needed to sign in to enable Task 7 (highlighting text) to be completed using the *ebrary* system is taken into account.

Differences between the systems in terms of errors

The difference in the number of errors that occurred when using the two systems was only significant when the sign-in process of Task 7 in the *ebrary* system was taken into account ($F = 58.987$; $p < 0.0005$). In the latter case, more errors occurred with the *ebrary* system than with the *OverDrive* system; the mean difference between the two systems was 0.44 errors.

Significant differences were observed in the interaction between the tasks and the system ($F = 29.172$, $p < 0.0005$) (Figure 22.2). It is evident that the *ebrary* system differs significantly from the *OverDrive* system in Tasks 2, 3, (where more errors occurred in the *ebrary* system), 4 and 9 (where more errors occurred in the *OverDrive* system). In addition, users made significantly more errors when completing Task 7 using the *ebrary* system because of the difficult sign-in procedure that had to be completed.

It was not immediately obvious to some *ebrary* users how to browse by subject (Task 2) or how to use the search facility (Task 3), which resulted in errors. This was compounded by slow response times (for approximately 5–6 seconds, and in some cases of Task 2 more than 10 seconds). The main sources of errors with the *OverDrive* system were the lack of visibility of the download function, which was hidden under the 'add to basket' process, and the 'online help' system. The high number of errors using *ebrary* in Task 7, highlighting text, was caused by users either trying to use the wrong passwords to sign on to the bookshelf function, or trying to sign on without creating an account first.

Common sources of errors with both systems were:

- *the online help systems.* The linear structure of the online help systems does not facilitate flexible searching. As one expert user said, 'fewer errors would occur if adequate help systems were provided.'

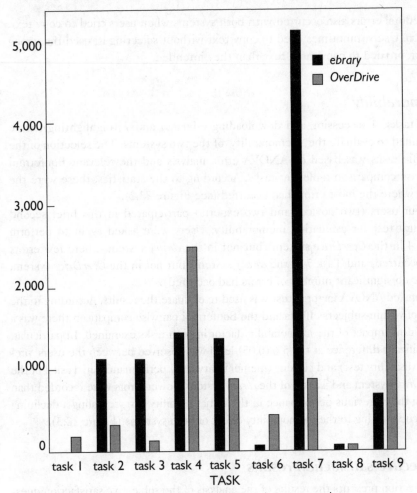

Figure 22.2   *Mean errors for the interaction between tasks x system*

- *e-book searching.* The small size of the query box does not permit users to search for long titles. This often resulted in typing or spelling errors.
- *mismatch of user and system models.* This was particularly the case for Task 7, high-lighting, with the *ebrary* system, and Task 4, borrowing, downloading, and accessing an e-book, in the *OverDrive* system.
- *backward and forward buttons.* These do not always align with users' expectations. For example, when trying to locate a part of a book (Task 5), *ebrary* users often tried to return to a previous page. Several users used the backward browser button to go back from the main contents to the table of contents page. This, confusingly, led users out of the e-book context to the results page.

Procedural errors also occurred with both systems when users tried to copy text, Task 6. Users sometimes tried to copy text without selecting it, used the wrong cursor, or tried to copy more text than they intended.

Memorability

Two tasks, 4 (accessing and downloading e-books) and 7 (highlighting), were examined to evaluate the 'memorability' of the two systems. The selection of the specific tasks was based on ANOVA error analysis and the relevant Bonferroni pairwise comparison tables for tasks. According to the statistics, these were the tasks where the most errors had occurred (see Figure 22.2).

Four users (two novices and two experts) participated in this brief second usability test for evaluating memorability. Users were asked again to perform Task 4 in the *OverDrive* system (but not in the *ebrary* system, where few errors had occurred) and Task 7 in the *ebrary* system (but not in the *OverDrive* system, where no significant number of errors had occurred).

A mixed ANOVA factorial test was used to evaluate the results. According to the tests of within-subjects effects and the Bonferroni pairwise comparison there was a significant impact of the memorability factor in both tasks examined. In particular, a significant difference at the 5% (0.05) level was observed between the users' previous (usability test) and current (memorability test) performances in Task 4 of the *OverDrive* system and Task 7 of the *ebrary* system. Fewer errors were recorded than during their previous performance in the initial usability test, revealing a declining error curve owing to the memorability effect of both systems (Figure 22.3).

Subjective satisfaction results

This section presents the results of the analysis of the subjective satisfaction questionnaire used to evaluate both systems by the participants in the usability session.

Expert users seemed to be generally more satisfied by both systems than were the novice users. Expert users favoured the *OverDrive* system but found the *ebrary* system more stimulating to use. On the other hand, novices were marginally in favour of the *ebrary* system but, conversely, found the *OverDrive* system more stimulating to use. It would appear, therefore, that users perceived the system they found more difficult to use to be stimulating.

The *OverDrive* system was rated friendlier and easier to use than *ebrary* for browsing by subject, searching for a particular title, and searching within e-books. However, *ebrary* was rated higher for reliability for the latter task. It is worth mentioning that for all three tasks the user-friendliness of both systems was rated lower than their reliability and ease of use.

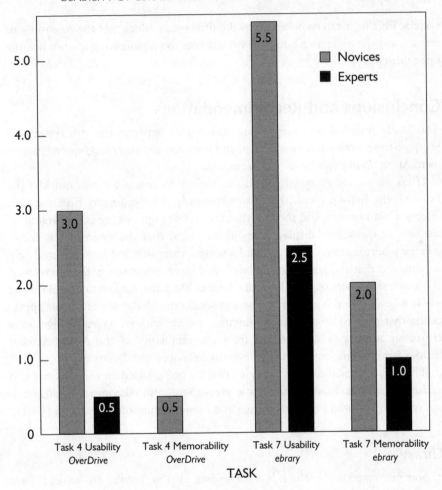

Figure 22.3   *The evaluation of memorability in task 4 of the Overdrive system and task 7 of the ebrary system between the two categories of participant*

Both expert and novice users found it easier to download e-books using the *OverDrive* system. The reasons for this are first, the downloading process in the *ebrary* system is ambiguous (the users had no indication whether or not they had accessed the whole e-book because of the download per page model, and they were confused by the lack of a more concrete download button instead of a vague 'view' link); and second, the downloading metaphor of one page at a time did not correlate with the mental model users have of expecting to download the whole document at once.

ebrary's copying feature was perceived by all users as being easier, but the highlighting and adjusting feature was regarded as more difficult than in the *OverDrive* system. Finally, it can be observed by the total mean values that the zoom-in/-out feature was the easiest task to perform whereas the highlighting feature was the most difficult.

Conclusions and Recommendations

This study revealed some significant differences between the two systems in terms of time, errors and satisfaction, and between the two categories of participant. All the null hypotheses were rejected.

Users of the *ebrary* system liked the facility to access e-books quickly, the Infotool, the pop-up menu that is automatically displayed every time the user selects a word or text, and the fact that the website options are concentrated on one side of the screen display. They also thought that the *ebrary* system incorporated a better search tool, provided a better structured and less cluttered help system, and that the general design included more 'white space' than *OverDrive*.

Conversely, users of the *OverDrive* system liked the facility to download the whole e-book, found it easy to browse and scroll through the whole e-book, appreciated that they could use the highlighting facility without having to sign on or create an account, and benefited from the familiarity of the Adobe Acrobat Reader family owing to prior use of e-journal services and databases.

The recommendations given below, despite being based on the usability test evaluation and the follow-up heuristic assessment, also take into account previous relevant research in e-book design and human computer interaction (HCI):

Ebrary

- *Searching across and within e-books.* The link to the 'browse by subject' page should be visible and highlighted so that users can find it easily. The search query boxes should also be long enough to enable users to control input backwards and forwards.
- *Downloading and accessing e-books.* Ideally, the system should provide users with the opportunity to download the whole e-book. This was a significant point mentioned by both novice and expert users during the usability test. If this cannot be achieved, then the one page at a time access model should be explicitly stated. Information could be provided, for example, through a pop-up menu or case-sensitive help feature.
- *Manipulating/added-value features.* Users should be able to use various manipulating facilities, such as accessing bookshelf features, without having to create personalized accounts.

- *Online help system.* Users should be able to perform keyword searches on the full text of the online documentation. In addition, an index of synonyms should be provided (Schneiderman and Plaisant, 2005, 540–1).

OverDrive system

- *Searching across and within e-books.* The simple search query box should be long enough to enable users to control input backwards and forwards. Also, hierarchical subject lists, when included, should be readable and placed on the left-hand side of the screen display, so that they can be always visible when a user accesses the system even when the interface is not designed for low-resolution screens, or even when the interface window is minimized (Nielsen, 2000, 28).
- *Downloading and accessing e-books.* The download button should be provided independently of the 'add to basket' personalization feature, where the download function is included. The download button should be visible and easily accessible.
- *Manipulating features.* The highlighting, copying and zoom features should be more visible and highlighted, as the Adobe Reader's interface is cluttered with functions and menus.
- *Online help.* The contents of the online help should be less cluttered. Ideally, information should be categorized into subject areas. Further, the help system should be visible and consistently displayed on the left-hand side of the screen display, and links in a standard colour (for example blue) should be provided (Nielsen, 2000). As with the *ebrary* system, users should be able to perform keyword searches on the full text of the online documentation and have the option to use synonyms.

Although not covered by the usability testing, further use of added-value features such as cross-referencing, within and between e-books, multimedia applications and advanced content personalization might be beneficial in creating a more stimulating environment for users.

It is clear from the usability testing that, although improvements can be made, both the *ebrary* and *OverDrive* systems are generally easy to use. However, the subjective rating of on-screen reading for both systems shows that this remains one of the major pitfalls for e-books.

References

Armstrong, C., Edwards, L. and Lonsdale, R. (2002) Virtually there? E-books in UK academic libraries, *Program*, **36** (4), 216–17.

Bennett, L. and Landoni, M. (2005) E-books in Academic Libraries, *Electronic Library*, **23** (1), 9–16.

Dearnley, J., McKnight, C. and Morris, A. (2004) Electronic Book Usage in Public Libraries: a study of user and staff reactions to a PDA based collection, *Journal of Librarianship and Information Science*, **36** (4), 175–82, lis.sagepub.com/cgi/reprint/36/4/175 [accessed 10 June 2005].

Dearnley, J. A., Morris, A., McKnight, C., Berube, L. and Palmer, M. (2005) Electronic Books in Public Libraries: a feasibility study for developing usage models for web-based and hardware-based electronic books, Report to Laser Foundation, in press.

Henke, H. (2002) *Survey on Electronic Book Features*, Open e-book Forum, www.opene-book. org/doc_library/surveys/features/downloadformats/e-book_survey.pdf [accessed 26 May 2005].

JISC (2003) *Promoting the Uptake of E-books in Higher and Further Education*, Gold Leaf, 2003, www.jisc.ac.uk/uploaded_documents/Promotinge-booksReportB.pdf [accessed 23 May 2005].

Landoni, M., Wilson, R. and Gibb, F. (2000) From the Visual Book to the Web Book: the importance of the design, *Electronic Library*, **18** (6), 407–19.

Lee, K.-H., Guttenberg, N. and McCrary, V. (2002) Standardisation Aspects of E-book Content Formats, *Computer Standards and Interfaces*, **24**, 227–39.

Macworld (2004) E-book Sales Rocket, *Macworld*, (June 07), 2004, www.macworld.co.uk/ news/index.cfm?NewsID=8848&Page=1&pagePos=1 [accessed 23 March 2005].

McFall, R. (2005) Electronic Textbooks that Transform how Textbooks are Used, *Electronic Library*, **23** (1), 72–81.

McKnight, C. and Dearnley, J. (2003) Electronic Book Use in a Public Library, *Journal of Librarianship and Information Science*, **35** (4), 235–42, lis.sagepub.com/cgi/ reprint/35/4/235 [accessed 11 June 2005].

Nielsen, J. (1993) *Usability Engineering*, London, Morgan Kaufmann.

Nielsen, J. (1998) *Electronic Books – a bad idea*, www.useit.com/alertbox/980726.html [accessed 12 June 2005].

Nielsen, J. (2000) *Designing Web Usability*, Indianapolis, USA, New Riders.

Opene-book (2004) www.opene-book.org/pressroom/pressrelease/q104stats.htm [accessed 13 May 2005].

Schneiderman, B. and Plaisant, C. (2005) *Designing the User Interface*, London, Pearson.

Su, S.-F. (2005) Desirable Search Features of Web-based Scholarly E-book Systems, *Electronic Library*, **23** (1), www.emeraldinsight.com/Insight/viewPDF.jsp?Filename= html/Output/Published/EmeraldFullTextArticle/Pdf/2630230106.pdf [accessed 23 May 2005].

Wilson, R. and Landoni, M. (2003) Evaluating the Usability of Portable E-books. In *SAC 2003, Melbourne, Florida USA*, ACM, www.cis.strath.ac.uk/research/publications/papers/ strath_cis_publication_32.pdf [accessed 10 June 2005].

Wilson, R., Landoni, M. and Gibb, F. (2003) The Web Book Experiments in Electronic Textbook Design, *Journal of Documentation*, **59** (4), 454–77.

Wilson, R., Shortreed, J. and Landoni, M. (2004) A Study into the Usability of E-encyclopaedias. In *2004 ACM Symposium on Applied Computing*, 1688–92, www.cis.strath.ac.uk/research/publications/papers/strath_cis_publication_202.pdf [accessed 7 June 2005].

23
Tearing down the walls: demand for e-books in an academic library

Ellen Derey Safley

Introduction

Libraries are challenged to remain vital and dynamic in an age where users are addicted to the internet and demand that information be delivered electronically. Although the literature suggests that the substitution of electronic journals is fully established in most disciplines, the use of electronic books is often reported as flawed, limited, or largely unacceptable to library customers. Understanding how electronic books are used is fundamentally important for the future of libraries and the ultimate creation of a true library without walls.

This paper analyses the delivery models of electronic books and their integration into library collections. Usage statistics are presented, along with the results of two surveys in 2004 and 2005 which analysed customer knowledge and preferences for book formats.

Background

What do our learners want with respect to electronic books? There are a few surveys and use studies that indicate the growing importance of electronic books in academic libraries.

Croft and Bedi (2005) found that once students are introduced to the advantages of electronic books, they are more likely to use them again. Secondly, the librarians tested students' preferences between two models because of perceived difficulty with the *NetLibrary* delivery model, and showed that the users did not prefer one model to another. To test the assumption of preference for print or electronic books, the librarians referred students to both versions of certain texts. Students opted for the electronic version over print at a rate of 3:1. Students used e-books for research and reference, but not primarily for reading (Croft and Bedi, 2005, 95).

Dillon (2001a, b) wrote two papers on e-book purchases between libraries in the University of Texas system. Since 1999, the system librarians have selected the items although the materials were not acquired as they were published. Dillon (2001a) wrote that it was too soon to place much validity in usage statistics, but he outlined many of the problems intrinsic in comparing print and electronic usage.

> The printed book circulation data is particularly vexing in that, even though we know the patron checked the book out, we don't know how intensively they used each title, or whether they even opened the book at all. With the e-book data we don't know if the usage represents one user intensively reading a title in many different sessions, or if it represents brief examinations by many different people.
>
> (Dillon, 2001a, 116–17)

The e-book collection at the University of Texas at Dallas libraries

Created in 1969, the University of Texas at Dallas, a medium-sized largely commuter institution within the UT system, is known for programmes in the natural sciences, engineering/computer science and management. The Eugene McDermott Library contains over 1,000,000 volumes and complements this with over 35,000 electronic journals and 300,000 electronic books.

In 2001, the librarians regularly analysed the *NetLibrary* usage statistics and realized the growing popularity of e-books, although customers regularly complained about how the content was delivered. To explore the delivery of e-books, in 2004 the library subscribed to *ebrary* in 2004. The model provided for unlimited simultaneous use without the need for passwords. Titles were regularly added to the library catalogue and merged with existing materials. Usage was very high for books on computer science and business/economics. In March 2004 the library also purchased a small collection of Safari Tech titles in March 2004 which was expanded within a year.

The purchase of historical e-book collections provided a wealth of primary resource material for a young library. In addition to access to *Early English Books Online*, the UT system acquired the *Eighteenth Century Collection* (Gale) and several Alexander Street Press databases. The library purchased the *Evans Digital Library*, the *Shaw-Shoemaker Collection*, and the *Making of the Modern Economy*. Bibliographic records were added although the information was sometimes inaccurate.

In order to explore e-reference books, *Oxford Reference Online* and *Oxford Digital Library*, a portion of the Gale Virtual Reference Library and the *Oxford English Dictionary* were added. Although the literature suggests that e-books are particularly suited for reference use, the statistics provide no information about who is using the titles.

The collection consists of over 300,000 catalogued titles, with another 100,000 waiting for bibliographic records. Despite the proliferation of e-book purchases, the library has not curtailed its print book purchases, including an active approval programme and direct orders.

Electronic book usage at the University of Texas at Dallas libraries

As described earlier, analysing statistical use of electronic books is highly suspicious. Unlike COUNTER (undertaken to standardize the reporting of electronic journals usage), no standards for statistics on e-books exist. Suppliers may provide data about time online, the number of sessions, the items retrieved (number and title), items viewed, average time online, pages viewed and pages downloaded, to name but a few of the options. Making comparisons between products is as difficult as comparing online access to print circulation patterns. However, it is obvious that usage is increasing over time for all products.

During 2004 the library began to track usage of electronic books. Whenever possible, the statistics on the number of titles used was preferred over other indicators such as sessions, downloads or pages viewed, in an effort to try to compare checkouts of the print collection to the use of online books. Three collections, *NetLibrary* (49%), *Safari Tech* (15%), and *ebrary* (11%) constitute the majority of usage, yet the historical collections are finding an audience despite the lack of full cataloguing.

Figure 23.1 shows the dramatic increase in *NetLibrary* use since its initial creation in late 1999. Currently, the library has access to almost 36,000 titles, and the use of the collection is slowing as more collections are acquired. The breakdown by subject is consistent over time and is presented in Figure 23.2. Computer science and engineering (39%) and business, economics, and management (17%) constitute the majority of the demand. These numbers correlate with the usage of the print collection.

Safari Tech provides statistics on the number of successful queries (something retrieved), on the time spent online during an average session, on the number of turnaways and the number of sections retrieved (generally chapters of a book). Remarkably, the average session length is approximately 8½ minutes. *Safari Tech* showed a 300% increase in sessions and a 269% increase in sections retrieved from 2003/2004 to 2004/2005 (July).

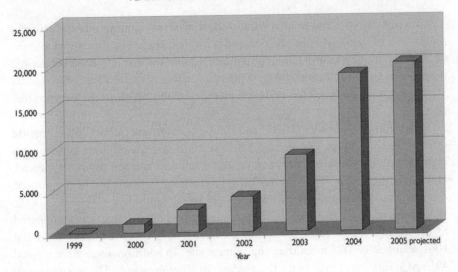

Figure 23.1   *NetLibrary use, 1999 to July 2005*

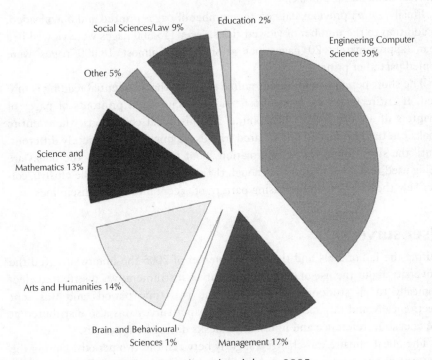

Figure 23.2   *NetLibrary use: subject breakdown 2005*

Although the user community for historical materials is limited because of the orientation of the university, the demand is impressive. In the first seven months of 2005 the usage of these titles constituted 12% of the entire e-book collection, despite the lack of full cataloguing. While the loading of the bibliographic records is pending, the databases are being promoted and add depth to the print collection.

Oxford English Dictionary (OED) and the *Oxford Reference Online* (ORO) provide other usage indicators. On average, OED sessions last 6½ minutes and learners view four pages, whereas ORO sessions last 7 minutes and ten pages are viewed. During the next year, reference staff will be scanning in-house use of the printed collection to compare the demand for its electronic equivalent.

The use of *ACLS History E-Book Project* exhibits above average usage compared to the average of all subscribers. Since March 2004, UTD learners conducted 1061 searches, or 18% more than the average site. In addition, users have viewed 4016 page images, or over twice the average for all project sites. Despite the small size of the programmes in arts and humanities, these statistics illustrate the unusual demand for e-books.

Finally, *ebrary* provides data on the number of pages printed and downloaded, in addition to the number of viewed titles. Over 115,300 pages were viewed in a year (approximately 20 pages per session) and almost 18,000 pages were copied/pasted or printed.

The short period of time spent online suggests that sequential reading is limited. If entire books are read, most reading occurs from printouts of pages or chapters of a work rather than online. For historical collections where entire books can be downloaded and printed, the usage might be completely different. Until the sites provide more information about the sessions, how the books are being used remains a mystery. Although the statistics continue to be elusive, collectively they suggest an increasing pattern of acceptance across disciplines.

User surveys

During the fall of 2004 and the spring/summer of 2005 the library surveyed the university about the use of e-books. The survey instrument was distributed electronically to all students twice during the two time periods and was sent electronically and in paper to faculty. The paper survey was also distributed at the checkout, reference and information desks during both periods.

The questionnaire was changed slightly between the two periods. During the first survey, the questions asked about the subject of the e-book. During the second survey, questions analysed differences between the learner's programme of study and addressed preferences for e-book models. In both periods the questionnaire collected general comments concerning electronic books.

Over 3% of the university students and faculty completed the survey. Use of electronic books by faculty members was the lowest (39%), but was highest for graduate students (45%). The majority of undergraduates (57%) had not used an electronic book. It would appear that those not knowing about e-books might not be using the library, its catalogue or its collections because of the pervasive nature of the online monographic resources; however, the questionnaire did not ask about overall use of the library.

The 2005 survey collected the participants' affiliation by school/programme. The distribution of the non-users indicated that approximately 50% of the respondents in engineering/computer science and 60% of the respondents in management had not used an electronic book. Yet these are precisely the subjects best represented within the e-book collections. Learners affiliated with arts and humanities (61%), natural sciences and mathematics (59%) and social sciences (58%) were most familiar with e-books.

The survey results over-represent programmes in arts and humanities, brain and behavioral sciences, and social sciences and under-represent programmes in management, natural sciences and mathematics, and engineering/computer science. It is assumed that the distribution reflects the actual usage of the library, although the integrated library system does not collect information about the specific programme of borrowers by programme.

In the initial survey, 34% of the respondents were unaware that the library provided electronic books. Less than one year later, this statistic had declined to 21%. During the interval between surveys, the total number of respondents who had never used an electronic book declined by 6%. In the latest survey (2005), 53% of all respondents had never used one. Some participants who were aware of e-books either did not choose them because of the format or did not find any relevant e-books.

Both surveys addressed how the participant found the e-book and the results were consistent. The majority of the time the responder used the catalogue (56% in 2004 and 58% in 2005), whereas others used a link on the home page (30% in 2004 and 27% in 2005), suggesting their preference for electronic delivery. Approximately 14–15% of the users were directed to an e-book by a librarian or a faculty member.

Participants were looking for a particular title (38% in 2004 and 36% in 2005) or for works by a particular author (15–16%). Subject searching was the most popular (40% in 2004 and 43% in 2005). Only a small number of respondents were trying to find statistics (7% in 2004 and 5% in 2005). These results parallel usage numbers generated from monthly catalogue reports.

The surveys analysed how easy it was to find, connect to and use e-books. On a scale of 1–10, with a score of 5 being neutral, respondents rated using the electronic book as 6.6 and finding/connecting to a book at 7.3. The results reflect a number of concerns intrinsic to electronic books, including printing and downloading portions of the book, scanning/browsing within the item, cutting/pasting text, and password requirements.

For the 2005 survey, respondents were questioned about personal preferences. If the library did not own the print equivalent, 92% would use the e-book and 88% would use one to write a research paper or to complete a class assignment.

Survey participants in the arts and humanities responded that the subject of their research did not make a difference to their use of the e-book (53%), indicating that they were more directed towards a known item. All other groups responded that the subject of the research made a difference in whether they would use it. Respondents in engineering and computer science indicated that 83% of the time the subject of their search made a difference in whether they would elect to use an e-book.

The usage of electronic reference books was evaluated in a question concerning whether they would use an electronic resource to find a 'quick fact'. Of the participants who used electronic books, 80% would do so to find factual information. This finding supports the literature on demand for reference e-books.

Overwhelmingly, the participants indicated their overall preference for paper books (69%); however, a small percentage (4%) responded that it depended on their research. Almost one-third of the respondents preferred e-books over paper. Although interesting, this finding should be explored further to determine whether the results are biased towards users of electronic books. If e-book users were more likely to complete the survey, then the results are biased. However, given that the majority of respondents either did not know the library had electronic books or had never used them suggests that the survey was not biased towards e-book supporters. In addition, because learners in management and computer science/engineering were under-represented in the survey, it is assumed that the findings are not biased. Given the usage statistics, it is probable that e-book users are under-represented.

The survey asked whether the responders had used a catalogue feature that restricts a search to the electronic books, as this could indicate a preference for the format. Although 85% were not aware of the feature, 56% of the participants would be likely to use it in the future.

The 2005 survey asked which electronic book models they preferred, and these selections were matched against their overall rating for e-books and their school/programme. Overall, *Safari Tech* was rated the highest (7.11) while the *Eighteenth Century Collection Online* (5.7) and *PastMasters* (5.6) were rated the lowest (but slightly higher than neutral). These scores rate the model not the quality of the product.

Participants rated their e-book experience. On the 0–10 scale, the overall ranking was 6.1. Faculty members were less enthusiastic (5.45), whereas undergraduates were more accepting (6.5). The general comments indicated that e-books were more difficult to read or skim online, many users want to print large sections of the book, or download the entire item, and that the system kept asking them for a password or stating that the checkout period was not long enough. Many participants mentioned that the systems did not allow them to highlight text or save specific passages despite the fact that most have these capabilities. Additional promotion of and instruction in these special features is desirable for full use by students.

Although the overall rating was positive, the respondents were clearly inconvenienced by the printing and cutting/pasting functions. If these issues were resolved, many respondents indicated that they would print out the needed sections and read them offline or download them as they do articles from e-journals.

Library customers found e-books useful for their projects, efficient if away from campus, and non-competitive, as many people can use an e-book at one time (*ebrary* can, but *NetLibrary* cannot). Participants also contradicted each other in their praise and condemnation for e-books. Whereas several students did not want the library to substitute electronic for print materials, others indicated that e-book collections brought depth to the library, particularly for historical materials. Others suggested that the library provide more supporting information for using electronic collections. Finally, the participants were very supportive of the library and its staff and were generally thankful for being asked their opinions.

The surveys promoted the electronic book collection and the library. As the majority of the survey participants had never used the e-book collection, many students asked for specific instructions or assistance.

Although the circulation of paper books is relatively stable, the use of electronic information is escalating. During the next year, in-house use of paper titles will be analysed to complete the pattern of usage and determine how reference titles in particular are being used when the online equivalent is available.

Conclusion

Whereas other librarians are reluctant to consider e-books when developing library collections, the library found that some models of electronic books are more desirable than others, that additional training is wanted by many learners, and that the publishers will find a method to deliver books that captures the needs and demands of scholars. Learners still prefer to read paper, and limiting the printing and downloading complicates the delivery of the information. In the future, creative contracts can limit the conflicts involving rights management and can deliver information efficiently.

Although the jury is still out on sequential reading of electronic books, many learners will consult an electronic version if the print is not available, and many already prefer online delivery. Basic attributes are alluring to libraries: e-books do not need to be processed, do not wear out, and cannot get lost; they do not need to be checked in, checked out or shelved; and inventories are unnecessary.

The selection of electronic books is more complicated than for print. At the University of Texas at Dallas, librarians are developing two collections simultaneously: print and electronic. Sometimes the collections duplicate each other, but at other times they complement each other. At present, publishers are not enabling librarians to choose between formats at the time of publication, yet this condition will soon disappear. Many experts believe that e-books should be selected when demand warrants more than one copy. An equally compelling argument supports the selection of a title that might see little use. Selection does require some thought to determine when the library should buy one format over another, and there are even publisher models available to let the learner decide when the library should purchase the electronic version.

The statistics generated by publishers on electronic book usage are not satisfactory or standardized. Further development of the usage statistics is warranted to obtain a better idea of when electronic books are most useful for students. Overall, the convenience of searching across scholarly texts will allow the retrieval of relevant materials. Printed indexes cannot compare to the standard means of retrieval experienced in most electronic resources.

Whether a handheld/tablet device becomes the means of access or desktop delivery is preferred, electronic books are yet another format that will evolve to meet user demand and benefit libraries. Librarians can play an integral role in defining models for electronic book delivery and making them usable by all scholars.

References

Croft, R. and Bedi, S. (2005) eBooks for a Distributed Learning University: The Royal Roads University Case, *Journal of Library Administration*, **41** (1/2), 113–37.

Dillon, D. (2001a) E-books: the University of Texas experience, Part 1, *Library Hi Tech*, **19** (2), 113–24.

Dillon, D. (2001b) E-books: the University of Texas experience, Part 2, *Library Hi Tech*, **19** (4), 350–62.

INDEX